WITHDRAWN

D1376627

PLAYWRIGHTS AND PLAGIARISTS IN EARLY MODERN ENGLAND

PLAYWRIGHTS AND

PLAGIARISTS IN

EARLY MODERN ENGLAND

Gender, Authorship, Literary Property

LAURA J. ROSENTHAL

Cornell University Press

Ithaca and London

Copyright © 1996 by Cornell University

All rights reserved. Except for brief quotations in a review, this book, or parts thereof, must not be reproduced in any form without permission in writing from the publisher. For information, address Cornell University Press, Sage House, 512 East State Street, Ithaca, New York 14850.

First published 1996 by Cornell University Press.

Library of Congress Cataloging-in-Publication Data

Rosenthal, Laura J. (Laura Jean), 1960–
    Playwrights and plagiarists in early modern England : gender, authorship, literary property / Laura J. Rosenthal.
        p.   cm.
    Includes bibliographical references and index.
    ISBN 0-8014-3252-9 (alk. paper)
        1. English drama—Restoration, 1660–1700—History and criticism.
    2. English drama—Women authors—History and criticism.   3. English drama—18th century—History and criticism.   4. Plagiarism—England—History—17th century.   5. Plagiarism—England—History—18th century.   6. Literature and society—England.   7. Women and literature—England.   8. Authorship—Sex differences.   9. Theater—England.   10. Intertextuality.   11. Playwriting.   I. Title.
    PR698.W6R67   1996
    822'.409—dc20   96-22233

This book is printed on Lyons Falls Turin Book,
a paper that is totally chlorine-free and acid-free.

PR
698
.W6
R67
1996

100797-3516X8

for **Russell Mardon**

CONTENTS

ACKNOWLEDGMENTS

This project has benefited from support from several institutions to which I am grateful. The Monticello College Foundation Fellowship at the Newberry Library provided six crucial months of research and writing. Florida State University provided two summer research grants and generous support that allowed me to accept the Monticello Fellowship. A short-term fellowship from the Folger Shakespeare Library and a grant from the English-Speaking Union furnished the opportunity for my initial research. The Society for Critical Exchange's conference "The Construction of Authorship," organized by Peter Jaszi and Martha Woodmansee, introduced me to issues that I had not previously considered. I am grateful to the organizers and to my fellow participants. A seminar on literary property organized by Susan Staves at the William Andrews Clark Memorial Library offered me the first opportunity to exchange ideas with other scholars working in the field. I am grateful for all this institutional support and to the many colleagues who made the experiences so valuable.

Some of the material in this book has already appeared in print in earlier version. I thank Northwestern University Press for permission to use a revised version of "Owning Oroonoko: Behn, Southerne, and the Contingencies of Property" in Chapter 3; the essay first appeared in *Renaissance Drama* 1992. I am also grateful to AMS Press for permission to include a version of "The Author as Ghost in the Eighteenth Century," which will appear in the journal *1650–1850: Ideas, Aesthetics, and Inquiries in the Early Modern Era,* and has been incorporated into Chapter 1.

My most important individual debts remain with Leonard Barkan, Lawrence Lipking, Mary Beth Rose, and Richard Wendorf. While this book bears little resemblance to my graduate work, it continues to ask many of the same questions that these scholars, especially Leonard Barkan, encouraged me to consider. The current text has benefited from the generous readings of Bruce Boehrer, Helen Burke, Helen Deutsch,

Kathy King, Karen Laughlin, Mary Beth Rose, and Simon Stern. Valuable insights, questions, comments, and references have been offered over the years by Anna Battigelli, Karen Cunningham, Frances Dolan, Margaret W. Ferguson, Donna Heiland, Madeleine Kahn, Rosemary Kegl, Rip Lhamon, Joanna Lipking, John Marino, Stuart Sherman, Susan Staves, Valerie Traub, James Turner, and Cynthia Wall. Michael Dobson has been particularly generous in sharing information and ideas about adaptation. I am grateful to Cornell University Press's readers, Cynthia Lowenthal and Kristina Straub, for their thorough, encouraging, and challenging reports. Madelyn Kranis at Florida State University has been immensely helpful in the final preparations of the manuscript.

Finally, I am grateful to my mother, sister, and daughter—Evelyn Rosenthal, Helen Keaney, and Sophie Rosenthal—who continue to inspire and challenge my thinking about gender. Bernard, Daniel, and Rosalind Rosenthal have each offered different kinds of insight and support as well. No one has been more important, helpful, and patient through the research and writing of this book than my husband, Russell Mardon, to whom *Playwrights and Plagiarists in Early Modern England* is dedicated.

L. J. R.

PLAYWRIGHTS AND

PLAGIARISTS IN

EARLY MODERN ENGLAND

INTRODUCTION

Drama and
Cultural Location

Most playwrights discussed in this book were also known as plagiarists. I am less interested, however, in vindicating Margaret Cavendish, Aphra Behn, John Dryden, Susanna Centlivre, or Colley Cibber from the charge of stealing lines or plots than I am in exploring the cultural meaning of plagiarism in the late seventeenth and early eighteenth centuries. In fact, these dramatists clearly benefited from the works of others; we would be hard pressed, however, to find a playwright in this period who repeated nothing from the past. Nor do the playwrights accused of plagiarism seem necessarily to have copied significantly more or copied in less interesting ways, although the task of quantifying and qualifying literary repetition ultimately would be futile. I call attention to these dramatists not as unjustly slandered victims, but as writers who struggled with and negotiated the profound instabilities, ambiguities, and uneven forms of literary property.

Rejecting the romantic model that assumes true authors write for reasons that transcend the market, recent scholarship has revealed the ways in which changing legal and cultural definitions of literary property shape literary production. This observation has produced a variety of narratives about the emergence of a new kind of authorship in the eighteenth century.[1] Yet most studies, like the language of law and the

---

[1] Michel Foucault, "What Is an Author?" *Textual Strategies: Perspectives in Post-Structuralist Criticism*, ed. Josué V. Harari (Ithaca: Cornell University Press, 1979), 141–160; Alvin Kernan, *Printing Technology, Letters, and Samuel Johnson* (Princeton: Princeton University Press, 1987); Mark Rose, "The Author as Proprietor: *Donaldson v. Becket* and the Genealogy of Modern Authorship," *Representations* 23 (Summer 1988): 51–85, and *Authors and Owners: The Invention of Copyright* (Cambridge: Harvard University

discourse of individualism, either tell this story without explicit attention to gender or attend to the particular history of women's authorship.[2] This book is neither a history of the legal ownership of writing nor a general study of women's literary history, although my debt to this scholarship is considerable. Rather, I have looked at the gendered cultural discourses that have challenged, threatened, and enabled the literary careers of women and men. I have attempted to show how Restoration and early eighteenth-century culture limited and enabled different writers in different ways, but that gendered cultural discourses compromised ownership and authorship for those signified as outside of the dominant masculine positions. This does not mean that women (and occluded others) remained outside of literary culture. In fact, *Playwrights and*

Press, 1993). Rose has argued that eighteenth-century disagreements over perpetual copyright—whether holding a copyright is legally permanent or whether it eventually reverts back to the author's estate or to the public domain—produced "a twin birth, the simultaneous emergence in the discourse of the law of the proprietary author and the literary work," and that "the distinguishing characteristic of the modern author . . . is that he is a proprietor, that he is conceived as the originator and therefore the owner of a special kind of commodity, the 'work' " ("Author as Proprietor," 65, 54). Before the eighteenth century, authors did not generally hold the copyrights to their own texts. See also Margreta de Grazia, *Shakespeare Verbatim: The Reproduction of Authenticity and the 1790 Apparatus* (Oxford: Clarendon Press, 1991); Martha Woodmansee, "The Genius and the Copyright: Economic and Legal Conditions of the Emergence of the 'Author,' " *Eighteenth-Century Studies* 17 (Summer 1984): 425–448; Jerome Christensen, *Practicing Enlightenment: Hume and the Formation of a Literary Career* (Madison: University of Wisconsin Press, 1987); Susan Stewart, *Crimes of Writing: Problems in the Containment of Representation* (New York: Oxford University Press, 1991); David Saunders and Ian Hunter, "Lessons from the 'Literatory': How to Historicise Authorship," *Critical Inquiry* 17 (Spring 1991): 479–505; Linda Zionkowski, "Territorial Disputes in the Republic of Letters: Canon Formation and the Literary Profession," *The Eighteenth Century: Theory and Interpretation* 31 (Spring 1990): 3–22; Jim Swan, "Touching Words: Helen Keller, Plagiarism, Authorship," in *The Construction of Authorship: Textual Appropriation in Law and Literature*, ed. Martha Woodmansee and Peter Jaszi (Durham, NC: Duke University Press, 1994), 57–100.

[2] On women writers, see Catherine Gallagher, *Nobody's Story: The Vanishing Acts of Women Writers in the Marketplace, 1670–1820* (Berkeley: University of California Press, 1994); Janet Todd, *The Sign of Angellica: Women, Writing and Fiction, 1660–1800* (New York: Columbia University Press, 1989); Elaine Hobby, *Virtue of Necessity: English Women's Writing, 1649–1688* (Ann Arbor: University of Michigan Press, 1988); Nancy Cotton, *Women Playwrights in England, c.1363–1750* (Lewisburg: Bucknell University Press, 1980); Jacqueline Pearson, *The Prostituted Muse: Images of Women and Women Dramatists, 1642–1737* (New York: Harvester Wheatsheaf, 1988).

Plagiarists in Early Modern England explores the work of women and men who became signified as illegitimate owners of text—that is, plagiarists—but who nevertheless found strategies for claiming property in their work and in themselves.

I have attempted to offer insights about Restoration and early eighteenth century dramatic authorship by making gender and culture, as distinct from women and legal rights, my primary categories of investigation. Legal debates remain crucial for understanding authorship during this time, but they tend either to disguise gender differences or fail to recognize women as full legal subjects.[3] Further, while plagiarism clearly describes a violation of property, rarely did it come to legal action.[4] Plagiarism, it seems to me, functioned more as a cultural category defining the borders between texts and policing the accumulation of cultural capital.[5] I argue that while individual differences do shape the playwright's relationship to the market and while authorship as an institution changes, however unevenly, over time, gender and class shape critical judgments about what stories a playwright can own or use, about who can be praised as an heir to Shakespeare or Jonson, and who appears as a violator of textual boundaries. This period defined authorship not just through a material economy of literary property, but through the symbolic economies of social and cultural capital. Authorship becomes meaningful through both material ownership and culturally contingent gestures of attribution. Those interested in the gendered history of authorship, then, need to consider not just material success or failure but cultural location as well.

Once we start thinking about literary property as a cultural as well as a legal issue, it becomes possible to see the problem of plagiarism as a problem of social subjectivity—and thus a problem of gender. In Chap-

---

[3] Susan Staves's *Married Women's Separate Property in England, 1660–1833* (Cambridge: Harvard University Press, 1990) provides a superb model for critical readings of the law. While my approach has been quite different, I am nevertheless greatly indebted to Staves's work. For a brilliant discussion of the limits of legal rights, see Patricia J. Williams, *The Alchemy of Race and Rights* (Cambridge: Harvard University Press, 1991).

[4] The "piracy" of entire books later in the eighteenth century, however, demanded some legal decisions.

[5] Even now, Susan Stewart points out, plagiarism has more to do with community self-regulation than with legal boundaries. See *Crimes of Writing*, 24. See also Thomas Mallon, *Stolen Words: Forays into the Origins and Ravages of Plagiarism* (New York: Penguin, 1989).

3

ter 1, I explore the various discourses through which the position of owner emerges as non-normative, as tenuous for most people and sometimes explicitly unavailable to women and to men outside of dominant masculinity or elite status. The capacity to be understood as an owner of cultural property can rarely be taken for granted, and the difference between legitimate and illegitimate forms of appropriation often has less to do with the amount of text repeated than with the identity of the author. Women writers articulate an awareness of this problem, but they were not the only ones affected. John Dryden also found that his unstable location as both professional and aspiring elite amateur brought challenges to his legitimacy in similar terms.

For women writers who understood that they could not always count on owning literary property because they did not necessarily own themselves, authorship demanded a consideration of social subjectivity.[6] Full social subjectivity—the capacity to be constituted in terms of civil personhood, potential authority, and one's distinction from the status of possessed object—remained elusive for most women (and many men). Margaret Cavendish, the duchess of Newcastle, negotiated this problem by imagining alternatives and creating imaginary property. Empowered by her elite status but excluded from many forms of ownership by her gender, Cavendish constructed in her plays, essays, and fictional narratives a social subjectivity that avoided transgressive appropriation by claiming originality. While most histories of authorship connect the valuation of originality to copyright law in the mid-eighteenth century, *Playwrights and Plagiarists in Early Modern England* argues that originality became a strategy for (self-)ownership one hundred years earlier in response to reconceptualizations of property that emphasized individual ownership but limited who could inhabit the position of owner.

While the duchess of Newcastle constructed her social subjectivity from the advantage of her elite amateur status, Aphra Behn fully participated in a literary marketplace that commodified writing and implicitly commodified any woman who entered it. Behn, I argue, negotiated her position as plagiarist by both challenging gendered property relations and by, contradictorily, representing herself as both in and above the

---

[6] My readings of gender and property are greatly indebted to Carole Pateman, *The Sexual Contract* (Stanford: Stanford University Press, 1988) and in less obvious ways to Staves's *Married Women's Separate Property*.

marketplace. In *The Rover*, she disputes masculine claims to sexual in-alienability through her appropriation of Thomas Killigrew's *Thomaso; or, The Wanderer*; in *Oroonoko*, she imagines both "Africa" and her own career as outside of commercial exchange. In turn, Thomas Southerne's dramatic appropriation of *Oroonoko* represents Behn herself as unable legitimately to own literary property.

By the early eighteenth century, British law recognized the author as an owner of literary property. As many scholars have pointed out, this represents only one of the many ways in which the 1690s ushered in an economy of commodification, professionalization, and exchange. While J. G. A. Pocock's influential essays have demonstrated that with England's financial revolution exchange was understood by some as promoting the civilization of passions and thus proper refinement,[7] Dustin Griffin has pointed out that this highly uneven transition elicited great ambivalence among authors, who "negotiated a balance among the claims of occasion, audience, patron, bookseller, immediate financial need"; further, "there was no simple and steady progress from a court-based to a marketplace-based literature, from poem as amusement, gift, or tribute to poem as commodity."[8] In spite of (or perhaps because of) the commodification of writing, the idealized literary career (re)emerged as that of the gentleman-scholar who could transcend the marketplace but nevertheless claim property in his writing. I have found Pierre Bourdieu's distinction between economic, social, and cultural capital useful in understanding this change, as well as Peter Stallybrass and Allon White's observation of the widening split between elite and popular culture in the theaters of this time.[9] The insistent distinction between hacks and

[7] J. G. A. Pocock, *Virtue, Commerce, and History: Essays on Political Thought and History, Chiefly in the Eighteenth Century* (Cambridge: Cambridge University Press, 1985), especially "Virtues, Rights, and Manners: A Model for Historians of Political Thought," 47–50. See also Gallagher, *Nobody's Story*, chap. 3.

[8] Dustin Griffin, "The Beginnings of Modern Authorship: Milton and Dryden," *Milton Quarterly* 24 (March 1990), 6. To quote Griffin further, "Pope manipulated the new world of bookselling to his own advantage, but liked to think himself a gentleman writing for his friends. Johnson, who plainly and proudly wrote 'for money' accepted a pension from George III." See also Christensen, *Practicing Enlightenment*.

[9] Pierre Bourdieu, *Distinction: A Social Critique of the Judgement of Taste*, trans. Richard Nice (Cambridge: Harvard University Press, 1984); Peter Stallybrass and Allon White, *The Politics and Poetics of Transgression* (Ithaca: Cornell University Press, 1986). My debt to both of these works is considerable.

true authors—those whose writing circulated cultural capital, but by this time not necessarily to the exclusion of economic capital—both undermined and enabled the careers of women playwrights, who not only found new successes on the public stage but also endured new kinds of satire against them. The post–Glorious Revolution possibility that women could potentially become rights-bearing individuals seems to have enabled their greater participation in the literary marketplace; nonetheless, emergent discourses distinguishing authors from "hacks" occluded many women (and some men) from both cultural legitimacy and full individuality. In this context, Colley Cibber becomes Pope's quintessential plagiarist for constructing his persona at the confluence of "hack" authorship and positions outside of dominant masculinity. Susanna Centlivre succeeded through her own form of feminist individualism, whose possibilities and limitations I explore. She combined Cavendish's claim to originality, only without the aristocratic singularity, and Behn's professionalism, only without the ambivalence. Centlivre owed her success, I contend, to both her talent and her avoidance of any claim to cultural capital.

This book, as the title suggests, is about both playwrights and plagiarists. My concentration on drama warrants some explanation, since most studies of gender and authorship during this period explore the novel. All the playwrights I discuss worked in other genres as well, and I have drawn on poems and prose narratives when I felt they could illuminate the issues at hand. The particular complexities of writing for the stage, however, offer distinct and enlightening perspectives on literary property, authorship, and gender that have remained overshadowed by the study of the novel.[10] In fact, no genre illustrates the significance of literary property as a *cultural* category quite so much as drama. While the novel, as Catherine Gallagher and J. Paul Hunter have in different ways demonstrated, emerges out of popular, scandalous, and Grub Street narratives,[11] drama had long held meaning as both an "elite" and a "popular" art.

[10] For the significance of the stage to authorship, see Julie Stone Peters, *Congreve, the Drama and the Printed Word* (Stanford: Stanford University Press, 1990); Michael Dobson, *The Making of the National Poet: Shakespeare, Adaptation, and Authorship 1660–1769* (Oxford: Clarendon Press, 1992); Margreta de Grazia, *Shakespeare Verbatim: The Reproduction of Authenticity and the 1790 Apparatus* (Oxford: Clarendon Press, 1991); Stallybrass and White, *The Politics and Poetics of Transgression.*

[11] Gallagher, *Nobody's Story*; J. Paul Hunter, *Before Novels: The Cultural Contexts of Eighteenth Century English Fiction* (New York: W. W. Norton, 1990).

At the same time, while circulating poems as commodities rather than gifts or bids for patronage becomes a significant source of income only in the eighteenth century, dramatic authorship already carried a long history of participation in the marketplace. To locate the emergence of "professional authorship" in the eighteenth century, in fact, makes only limited sense in the study of drama. Because of this complex history as well as its public status, the drama becomes a privileged site of contestation over cultural authority. The novel and the poem become significant sites as well, but those genres tend to express an initial allegiance to the "popular" and the "elite," respectively.

Further, dramatic writing raises particular ambiguities of intertextuality and originality. Much poetry of this time self-consciously locates itself in a learned tradition and even depends upon knowledge of this tradition for its meaning. The novel, by contrast, tells "new" stories, as its name indicates. As a commercial genre, theater had since the Renaissance been under some pressure to offer something that the audience had not seen the previous week;[12] still, retelling familiar stories had also been customary and rarely understood as plagiarism. While praise of invention appears during the Renaissance, such statements can mean, as Harold Ogden White put it, "finding quotations with which to fill note-books, and selecting from them as occasion demands."[13] Similarly, not until the early seventeenth century, Stephen Orgel points out, did art patrons begin to distinguish between works made by the master and those made by pupils in his workshop. The Renaissance artist, he argues, regularly practiced forms of writing that we might consider plagiarism: "The entire creative career was often conceived to be imitative."[14] The rare charges of plagiarism one finds in the Renaissance tend to accuse the artist of a "pernicious adherence to authority" rather than

[12] See Gerald Eades Bentley, *The Profession of Dramatist in Shakespeare's Time, 1590–1642* (Princeton: Princeton University Press, 1971).

[13] Harold Ogden White, *Plagiarism and Imitation during the English Renaissance*, Harvard Studies in English, Vol. 12 (Cambridge: Harvard University Press, 1935), 38. White credits Joseph Hall for bringing the word "plagiarism" (from the Latin word meaning kidnapping) into English. But White believes that even Hall objected only to servile imitation rather than to the modern sense of property violation (120–122). A. J. Minnis's *Medieval Theory of Authorship: Scholastic Literary Attitudes in the Later Middle Ages* (Philadelphia: University of Pennsylvania Press, 1984) confirms White's perspective on the acceptability of imitative authorship.

[14] Stephen Orgel, "The Renaissance Artist as Plagiarist" *ELH* 48 (Fall 1981): 479.

of a violation of property.[15] But perhaps it is no coincidence that the first English author to consider the problem of plagiarism extensively—Ben Jonson—was a playwright negotiating the boundaries between professionalism and an elite amateur community. Joseph Loewenstein has astutely described Jonson's authorial project as "neoconservative": "a groping forward toward later authorial property rights within a bourgeois cultural marketplace, but modeled on the ethos of the classical *auctor* and the economics of patronage."[16] While the novel arose as a genre of the marketplace and poetry carried at least its history of association with both patronage and privileged amateur careers, drama continually demanded the negotiation of both these possibilities.

Institutional changes brought by the Restoration complicated the collaboration and intertextuality that had long been part of dramatic writing and began a movement toward the reconceptualization of the playwright as independent and individually creative. Rather than working as a "house playwright" such as Shakespeare—although some dramatists established long-term contracts with a theater—Restoration playwrights had to hope that their plays would last until the author's benefit each third night. In the early part of the Restoration period, publication earned the author only a modest profit compared to a good benefit and a nice gift from a patron. By the end of the seventeenth century, however, dramatists understood the sale of their plays to publishers as an important source of profit; plays appeared in print sooner and sooner after their

[15] Ibid., 492–493. See also Elisabeth M. Magnus, "Originality and Plagiarism in *Areopagitica* and *Eikonoklastes,*" *English Literary Renaissance* 21 (Winter 1991): 87–101. Magnus offers a wonderful reading of Milton's objections to plagiarism that unites Orgel's insight about adherence to authority with Milton's politics. David Quint considers the case of Milton to suggest "that a shift in literary values had taken place by the end of the Renaissance, so that the writer's originality would replace a transcendent allegorical origin as the literary text's principal criterion of worth" (x). See his *Origin and Originality in Renaissance Literature: Versions of the Source* (New Haven: Yale University Press, 1983). In the tradition of popular fiction, J. Paul Hunter in *Before Novels* notes the "extraordinary attention to novelty and innovation that [John] Dunton and many others articulated around the turn of the [seventeenth to eighteenth] century" (14).

[16] Joseph Loewenstein, "The Script in the Marketplace," *Representations* 12 (Fall 1985), 109. See also David Riggs, *Ben Jonson: A Life* (Cambridge: Harvard University Press, 1989), and Richard Helgerson, *Self-Crowned Laureates: Spenser, Jonson, Milton, and the Literary System* (Berkeley: University of California Press, 1983), chap. 3.

opening on stage.[17] Julie Stone Peters's study of Congreve traces this change in one writer's career. Congreve displayed, she writes, an increasing concern for the printed page: his "move from work for the active stage in the seventeenth century to work on editions and on his own library in the eighteenth century parallels [a] shift in the idea of the drama"[18] from performed orality to print. Like Dryden, Congreve insisted on calling himself a *dramatic poet*;[19] Dryden repeatedly advocated the high culture status of drama as opposed to the "popular" culture status of the theater.[20] This authorial individualization, which contributed to the construction of the bourgeois "public" sphere, demanded the demarcation of the edges of the text before the legal codification of authorship as ownership.

Upon the Restoration, theater also emerges as a highly charged arena for the formation of gender ideology and the expression of cultural anxieties over gender. The employment of women actors, as has been widely recognized, made a significant institutional difference. It was not until the 1690s, however, that women began to sustain careers as professional playwrights.[21] Because of both her elite status and the meaning of the stage itself, Margaret Cavendish wrote in the tradition of court masques and never produced a play in the public theater. Aphra Behn, of course, survived as a professional female playwright in the early Restoration; no other women, however, enjoyed sustained careers at that time. The triumph of both liberal individualism (symbolized by the Glorious Revolution) and finance capitalism by the end of the century proved enabling in some ways to women's authorship. Lockean liberalism articulated the possibility that anyone could potentially inhabit the position of a possessing individual; at the same time, this rhetoric defined the

[17] Shirley Strum Kenny, "The Publication of Plays," in *The London Theatre World, 1660–1800*, ed. Robert D. Hume (Carbondale: Southern Illinois University Press, 1980), 309–336.

[18] Peters, *Congreve*, 73–74.

[19] "The use of *poet* to denote *dramatist* is at its height at the end of the seventeenth century," ibid., 71.

[20] For an important discussion of the Restoration division of high culture from popular culture, to which mine is indebted, see Stallybrass and White, *The Politics and Poetics of Transgression*, chap. 2.

[21] See Paula R. Backscheider, *Spectacular Politics: Theatrical Power and Mass Culture in Early Modern England* (Baltimore: Johns Hopkins University Press, 1993).

position of individual so narrowly that women and Grub Street professionals had to defend themselves continually against the charge of plagiarism. The emergence of cultural capital as a category potentially independent of elite status offered unprecedented opportunities, but also new ways of distinguishing "true authors" from hacks. Thus women playwrights found new possibilities and faced new structures of limitation. Contradictory as this may appear to those looking for either a linear history or an epistemic rupture, I have found both the possibilities and limitations important to an understanding of dramatic authorship, particular cases of plagiarism, and the forms of social subjectivity the plays represent.

I do not put the word "plagiarism" in quotation marks most of the time, but perhaps those quotations marks should be imagined. Part of my purpose here is to defamiliarize Restoration and early eighteenth-century intertextuality and to question differences between plagiarism, imitation, adaptation, repetition, and originality. To accuse someone of plagiarism was to accuse him or her of repeating the literary property of another, for it is not just the taking of property or "kidnapping," as plagiarism's literal meaning suggests, that constitutes the violation, but the property's (re)use in some kind of a public context. Originality, I argue, is both relative and ultimately inconceivable; I have been interested, then, in cultural distinctions between legitimate and illegitimate forms of appropriation. For this reason, I may have used the term "plagiarism" to describe a wider range of transgressive appropriations than perhaps the word ordinarily signifies. The common charge against women writers of trying to pass off a man's text as their own, for example, strikes me as sufficiently like the charge that Behn used too much of *Thomaso; or, The Wanderer* to call them both accusations of plagiarism. Similarly, when Cavendish insists that learned male authors merely repeat the insights of other poets, she accuses them of a version of plagiarism as well.

While accusations of plagiarism appear in many different locations, the theater seems to have been understood as a particularly dangerous place for the circulation of literary property. "The *Play-house* is an inchanted island," according to Thomas Brown, "where nothing appears in reality what it is, nor what it should be. 'Tis frequented by persons of all degrees and qualities what [s]oever, that have a great deal of idle time lying upon their hands, and can't tell how to employ it worse."

Brown connects this promiscuous social mixing to rampant plagiarism: "What are all their new plays but dam'd insipid, dull *farces,* confounded toothless *satyr,* or plaguy *rhimy plays,* with scurvy heroes, worse than the *knight of the sun,* or *Amadis de Gaul?* They are all the arrantest *plagiaries* in nature; and, like our common *news-writers,* steal from one another."[22] Thomas Brown, of course, *was* one of these common newswriters, and while here he repeats the commonplace of the popular culture playwright as having no respect for the legitimate boundaries of literary property, elsewhere he questions the difference between plagiarism and imitation. His interrogation of this distinction has a comic and ironic edge; nevertheless, he raises the possibility of its arbitrariness:

> Some of our modern writers, that have built upon the *foundation* of the *ancients,* have so far excell'd in disguising their notions, and improving their first essays, that they have acquir'd more glory and reputation than even was given to the *original* authors; nay, have utterly effaced their memories. Those who rob the *modern writers* study to hide their thefts; those who filch from the *ancients,* account it their glory: but why the first shoud be more reproach'd than the latter, I can't imagine, since there is more wit in disguising a thought of Mr. *Locke*'s, than in a lucky *translation* of a passage of *Horace.* After all, it must be granted, that the *genius* of some men can never be brought to write correctly in this age, till they have formed their judgments from the standards of the *ancients,* and the delicacy of their expression from the variety and turns of the *moderns*; and I know *no reason* why it should be their disparagement, to capacitate themselves by these helps to serve the publick.
>
> Nothing will please some men but books stuff'd with *antiquity,* groaning under the weight of the learned quotations drawn from the *fountains.* And what is all this but pilfering?[23]

He himself claims to rob neither ancient nor modern books, but only to "pillage" from the "books of the world." So while Brown enforces the ideological distinction between elite and popular culture by representing the theater as a hotbed of plagiarism, when he reflects on his own authorial position he deconstructs the categories of legitimate and illegitimate intertextuality. In this instance taking the perspective of the

[22] *The Works of Mr. Thomas Brown,* 4 vols. (London, 1760), 3:34.
[23] Ibid., 3:3–4.

"modern," he claims a direct rather than textually mediated access to the world.[24]

Like Brown and like some of the writers discussed in this book, I have questioned the difference between robbing the ancients and stealing from the moderns. But I have also questioned why some (re)writers seem more vulnerable to the charge of plagiarism, and why some appear more vulnerable to being plagiarized *from*. Writing, I demonstrate throughout, is always an act of appropriation. Everyone whose work I read here is thus both a playwright *and* a plagiarist, but that is not what distinguishes them from the more traditionally celebrated dramatists of the time. Throughout this book I ask: when one's world defines social subjectivity in terms of self-ownership but at the same time does not grant everyone full rights in themselves, how does one construct an alternative subject position? Does one attempt to claim property on the terms that the culture offers, or does one renegotiate those terms themselves? Most of the writers considered here renegotiate the terms, and their astute and creative reconfigurations of positionality, social subjectivity, and property surface in the drama they live and the drama they write. This, and not their originality or lack thereof, is what makes them worth reading.

[24] Elsewhere, though, Brown aligned himself with the ancients. See Joseph M. Levine, *The Battle of the Books: History and Literature in the Augustan Age* (Ithaca: Cornell University Press, 1991), 65.

ONE

Rewriting Distinctions:
Property, Plagiarism, Position

Plagiarism, suggests the *Grub Street Journal,* is the Grub Street version of imitation.[1] The *Journal* clearly satirizes the pilfering that apparently distinguishes the hack from the learned author. Yet we might also read another consequence: the intertextual freedoms of the educated poet constitute imitation, while similar kinds of repetition by Grub Street professionals go by the name of plagiarism. In the first (and more likely intended) reading, the difference between plagiarism and imitation remains natural and obvious: true poets repeat with artistic purpose, but Grub Street writers simply steal. The second possibility, however, denaturalizes the distinction between imitation and plagiarism, locating difference in the position of the author rather than in the activity of rewriting itself. Thus all intertextuality in the works of Grub Street denizens becomes signified as plagiarism, for such writers cannot by definition transmit texts legitimately. Any inherent difference between these two forms of rewriting gives way to a distinction between legitimate and illegitimate intertextuality shaped by the cultural location of the text and the position of the author.

The *Journal*'s satire opens up the possibility of denaturalizing distinctions not only between imitation and plagiarism, but also between adaptation, revision, imitation, translation, and even originality. Restoration and early eighteenth-century critics devoted much energy to distinguish-

---

[1] *Grub Street Journal,* no. 5, 5 Feb. 1730. Cited by Pat Rogers in *Grub Street: Studies in a Subculture* (London: Methuen, 1972), 359.

ing these forms of intertextuality, perhaps because it was and remains an endless task of creating boundaries and defining legitimacy. Writers commonly expressed this legitimacy in terms of property: Grub Street authors violate the boundaries of property through plagiarism, yet others somehow come to own the texts they rewrite. The literary property at stake in the *Journal*'s remark and in this book cannot be understood in terms of copyright and payment for a manuscript alone, for this framework already assumes, however conflictually, the liberal, rights-bearing individual. I wish instead to explore the cultural economy of literary property that renders one intertextual act legitimate and another transgressive, and to demonstrate that this distinction commonly bears less relation to the extent of textual repetition than to the cultural location of the text and the subject position of its author. Especially by the early eighteenth century, literary property operates differently in the spheres of elite culture and popular culture, with the latter commonly and disparagingly represented by a dangerous absence of boundaries. In a sense, then, plagiarism *is* the Grub Street version of imitation.

In this chapter, I begin with Edward Young's *Conjectures on Original Composition*, for it demonstrates the fragility of the distinction between originality and appropriation. Young's essay does not explicitly engage questions of gender, but participates in a similar economy of difference with other constructions that do. Further, for Young originality separates true authorship from the "vulgar." These differences find their parallel and underpinnings in philosophical considerations of property itself: for both Locke and Hobbes, the position of owner defines the subject position of the individual. Still, while Locke argues that anyone can inhabit this position, upon closer inspection the capacity to do so emerges as limited by gender and class. The discourse of plagiarism reveals these differing capacities to own, as does some writing by women themselves. But it is not just gender that occludes writers from the subject position of owner, for the social anxieties raised by professional authorship become apparent as well; they are commonly articulated, however, in terms of gender as well through accusations of insufficient masculinity. Thus the cultural economy of literary property challenged the careers of some men just as profoundly, and while subsequent chapters will explore the ways in which several women negotiated their unstable positions, this chapter will end with a glance at the complexities faced by a poet laureate, John Dryden.

Originality

Edward Young's *Conjectures on Original Composition* claims to make the first argument for originality over imitation and to offer a clear distinction between them.[2] It actually accomplishes neither goal, but nevertheless remains important for its claim of critical innovation, for the frequency with which histories of criticism accept its benchmark status, and for its serious and eloquent consideration of this problem. Young had not actually chosen an original topic; his essay, however, proves instructive in its efforts to theorize the inferiority of imitation and for its contribution to moving originality into dominance as a critical value. Young *nearly* admits that originality has no intrinsic meaning when he declares early in the essay that he "shall not enter into the curious enquiry of what is, or is not, strictly speaking, *Original*, content with what all must allow, that some Compositions are more so than others; and the more they are so, I say, the better."[3] Joel Weinsheimer has effectively demonstrated how the *Conjectures* fails to reveal an essential difference between originality and imitation. Young's favorite examples of true originals—the ancients—are only in Young's argument "accidental originals" because their sources have been lost. Since "we cannot demonstrate the absence of precedent that would certify an original as real," Weinsheimer reasons, then "to us there is no difference per se between real and accidental

[2] See Edward Young, *Conjectures on Original Composition, In a Letter to the Author of Sir Charles Grandison*, 2d ed. (London, 1759), 4. Joel Weinsheimer in "Conjectures on Unoriginal Composition," *The Eighteenth Century: Theory and Interpretation* 22 (1981): 58–73, points out that this claim to originality of argument appears only in Young's revision for the second edition and constitutes the single substantial difference from the first. Clearly other writers had argued for originality previously; Young, in fact, alludes to those arguments. Yet he "feels compelled," as Weinsheimer points out, "for the sake of consistency to make the claim, however ill founded, of originality" (59). Future quotations from the *Conjectures* are cited in the text from the first edition reprinted in facsimile by the Scholar Press Limited (Leeds, England, 1966). See also Weinsheimer, *Imitation* (London: Routledge & Kegan Paul, 1984). Weinsheimer argues that three major movements in the eighteenth century that undercut imitation—empiricism, originalism, and historicism—are "mistaken in conception" (4).

[3] Young, *Conjectures*, 9–10. See also Weinsheimer ("Conjectures," 59) on this point. Weinsheimer takes this admission as a function of the weakness of the argument for originality itself.

originality, and hence none between a real original and an imitation."[4] Further, in Young both originals and imitations imitate; they differ only in their objects of imitation. To argue that originals imitate nature and imitations imitate art assumes "not only the aesthetic and anthropological distinction between nature and art but also the more fundamental distinction between objects and signs."[5] The essential difference between originality and imitation, then, depends upon the absolute distinction between sign and object as well as an impossible assurance of the absence of precedent. So if the very definition of originality that Young refuses to articulate directly depends upon a series of unconvincing binary oppositions, then the *Conjectures* reveals the eighteenth-century conception of originality as unstable and even arbitrary. If originality cannot function as an objective category, then neither can imitation—the legitimate form of intertextuality—or plagiarism, its illegitimate form.

The force of Young's *Conjectures* lies less in any logical distinction between imitations and originals than it does in "distinction" itself and in the ideological contradictions of authorship as a gentlemanly occupation.[6] In this sense, Young becomes, like so many eighteenth-century authors, a son of Ben, ambivalently negotiating between the rights necessary for composing for a market and the appearance of retired leisure. Writing at a time when authorship was becoming increasingly professionalized, Young represents *original* writing—the kind he grants the greatest approval—as effortless.[7] His favorite metaphor is organic: "An *Original* may be said to be of a *vegetable* nature; it rises spontaneously from the vital root of Genius; it *grows*, it is not *made*: *Imitations* are often a sort of *Manufacture* wrought up by those *Mechanics*, *Art*, and *Labour*, out of pre-existent materials not their own" (12). The organic and vital root of

[4] Weinsheimer, "Conjectures," 60–61.

[5] Ibid., 62.

[6] Distinctions in taste, Pierre Bourdieu argues, serve to signify the social and cultural capitals that indicate one's class fraction. See *Distinction: A Social Critique of the Judgement of Taste*, trans. Richard Nice (Cambridge: Harvard University Press, 1984). I have depended on Bourdieu's insights throughout. For a brilliant exploration of the contradictions of eighteenth-century authorship, see Jerome Christensen, *Practicing Enlightenment: Hume and the Formation of a Literary Career* (Madison: University of Wisconsin Press, 1987). Christensen observes that these contradictions do not necessarily force a crisis; rather, they can sustain themselves indefinitely.

[7] See, for example, Alvin Kernan, *Printing Technology, Letters, and Samuel Johnson* (Princeton: Princeton University Press, 1987).

genius becomes desirable for its distinction from the necessity of labor. Even if originally pure, text becomes contaminated through repetition by "common" people: "It is with Thoughts, as it is with Words; and with both, as with Men; they may grow old, and die. Words tarnished, by passing thro' the mouths of the Vulgar, are laid aside as inelegant, and obsolete. So Thoughts, when become too common, should lose their Currency; and we should send new metal to the Mint, that is, new meaning to the Press" (13–14). As much as Young attempts to separate writing from the marketplace, a consciousness of the financial value of literature intrudes through his metaphors.

While Young opposes original, organic genius to mechanical labor, thus placing genius outside of the marketplace, the imitator ultimately violates property above all else: "We may as well grow good by another's Virtue, or fat by another's Food, as famous by another's Thought. The World will pay its Debt of Praise but once; and instead of applauding, explode a second Demand, as a Cheat" (14). Young's tropes offer contradictory representations of the status of ideas, although virtue, food, and thought each becomes a kind of capital. But while the circulation of virtue to make another person good is impossible, the circulation of food to make another fat is comprehensible. Is literary property, then, like virtue in that it adheres to the person and could not possibly add to another's stock of symbolic capital, or is it like food, easily circulated and converted to material capital? Or is it, to recall his previous metaphor, like currency itself? The ideological work of Young's *Conjectures* lies precisely in this elision of virtue and food: literary property becomes alternately inalienable and alienable. This contradictory status of literary property permits Young to associate eighteenth-century authorship with earlier, aristocratic modes, and at the same time not ignore the demands of professionalism. The status of writing as alienable property surfaces in Young's fragile distinction between imitation and originality. Latin and Greek authors, he argues, "tho' not *real*, are *accidental Originals*; the works they imitated, few excepted, are lost: They, on their Fathers' Decease, enter, as lawful Heirs, on their Estates in Fame: The Fathers of our Copyists are still in possession; and secured in it, in spite of *Goths*, and Flames, by the perpetuating power of the Press. Very late must a modern *Imitator's* Fame arrive, if it waits for their Decease" (15). Originality, then, turns out to be a matter of property indeed, for otherwise what difference would it make whether or not the earlier text remained in existence? Classical authors inherit the estates of their dead fathers, but modern writers suffer under the technologically prolonged lives of their ancestors.[8]

Young's plea for original genius constructs authorship in terms of a limited capacity to appropriate. He begins the *Conjectures*, after all, with the question of how to keep writing elite: while he does not lodge the blanket complaint, as do others, of an overcharged press, he insists that only a small number of publications contribute to "*sound Understanding, and the Public Good*" (4). The press thus "should sacrifice its most darling Offspring to the sacred interest of Virtue, and real Service of mankind" (4). Original genius draws the line between these troublesome literary excrescences and writing of genuine value; originality itself, however, functions as a signifier of difference with no intrinsic meaning.[9] For Young, originality serves as an indication of entitlement: the original author already inhabits the position of owner.

Young mentions no female original genius and does not enter into the eighteenth-century debate over whether women possess this capacity;

[8] See Margaret W. Ferguson's richly suggestive reading of Du Bellay in *Trials of Desire: Renaissance Defenses of Poetry* (New Haven: Yale University Press, 1983), in which some similar issues of appropriation become apparent. Du Bellay's "Deffence," Ferguson observes, "oscillates between presenting imitation as an act of reverent homage and as an act of aggressive theft" (23). Further, she points out, Du Bellay's organic defense "serves to legitimize and naturalize imitation as an appropriation of foreign riches" and "legitimizes the transfer of property from ancient to modern" (34–35).

[9] Young's use of "originality" as an evaluative term becomes clear again in his comparison of Shakespeare and Jonson. "*Johnson*," he writes, "in the serious drama, is as much an Imitator, as *Shakespeare* is an Original" (80). As a post-print author, though, Jonson cannot erase the literary past, as Young claims his classical precursors could: "*Cataline* might have been a good play, if *Salust* had never writ" (80). The cultural presence of Salust makes it impossible for Jonson to claim originality, even if Young simultaneously accuses Jonson of killing his precursors: in Jonson's plays, "we see nothing of *Johnson*, nor indeed, of his admired (but also murdered) antients" (80). If he murdered them, though, he did not succeed in hiding the body. Jonson offers nothing that Young can recognize as the imprint of a distinct personality—either his own or that of his precursors. Shakespeare, on the other hand, remains the poet of nature: he wrote so well and with such originality, Young argues, because he read so little (81). Shakespeare's books were the book of Nature and the book of Man, from which he transcribed his plays. Once again, though, originality differs from invention, for Shakespeare became so great by copying what he saw most exactly. Young erases all of Shakespeare's sources in order to transform Shakespeare himself into the origin.

others, however, defined genius as an exclusively masculine possibility. William Duff, who responded to Young's *Conjectures* with his own *Essay on Original Genius*, argues in his *Letters on the Intellectual and Moral Characters of Women* that genius eludes the female sex.[10] According to Christine Battersby, the concept of genius itself has historically assumed and even been quite literally defined by masculinity.[11] Battersby traces the Western concept of genius to the Romans, who associate genius with place and property, which men inherited and owned. Romans commonly represented Genius, Leo Braudy observes, "by a phallic column akin to the Greek *herm*, in which a column was topped with a human head and featured a penis, but no other physical features."[12] Genius, Battersby argues, has thus historically been a property that adheres to the male body itself, in spite of the changing constructions of the legitimate artist. Renaissance science defined female bodies as vulnerable to "vapours" that led to delusion and obscured the truth; women were thus *too* creative for genius. In the eighteenth century, genius changed from something one could have to something one could be. Male geniuses of the Romantic period appropriated the feminine position of extreme subjecthood, tendency toward madness, and excessive creativity; the emotional capacity expected of women could potentially signify genius in men. But "just when the primitive and the wild came to be valued," Battersby asserts, "women themselves were being prized precisely in so far as they were domesticated."[13]

While Battersby convincingly demonstrates that genius has historically been a property of masculinity and even physical maleness, the opulence of her evidence points to a relationship between genius and the specific (masculine) capacity to own. Romantic "geniuses," she points out, upheld their own work (as we saw in Young) as natural and organic, opposing their productions to the mechanical result of labor. It takes more than biological maleness, then, to claim genius. As Battersby observes, in Rome *genius* signified sperm, but "not simply mundane (physical) sperm; it was a seed that was ripened in the bodies of heroic male

[10] William Duff, *Letters on the Intellectual and Moral Character of Women* (1807), facsimile; intro. Gina Luria (New York: Garland, 1974), letters 3 and 17.

[11] Christine Battersby, *Gender and Genius: Toward a Feminist Aesthetics* (Bloomington: Indiana University Press, 1989).

[12] Leo Brandy, *The Frenzy of Renown: Fame and Its History* (Oxford: Oxford University Press, 1986), 108.

[13] Battersby, *Gender and Genius*, 82.

ancestors, and in the soil that has been cleared and planted by genera-tions of males. *Genius* was a sort of genetic coding that entitled a male to property, lands, rights and power over women and slaves."[14] Not *all* men, then, could possess genius, for the sperm of a male slave did not give him the right to share in this privilege. Throughout the eighteenth century, genius retains its associations with a place, a location, and thus with property. Genius signifies not only a capacity, but also a position.

Neither "original" nor "genius" are thus innocent terms in Young's *Conjectures.* Genius has been long understood to connote a subjective evaluation; the instability of originality, however, has come under scru-tiny as well. Jacques Derrida offers the most radical critique of originality as the metaphysics of presence. In Lévi-Strauss, Derrida argues, presence consists of speech, which writing records in certain cultures; writing marks the difference between two kinds of social organizations. For Derrida, however, the hierarchies whose possibility Lévi-Strauss attrib-uted to alphabetic writing have already appeared with "arche-writing," the concept of representation itself. As long as a system of representation exists, no single system creates presence any more than another. In his reading of Rousseau, Derrida notices a similar structure. For Rousseau, Derrida argues, masturbation poses the same problem as writing does in relation to speech: as an imaginary seduction, masturbation weakens the vitality of the thing itself. This problem appears in all forms of mimesis: "Since the supplementary mimesis adds *nothing,*" Derrida com-ments, "is it not useless? And if nevertheless, adding itself to the repre-sented, it is not nothing, is that imitative supplement not dangerous to the integrity of what is represented and to the original purity of nature?"[15] Rousseau must consistently contradict himself: "Imitation is therefore at the same time the life and death of art. Art and death, art and its death are comprised in the space of the *alteration* of the originary *iteration;* . . . : of repetition, reproduction, representation; or also in space as the possibility of iteration and the exit from life placed outside of itself" (209).

We find a similar problem in Young: the *Conjectures* condemns imita-tion, but at the same time cannot conceptualize art without it. Young

[14] Ibid., 57.

[15] Jacques Derrida, *Of Grammatology,* trans. Gayatri Chakravorty Spivak (Baltimore: Johns Hopkins University Press, 1974), 203. Future references are from this edition and are cited in the text.

identifies nature as the originary iteration; Shakespeare achieves his greatness by repeating it. If there were no alteration in Shakespeare's repetition, however, the imitation of Shakespeare (an author) would not differ from the imitation of nature. So either Shakespeare alters nature—one form of violation in Young—or the difference between originality and imitation, which Young describes as really two kinds of imitation, is nothing. The ambivalence toward imitation that Derrida finds in Rousseau appears just as powerfully in Young and perhaps in any attempt to distinguish originality from imitation in art. For as long as originality does not (and cannot) mean pure invention, it signifies some form of successful appropriation. Young's contention that the ancients can be original because their originary texts no longer exist makes sense only if writing is considered as a form of appropriation.

In Young's *Conjectures*, then, the legitimate author emerges as the successful appropriator rather than as the originator. To observe this, however, is not the same as observing the author's "death": Foucault wisely warns against imagining "an absolutely free state, in which fiction would be put at the disposal of everyone and would develop without passing through something like a necessary or constraining figure."[16] The celebration of the "death of the author" and the viewing of a text as "a tissue of quotations," as articulated by Roland Barthes, has been challenged by feminists.[17] For Nancy K. Miller, Foucault's apparent indifference to "who's speaking" actually functions as a mask "behind which phallocentrism hides its fictions": "What matter who's speaking? I would answer that it matters, for example, to women who have lost and still routinely lose their proper name in marriage and whose signature . . . has not been worth the paper it was written on; women for whom signature—by virtue of its power in the world of circulation—is *not* immaterial. Only those who have it can play with not having it."[18] Simi-

---

[16] Michel Foucault, "What Is an Author?" in *Textual Strategies: Perspectives in Post-Structuralist Criticism*, ed. Josué Harari (Ithaca: Cornell University Press, 1979), 159.

[17] Roland Barthes, "The Death of the Author," in *Literature in the Modern World*, ed. Dennis Walder (Oxford: Oxford University Press, 1990), 228–232. In this well-known essay, Barthes praises some contemporary writers for relinquishing the position of the controlling author; while the traditional author precedes or "fathers" the text, the modern "scriptor" is born simultaneously with the text.

[18] Nancy K. Miller, "The Text's Heroine," *Diacritics* 12 (Summer 1982), 53. Quoted by Tania Modleski, *Feminism without Women: Culture and Criticism in a "Postfeminist" Age* (New York: Routledge, 1991), 33.

larly, Tania Modleski argues that the subsequent "death of the social" must be interrogated as "another of phallocentrism's masks, likewise authorizing the 'end of woman' without consulting her."[19] Battersby agrees that "it is premature to announce the death of the female author" because "feminists have to concern themselves with what is involved in writing or creating *as a female*;"[20] further, "it is disturbing that, at the historical moment that second-wave feminism has brought to the surface a rich hidden history of female authors and artists, the very concepts of 'individuality' and 'authorship' have come under attack by an élite group of critics who draw on recent French theories of writing and language."[21] Women need to respond, she contends, by claiming the position of original genius for themselves.

But a critique of original genius, "authorship, and "individuality" does not necessarily preclude a feminist analysis. Suppose we take Foucault's question literally: what *does* it matter who is speaking? As Young's *Conjectures* inadvertently reveals, the origin of the story does not matter; what matters is *who gets to claim literary property*. Once we understand writing as appropriation, we can see "the author" as a subject position defined by the contingencies of ownership itself. Thus, a feminist analysis of the author/subject need not be a matter of life or "death." While I agree with Miller and Modleski that some poststructuralist formulations obscure gender difference, I find Battersby's solution—to claim original genius for women—unsatisfying in its necessary return to liberal individualism. Understanding the author as an appropriator, however, rejects traditional constructions of authorship but at the same time reveals the

[19] Modleski, *Feminism without Women*, 33.

[20] Battersby, *Gender and Genius*, 148. See also Sandra M. Gilbert and Susan Gubar, *The Madwoman in the Attic: The Woman Writer and the Nineteenth-Century Literary Imagination* (New Haven: Yale University Press, 1979). For studies of early modern authorship and women's social subjectivity, see Mary Ellen Lamb, *Gender and Authorship in the Sidney Circle* (Madison: University of Wisconsin Press, 1990); Ruth Perry, *The Celebrated Mary Astell: An Early English Feminist* (Chicago: University of Chicago Press, 1986); Elaine Hobby, *Virtue of Necessity: English Women's Writing, 1649–88* (Ann Arbor: University of Michigan Press, 1988); Donna Landry, *The Muses of Resistance: Laboring-Class Women's Poetry in Britain, 1739–1796* (Cambridge: Cambridge University Press, 1990).

[21] Battersby, *Gender and Genius*, 151. If these developments—poststructuralism criticism and the "discovery" of women writers—happened at the same time, couldn't the former just as likely have *enabled* the latter?

various ways in which gender, class, and other structures that define social subjectivity shape the capacity to claim property in writing.

Property

The cultural economy of literary property reinscribed seventeenth-century ideologies of material property. Even in the eighteenth century, as Susan Staves has so forcefully demonstrated, married women never fully achieved the capacity to control separate property.[22] The ironically titled *Womens Advocate* (1683), in fact, compares marriage itself to an act of enclosure and represents women *as* property:

> Matrimony is like a good hedge about a piece of Pasture; it keeps a Man from treading over my ground. Or if any Swash-buckler will be so eager after his game, as to break my Quick-set, and ride over my Corn, *a pedibus ambulando*, presently lays him by his heels for his daring presumption.
>
> Then again, a Woman is like a House; the Law gives a man a Lease of her; and he that takes a Lease of a House, is bound to keep the Tenement in repair. . . .
>
> [W]hen a man has got a woman within the Pale of Matrimony, she is then like a Mess of Porridge. And there is no man has got his dish of broth well crumm'd and season'd for his own Palate, but will be very angry if another come with his long spoon to eat it up from him. The most surly maintainer of *Liberty and Property*, in the case of Matrimony, will not allow those two words to *associate* together; for assuming all the property to himself, he will not admit of any liberty to the woman.[23]

Few texts represent women as quite so consumable or explicitly excluded from "liberty and property." Seventeenth-century writers, however, devoted much thought to this very issue: the burgeoning of plagiarism-hunting, not coincidentally, takes place in the context of crucial debates over ownership.

---

[22] Susan Staves, *Married Women's Separate Property in England, 1660–1833* (Cambridge: Harvard University Press, 1990).

[23] [M. Marsin], *The Womens Advocate; Or, Fifteen Real Comforts of Matrimony . . . Written by a Person of Quality* (London, 1683), 1, 29.

According to C. B. Macpherson, in the late seventeenth century England's status society, in which each rank remains confined to certain kinds of authoritatively regulated work, gave way to a "possessive market society," which demands the alienation of labor.[24] Joyce Oldham Appleby, however, has pointed out the complexities of this transition and challenged Macpherson's economic determinism: "The acceptance of a market in land and labor represents a crucial cultural change rather than an automatic response to the existence of a mechanism for exchanging goods."[25] Appleby observes that several areas critical to the development of a market economy "remained vulnerable to the scrutiny of moralists," including "the grain trade, the conversion of commonly held land to private property, and the lending of money for interest."[26] The reconceptualization of food as a commodity challenged the traditional perspective of the farmer as less of an owner than one working under a moral obligation to shepherd food through production. The seventeenth century, Appleby argues, saw both the emergence of food as a commodity like any other as well as vigorous debates over this transition by economists and moralists: "The very success of food production in England and the Netherlands in the seventeenth century," she asserts, "broke the vital connection between social needs and individual responsibility which had so long kept work and profit subordinated to the subsistence needs of society."[27]

Events leading up to the Glorious Revolution produced debates about authority that also reveal conflicting conceptions of property.[28] Sir Robert Filmer's treatise *Patriarcha* defended the Stuart monarchy in terms of natural authority. The king, he argued, inherits the right to rule through his direct line of descent from Adam, who ruled over Eve and their children. Filmer takes the father's rule over the rest of the family as a nonpolitical given; thus the king rules the country as a father rules the family. Only the father inhabits the position of owner, and each family

[24] C. B. Macpherson, *The Political Theory of Possessive Individualism: Hobbes to Locke* (1962; reprint Oxford: Oxford University Press, 1990).

[25] Joyce Oldham Appleby, *Economic Thought and Ideology in Seventeenth-Century England* (Princeton: Princeton University Press, 1978), 15–16.

[26] Ibid., 53.

[27] Ibid., 84, 85.

[28] For a study of the ideological conflicts of this time see Michael McKeon, *The Origins of the English Novel, 1660–1740* (Baltimore: Johns Hopkins University Press, 1987).

functions as a miniature kingdom. Though contested, Filmer's position had more than a nostalgic force when it was published in the late seventeenth century; no doubt, the persistence and significance of patriarchal thought, as Gordon J. Schochet contends, has been underestimated.[29] Filmer's political opponents provided the philosophical justification for what Macpherson calls "possessive individualism," for as individual property in land reached its limits, a greater proportion of the population became dependent on selling its labor.[30] Hobbes, Harrington, and Locke, according to Macpherson, all describe this kind of society. Schochet, however, finds in both Hobbes and Locke powerful vestiges of the very patriarchalism against which they argue. Hobbes represents the state of nature not as a group of individuals, but as a group of family units in which the father has sovereign-like power; Locke attacks Filmer's derivation of political power from patriarchal power, but does not attack fatherly authority as such.[31]

As noted, many aspects of C. B. Macpherson's arguments have been productively challenged.[32] We need not necessarily agree that the late seventeenth century had fully become a market society or that possessive individualism (as opposed to exchange, which Pocock emphasizes) best describes early capitalism in order to recognize in Macpherson's work some important insights into the formation of subject positions through narratives of property. While Macpherson never articulates the problem in these terms, his reading of Locke reveals the limits of who can inhabit the position of owner. The gendered occlusions of Filmer's traditional patriarchalism require little analysis, but both Macpherson and Carole

[29] Gordon J. Schochet, *Patriarchalism in Political Thought: The Authoritarian Family and Political Speculation and Attitudes Especially in Seventeenth-Century England* (New York: Basic Books, 1975).

[30] Macpherson, *Possessive Individualism*, 55. Future references are cited in the text.

[31] See Schochet, *Patriarchalism in Political Thought*, chaps. 12 and 13. Hobbes, however, "was unique in attempting to derive the father's power over his children from their consents" (241). Locke differed from Filmer on the family in his belief that the father's power over the children ended with their mature independence and development of reason.

[32] See, e.g., Appleby, *Economic Thought and Ideology*; James Tully, *An Approach to Political Philosophy: Locke in Context* (Cambridge: Cambridge University Press, 1993); J. G. A. Pocock, *Virtue, Commerce, and History: Essays on Political Thought and History, Chiefly in the Eighteenth Century* (Cambridge: Cambridge University Press, 1985). Tully is especially good at pointing out the limits of Macpherson's critique while retaining the best of Macpherson's insights.

Pateman offer insight into the formation of differing subject positions in liberal individualism.[33] Locke's *Two Treatises on Government* defined the right to own as natural, although limited by how much one could actually use. For Locke, appropriation consists of mixing nature with labor, which transforms the natural object. Someone who picks an apple from a tree, for example, comes to own the apple. This right may have limits—no one has the right to appropriate more than he can use—but it is apparently available to all. Macpherson shows that in spite of this declared equality of access, Locke silently assumes differences between individuals and non-individuals. Full individuality for some in Locke, Macpherson argues, "was produced only at the expense of the individuality of the others" (255–257). The capacity to reason divides the consumers from the consumed. But as Macpherson asserts: "The seventeenth-century bourgeois observer could scarcely fail to see a deep-rooted difference between the rationality of the poor and that of the men of some property. The difference was in fact a difference in their ability or willingness to order their own lives according to the bourgeois moral code. But to the bourgeois observer this appeared to be a difference in men's ability to order their lives by moral rules as such" (245–246). Locke reveals his belief that "members of the labouring class are in too low a position to be capable of a rational life" when he argues that Christianity should be reduced to a few simple articles "'that the labouring and illiterate man may comprehend'" (224). Property in oneself becomes dependent on reason, and reason dependent on class. As Macpherson points out, only by taking the alienability of a worker's labor for granted can Lockean passages such as the following escape blatant contradiction: "Thus the Grass my Horse had Bit; the Turfs my Servant has cut; and the Ore I have digg'd in any place where I have a right to them in common with others, become my *Property*, without the assignment or consent of any body. The *labour* that was mine, removing them out of the common state they were in, hath *fixed* my *Property* in them."[34] The servant no more owns the turfs he cuts than the horse owns the grass

[33] Carole Pateman, *The Sexual Contract* (Stanford: Stanford University Press, 1988). I have also relied on Ellen Pollak's fine account of the way social, cultural, and economic changes affected women in the late seventeenth century. See *The Poetics of Sexual Myth: Gender and Ideology in the Verse of Swift and Pope* (Chicago: University of Chicago Press, 1985), chap. 2.

[34] Locke, Second Treatise, sec. 28. Quoted by Macpherson, *Possessive Individualism*, 215.

26

it bites: laborers can no more own than animals. Members of the laboring class, then, implicitly defined by Locke as lacking in reason, do not fall into the category of those who can appropriate nature by adding labor.

Locke's defense of slavery further reveals that not everyone has the capacity to own even themselves. A seventeenth-century reader of Locke would most likely associate slaves with the African slave trade or possibly the traffic in American natives, although some English people were enslaved as criminals.[35] A slave, then, was either a cultural "other" to the English reader or a person who had lost rights of citizenship through a violation of the law. (It seems likely that Locke himself may have had the English trade in African slaves in mind, for he held stock in the Royal African Company and promoted its interests in the 1690s from his position at the Board of Trade.[36]) In spite of his central tenet that all people own their own bodies, Locke defends slavery with the following logic. First, an individual has the right to kill someone who infringes on his property rights, for this infringement initiates a state of war in which the conqueror has the right to kill the conquered. The conqueror, however, can choose to delay this death and enslave the conquered. Locke, however, fails to explain how this enslavement can be transferred to a third party who was never a victim of an attempted theft and thus does not necessarily possess the right to kill the slave. The master/slave relationship, as Carole Pateman points out, falls outside of civil society in Locke, stuck in a state of war.[37] Macpherson's reading of the *Two Treatises*, in which despite the claim of universal self-ownership the laboring class cannot appropriate, offers insight into Locke's contradictory representation of slavery as well. The original violent act—the state of war—parallels the laborer's irrationality, and both reveal the incapacity for self-ownership. The *Two Treatises*, then, states the universality of self-possession and the right to own, while at the same time taking for granted their contingency. For in Locke, the right of self-possession extends only to the self-possessed.

By rendering the capacity to own one's body and self contingent on reason, Locke, in spite of his explicit argument, actually represents the

[35] See David Brion Davis, *The Problem of Slavery in Western Culture* (Ithaca: Cornell University Press, 1966).

[36] Pateman, *The Sexual Contract*, 71.

[37] Ultimately, though, Pateman argues that "the limitation on the duration of the contract appears to be the only thing that divides a slave from a servant or wage labourer" (Ibid., 71).

possibility of self-possession as rare. "We are born free as we are born rational," Locke claims. Children temporarily lack self-possession and thus remain under the control of others; "Lunatics and idiots are never set free from the government of their parents."[38] Laborers and slaves, as we have seen, can appropriate only on behalf of others. Common property exists only temporarily: "As much land as a man tills, plants, improves, cultivates, and can use the product of, so much is his property. He by his labour does, as it were, enclose it from the common. . . . He that encloses land, and has a greater plenty of the conveniences of life from ten acres than he could have from a hundred left to nature, may truly be said to give ninety acres to mankind; for his labour now supplies him with provisions out of ten acres which were by the product of a hundred lying in common" (Second Treatise, sec. 32, 37, pp. 136, 139). Native Americans clearly do not have the capacity to own according to Locke's logic, for he describes America as "wild woods and uncultivated waste" (Second Treatise, sec. 37, p. 139). Thus Locke gives positive moral values to enclosure and colonization, representing them as the creation of property where none existed before. Communities, especially those failing to cultivate in Western agricultural style, do not have the capacity to own.

Finally, Locke excepts all women from full rights of self-possession and thus from the capacity to inhabit the position of owner. Even though Locke distinguishes his position on the family from that of Filmer by declaring that mothers have rights over children as well as fathers, he also argues that in a marriage the rule "naturally falls to the man's share, as the abler and the stronger" (Second Treatise, sec. 82, p.161). Both Locke and Hobbes, Carole Pateman asserts, articulated the important philosophical underpinnings of the seventeenth-century transition from what she calls "classical patriarchy" to its modern "fraternal" incarnation. While other feminists have abandoned the term "patriarchy" as anachronistic, Pateman holds that in these texts, "political right originates in sexright or conjugal right. Paternal right is only one, and not the original, dimension of patriarchal power. A man's power as a father comes after he has exercised the patriarchal right of a man (a husband) over a woman (wife)."[39] Locke opposes Filmer in his advocacy of contractual

---

[38] John Locke, *Two Treatises of Government*, ed. Thomas I. Cook (New York: Hafner Press, 1947), Second Treatise, 150.

[39] Pateman, *The Sexual Contract*, 3. Future references are cited in the text.

rights. But not everyone, Pateman observes, enters these contracts equally: "For all the classic writers (except Hobbes), a difference in rationality follows from natural sexual difference. . . . Only masculine beings are endowed with the attributes and capacities necessary to enter into contracts, the most important of which is ownership of property in the person; only men, that is to say, are 'individuals' " (5–6). Pateman points out that while seventeenth-century contractarians mobilize a rhetoric of equality, contracts between unequals necessarily establish hierarchical relationships.

Modern patriarchy subordinates women by representing masculine domination as nonpolitical. Locke disagrees with Filmer's reading of the Adam and Eve story, as Pateman shows, on the basis of the character of Adam's power, not its existence. Eve's subjection, according to Locke, "can be no other Subjection than what every Wife owes her Husband . . . [Adam's] can be only a Conjugal Power, not Political, the Power that every Husband hath to order the things of private Concernment in his Family, as Proprietor of the Goods and Lands there, and to have his Will take place before that of his wife in all things of their common Concernment; but not a Political Power of Life and Death over her, much less over anybody else."[40] For Locke, Adam dominates Eve in a pre-political state. As Pateman notes, Locke, like most contract theorists, represents marriage as retaining a "natural status even in civil society" (55). The marriage contract, then, necessarily differs from other contracts because it establishes a relationship not between two individuals, but between an individual and a natural subordinate. Women, then, as subordinates, wives, and potential wives, apparently do not own themselves. Women are themselves property, but also persons; they "are held both to possess and to lack the capacities required for contract" (60).[41] For Pateman, Locke's significant political difference from Filmer lies in his insistence on Adam's masculine, sexual authority rather than on his paternal authority. But even in Filmer, Pateman asserts, patriarchy consists of more than a father's political power over his sons: "Filmer's apparently straightforward statements obscure the foundation of patriarchal right. Sons do not spring up like mushrooms, as Filmer was quick

[40] Locke, First Treatise, 48. Quoted by Pateman, ibid., 53.
[41] See also Gayle Rubin, "The Traffic in Women: Notes on the 'Political Economy' of Sex," in *Toward an Anthropology of Women*, ed. Rayna R. Reiter (New York: Monthly Review Press, 1975), 157–210.

to remind Hobbes. If Adam was to be a father, Eve had to become a mother. In other words, *sex-right or conjugal right must necessarily precede the right of fatherhood.* The genesis of political power lies in Adam's sex-right or conjugal right, not in his fatherhood. Adam's political title is granted *before* he becomes a father" (87, emphasis in the original).

Hobbes differs from all other seventeenth-century contract theorists, Pateman argues, by representing the husband's authority as political. In the war of all against all, no one can protect themselves alone; thus, they form families. But in Hobbes, men form these families through conquest, a point underscored by the inclusion of both sons and servants as family members under the father's power. On the one hand, Hobbes insists that all individuals remain free and equal in the state of nature; on the other hand, women become subordinate to men through marriage just as children and servants become subordinate to the father through the family. Pateman shows, however, that the apparent inconsistency disappears when one recognizes Hobbes's "identification of enforced submission with voluntary agreement, . . . his assimilation of conquest and consent" (45). For example, a mother has the choice of whether to expose or nurture her child. If she decides to take care of it, the infant enters into a contract with her in which it trades submission for protection. It is easy to see in this example how in Hobbes a "contract" between unequals forms a relationship of subordination that an infant would nevertheless "willingly" enter. Less obvious, given Hobbes's assertion of a natural equality between the sexes, is why any woman would enter into a marriage contract in which husbands have domination, "because for the most part commonwealths have been erected by the fathers, not by the mothers of families." "Domestical command," Hobbes contends, "belongs to the man; and such a contract, if it be made according to the civil laws, is called matrimony."[42] Pateman concludes, "The assumption must necessarily be made that, by the time the social contract is made, all the women in the natural condition have been conquered by men and are now their subjects (servants). If any men have also been subjected and are in servitude, then they, too, will be excluded from the social contract. Only men who stand to each other as free and equal masters of 'families' will take part" (49).

As seventeenth-century philosophers re-theorize property, then, they

---

[42] Hobbes, *Leviathan* XV and *Philosophical Rudiments* IX, quoted by Pateman, *The Sexual Contract*, 48. Hobbes grants that the mother initially has power over the infant,

inscribe specific limitations on who can inhabit the position of the property-owning, contract-making, rational, self-possessing individual. For Hobbes, the ownership of language defines personhood itself:

> A Person is he, *whose words or actions are considered, either as his own, or as representing the words or actions of an other man, or of any other thing to whom they are attributed, whether Truly or by Fiction.*
>
> When they are considered his owne, then is he called a *Naturall Person*: And when they are considered as representing the words and actions of an other, then is he a *Feigned* or *Artificiall person* . . . . Of Person Artificall, some have their words and actions *Owned* by those whom they represent. And then the Person is the *Actor*; and he that owneth his words and actions, is the AUTHOR.[43]

Authorship in Hobbes consists of owning one's actions and words, but the ownership of language also defines natural personhood. Those who have no use of reason, such as "Children, Fooles, and Mad-men" cannot be authors.[44] Plagiarism and originality become such important issues in the late seventeenth century because of this close relationship between the ownership of words and personhood itself.

Plagiarism

Women writers at the time commonly expressed their own sense of a limited access to the position of full individuality. But before turning to their observations, I would like briefly to examine the different kinds of access within masculinity. For both genders, professional writing raised the suspicion of transgressive appropriation, and public spaces themselves were seen as intensifying the danger of plagiarism. Thomas Flatman reveals this anxiety in his *Poems and Songs* when he describes the kind of poet whose practice it was each night "*to digest all that he had pirated that Day, under proper Heads*":

---

but then quickly points out that if the mother is herself subordinate to a husband, then the child is under the father's power as well.

[43] Thomas Hobbes, *Leviathan*, ed. Richard Tuck (Cambridge: Cambridge University Press, 1991), chapter 16, 111–112.

[44] Ibid., 113.

I never saw but One of this Author's Compositions, and really It troubled me, because It put me in mind, how much time I had mispent in Coffee-Houses, for there was nothing in It, but what I could find a Father for There; Nay, (with a little recollection,) a man might name most of the Birds from whence he had pluckt his Feathers. Some there are that Beseech, Others that Hector their *Muses*: Some Diet their *Pegasus*, give him his Heats and Ayrings for the Course; Others that endeavor to stop up his broken wind with Medicinal Ale and Bisquet; But there for the most part are men of *Industry*; Rhiming is their proper Business, they are fain to labour hard, and use much Artifice for a poor Livelihood, I wish 'em good Trading.

Flatman follows his sneer at the property-conscious yet plagiarizing professional with an insistence upon his own amateur status:

I profess I never had design to be incorporated into the Society; my utmost End was merely for Diversion of my self and a few Friends whom I very well love: and if the question should be ask'd why these Productions are expos'd, I may truly say, I could not help it; One unlucky Copy, like a Bellweather, stole from me into the Common, and the rest of the Flock took their opporunity to leave the Enclosure.[45]

Flatman regrets his ability to "enclose" his words; further, he defines professionals by their tendency to plagiarize. Those with the greatest economic stake in writing as property come under the most suspicion for refusing to recognize proper(ty) boundaries. Flatman, then, does not experience the new forms of authorship as the professional demand for the protection of literary property; rather, he represents professionals themselves as violators, as unable truly to inhabit the position of owner. The coffee house, which provided a rare location for male cross-class socialization and played a central role in defining a "public" sphere, becomes in Flatman the place where true wits risk having their feathers plucked by professionals and where professionals all pluck each other's.[46]

No other work, however, provides such an extensive catalog of plagia-

[45] Thomas Flatman, "To the Reader," Preface to *Poems and Songs* (London, 1686). I thank Kathy King for calling this passage to my attention.

[46] See Jürgen Habermas, *The Structural Transformation of the Public Sphere: An Inquiry into a Category of Bourgeois Society*, trans. Thomas Burger (Cambridge: MIT Press, 1989).

rists as does Gerard Langbaine's *Account of the English Dramatic Poets*, first published in an earlier version, in apparent ridicule of the project, as *Momus Triumphans, Or, the Plagiaries of the English Stage.* Like the coffee house, the public theater threatens to confuse or dissolve the boundaries of literary property. Langbaine's identification of these plagiarists, however, has more to do with the subject positions of the authors and the cultural location of their plays than with the amount of writing repeated: women, male professionals, and those understood to please popular rather than elite audiences emerge as the most egregious plagiarists. For overlapping personal and ideological reasons, Langbaine leveled his most dogged attack against Dryden, to whose case I will return. John Crowne, however, earns the title of plagiarist for his intertextuality and his professionalism (although Langbaine may have held his friendship with Dryden against him as well).[47] Of Crowne's *Country Wit*, Langbaine writes that he "must take the freedome to tell our English Author, that part of the Language, as well as the Plot is stollen from [Molière]." Crowne, the critic contends, could not fulfill his own requirement for adaptation that "all Foreign Coin must be melted down, and receive a new Stamp, if not addition of Mettal, before it will pass currant in *England*, and be judged *Sterling.*"[48] Of Crowne's *Darius of Persia*, Langbaine comments that the author "has copyed, or at least imitated, *Euripides*" (95). Finally, Langbaine complains that Crowne's *Henry VI* "is (if I mistake not) very much borrow'd from the Second Part of *Shakespear's Henry the Sixth*; tho' Mr. *Crown* with a little too much assurance affirms, that he has no Title to the Fortieth part of it" (96). Crowne depended for his living on money from writing and the occasional "Princely bounty of K. *Charles.*" Uncomfortable with his own professional status, Crowne insisted on his birth to a family of property and complained bitterly of having been cheated out of his inheritance: "The Favour, or rather Authority, which a mighty Neighbouring Kingdom, had in our Court some years ago, got my Inheritance, which, tho' it lay in the Desarts of

---

[47] For a discussion of the enmity between Dryden and Langbaine, see James Anderson Winn, *John Dryden and His World* (New Haven: Yale University Press, 1987), 456, 460–461.

[48] Gerard Langbaine, *An Account of the English Dramatick Poets* (1691), facsimile (New York: Garland, 1973), 94. Langbaine quotes from Crowne's Epistle to the *Destruction of Jerusalem.* Future references to Langbaine's *Account* are from this edition and are cited in the text.

America, would have enabled me (if I cou'd have kept it) to have liv'd at my ease."[49] Noting this unfortunate turn of events in the preface to a play, Crowne indirectly apologizes for his dependence on the third night and longs for "ease."

Thomas D'Urfey, another professional, also earns Langbaine's scorn as a plagiarist: "He is accounted by some for an Admirable Poet, but it is by those who are not acquainted much with Authors, and therefore are deceiv'd by Appearances, taking that for his own Wit, which he only borrows from Others: for Mr. *Durfey* like the *Cuckow*, makes it his business to suck other Birds Eggs" (179). The less educated the audience, the more easily a plagiarist can escape notice. D'Urfey not only wrote for money, but also had the reputation of writing for the gallery: one detractor calls his writing "mere *Billings-gate* Discourse" and "more fit for *Bartholomew Fair*, than the *Theatre*."[50] "Patching" becomes Langbaine's favorite trope for D'Urfey's composition: in his *Common-wealth of Women*, "what is either alter'd or added may be as easily discern'd from the Original, as Patches on a Coat from the main Piece"; similarly, *Madam Fickle* is "patcht up from several other Comedies" (180, 182). In his comments on the *Fool's Preferment*, Langbaine not only insists on D'Urfey's humble rank, but he also accuses him of attempting to reach beyond its boundaries. D'Urfey dedicated the play "to the Honourable *Charles* Lord *Morpeth*, with this familiar Title, *My Dear Lord*, and subscrib'd like a Person of Quality, only with his Sir-name *D'urfey*" (180–181). Langbaine *parallels* this violation of class propriety with D'Urfey's violation of literary property: "Nor is his Epistle less presumptuous, where he arrogates to himself a Play, which was writ by another, and owns only a hint from an old Comedy of *Fletcher's*, when the whole Play is in a manner transcrib'd from the *Noble Gentleman*" (181). Even the first paragraph of the dedica-

[49] John Crowne, from the dedications to *The English Friar* (London, 1690) and *Caligula* (London, 1698).

[50] *Poeta Infamis: or, a Poet not worth Hanging* (London, 1692), 4, 12, quoted by Michael Dobson, *The Making of the National Poet: Shakespeare, Adaptation and Authorship, 1660–1769* (Oxford: Clarendon Press, 1992). Dobson astutely points out that D'Urfey "is only one of the more conspicuous victims of what Peter Stallybrass and Allon White have identified as a general movement within early eighteenth-century culture to stigmatize and repudiate the expressions of earlier popular culture" (102). Dr. Kenrick also accuses D'Urfey of plagiarism in his "New Session of Poets," in *The Grove. Or, A Collection of Original Poems and Translations* (London, 1721), 131: "*Tom Durfey* first endeavour'd at the Bays, / With twice five hundred Songs, and twenty Plays. / The dangling Doggrel hung like Pantaloons, / Set by himself to other People's Tunes."

tion, Langbaine complains, is borrowed from the earl of Rochester's translation of Horace's Tenth Satire. In another author, such repetition might be understood as a witty reference. The comments on D'Urfey resemble an expanded version of the critic's terse evaluation of Thomas Thomson: "Another Author of the meanest Rank, and a great Plagiary" (503). Stated this plainly, the second judgment appears to follow from the first.

Edward Ravenscroft, another playwright whom Langbaine scorns, occupies a slightly different position. Langbaine acknowledges Ravenscroft "a Gentleman," but nevertheless declares he is "One who with the Vulgar passes for a Writer" (417). The attack on Ravenscroft has less to do with his own position (he does not occupy the meanest rank) than it has to do with the cultural location of his plays, which, like D'Urfey's, smack of Bartholomew Fair in Langbaine's opinion. Langbaine extends this association with the "vulgar" in his description of Ravenscroft's writing: "Tho' he would be thought to imitate the *Silk worm*, that spins its Web from its own Bowels; yet I shall make him appear like the *Leech* that lives upon the Blood of Men, drawn from the Gums; and when he is rubb'd with Salt, spues it up again" (417–418). Langbaine excludes Ravenscroft from those who might associate their texts with the luxurious commodity of silk, and instead compares his writing with a bleeding, vomiting, cannibalistic blood-sucking body. As Peter Stallybrass and Allon White demonstrate, late seventeenth-century England distinguished high culture from "popular" culture through precisely this kind of opposition between refinement (silk) and the "grotesque body."[51]

Not surprisingly, Langbaine represents Ravenscroft as an egregious plagiarist in nearly all his entries on the plays. He calls *The London Cuckolds* "the most diverting of any that he has writ," though "patcht up from several Novels" (421). Of *Scaramouch a Philosopher*, Langbaine declares that Ravenscroft cannot claim "any Part of a Scene as the Genuine Offspring of his own Brain," and *Mamamouchi* is simply "a whole Play borrow'd" (422). When he comes to Ravenscoft's adaptation of Shakespeare's *Titus Andronicus*, he reminds readers of the author's own comments on plagiarism and profit: "In [Ravenscroft's] Preface to the Reader, he says, *That he thinks it a greater theft to rob the Dead of their Praise, than the Living of their Money*: Whether his Practice agree with his

---

[51] Peter Stallybrass and Allon White, *The Politics and Poetics of Transgression* (Ithaca: Cornell University Press, 1986).

Protestation, I leave to the Comparison of his Works, with those of *Molliere*" (464). Langbaine then quotes Shadwell, who characterizes Ravenscroft as one of the writers who "make a common practice of stealing other Men's Wit" (464).

It might be objected here that Ravenscroft *did* adapt Shakespeare's play and helped himself to Molière as well. This is indisputable. But might not the same charge—that the plays were patched together from several novels—be made against Shakespeare as well? No critic seriously raises this point until Charlotte Lennox in *Shakespear Illustrated* (1753), a work that accuses Shakespeare of copying and sometimes diminishing stories from the feminized genre of romance.[52] Comparing Langbaine's comments on Ravenscroft's adaptation to his comments on other, similar acts of intertextuality shows how literary property helps him construct separate cultural spheres. Regarding Sir William Davenant's *Law against Lovers*, a tragicomedy from *Measure for Measure* and *Much Ado about Nothing*, Langbaine writes, "Tho' not only the Characters, but the Language of the whole Play almost, be borrow'd from *Shakespear*: yet where the Language is rough or obsolete, our Author has taken care to polish it" (108).[53] Plagiarism in one writer constitutes improvement of an old play in another. Davenant's status clearly shapes this judgment: Langbaine does not fail to report that Davenant was "Poet *Laureate* to Two Kings" and that his widow dedicated Davenant's posthumous *Works* to "the late King *James*" (106–107). Langbaine further distinguishes Davenant by the audience at his masques: *Temple of Love* was "presented by the Queens Majesty, [Wife to King *Charles* the First] and her Ladies at *Whitehall*" and *Triumphs of the Prince D'Amour* was "presented by his Highness at his Pallace in the *Middle-Temple*" (110–111). He notes Hobbes's approval of *Gondibert* and that "the first and second Books were usher'd into the world, by the Pens of two of our best Poets: *viz.* Mr. *Waller*, and Mr. *Cowley*" (112).[54] Davenant's privilege comes partly from the cultural location of

[52] See Margaret Anne Doody, "Shakespeare's Novels: Charlotte Lennox Illustrated," *Studies in the Novel* 19 (Fall 1987): 296–310.

[53] Langbaine here articulates a widespread critical ideal that late seventeenth-century authors should improve the drama of the past as well as language itself. For the philosophical context of this ideal, see James Thompson, *Language in Wycherley's Plays: Seventeenth-Century Language Theory and Drama* (Tuscaloosa: University of Alabama Press, 1984).

[54] As a point of comparison, Langbaine reprints a short satire that attempts to locate Davenant in the lower stratum of authorship by associating him with the lower

his writing itself, which in turn empowers Davenant to become admirable for the same kind of project that reveals Ravenscroft as a plagiarist.[55]

In Langbaine's catalog, elite amateurs and well-patronized authors generally have a greater entitlement to literary property than do ordinary professionals. This presents a problem to Langbaine when he wishes to praise but cannot deny obvious instances of intertextuality. Of Sir Charles Sedley's *Mulberry Garden*, Langbaine writes that he "dare not say, that the Character of Sir *John Everyoung*, and Sir *Samuel Fore-cast*, are Copies of *Sganarelle* and *Ariste*, in *Molliere's L'Escole des Maris*; but I may say, that there is some Resemblance: tho' whoever understands both Languages, will readily, and with Justice give our *English* Wit the preference: and Sir *Charles* is not to learn to Copy Nature from the *French*" (487). Langbaine understands Sedley, whom he introduces as "A Gentleman whose Name speaks a greater *Panegyrick*, than I am able to express," as being entitled to literary property. Similarly, Sir George Etherege, "A Gentleman sufficiently eminent in the Town for his Wit and Parts" (186), transgresses no boundaries. (Langbaine does observe a song Etherege translated for *Man of Mode*, but does not accuse Etherege of stealing.) Unlike other playwrights who take their characters from previous plays, Etherege writes "Characters as well drawn to the Life, as any Play that has been Acted since the Restauration" (187). He wishes, in fact, for more plays from this "great Master," "which would put a stop to the crude and undigested Plays, which for want of better, cumber the Stage" (187–188). We may share Langbaine's admiration of Etherege, but be puzzled by his failure to identify any sources.

Women playwrights have different entitlements in Langbaine as well, although their capacity to own literary property cannot be understood outside of class difference and distinctions between professionals and amateurs. Aphra Behn's plagiarism, in fact, is for Langbaine a product of her professionalism. He praises Behn insofar as "her Comedies have had the good fortune to please," although "it must be confest that she

---

stratum of the body: in "The Author upon Himself," the fictional Davenant swears, "*Then no more I'll dabble, nor pump Fancy dry, / To compose a Fable, / Shall make* Will. Crofts *to cry, / O gentle Knight, / Thou writ'st to them that shite*" (113). He dismisses these and "other Railleries" as "trifles" (114).

[55] While Langbaine understands Davenant as a noble improver, Richard Flecknoe represents him as a profiteer and thus a violator of literary property. In Flecknoe's satire, *Sir William Davenant's Voyage to the Other World* (London, 1668), Davenant confesses that he only "studies to get Money" (7).

has borrow'd very much, not only from her own Country Men, but likewise from the French Poets: yet it may be said in her behalf, that she has often been forc'd to it through hast: and has borrow'd from others Stores, rather of Choice than for want of a f[u]nd of Wit of her own: it having been formerly her unhappiness to be necessitated to write for Bread" (17–18). Langbaine nevertheless argues that Behn often did improve her sources, and that if "her *Sex* may plead in her behalf, I doubt not but she will be allowed equal with several of our Poets her Contemporaries" (18). His comments on her individual plays, however, repeatedly accuse Behn of theft even though he only "condemn[s] this ingenious Authoress" (21) for outright plagiarism in the case of *The Rover*. Langbaine may not attack Behn with the vitriolic abandon that he reserves for Dryden, but he clearly considers her intertextuality illegitimate.

Like Behn, the duchess of Newcastle earns mixed praise, although none of her plays come under suspicion for plagiarism. Langbaine, however, defines the duchess in terms of her aristocratic husband: he calls her biography of the duke "the Crown of her Labours" (394) and introduces her as "a fit Consort for so Great a Wit" (390). Langbaine accepts and repeats Cavendish's own claims to originality, but at the expense of other women: "I know there are some that have but a mean Opinion of her Plays; but if it be consider'd that both the Language and Plots of them are all her own: I think she ought with Justice to be preferr'd to others of her Sex, which have built their Fame on other People's Foundations: sure I am, that whoever will consider well the several Epistles before her Books, and the General Prologue to all her Plays, if he have any spark of Generosity, or Good Breeding, will be favourable in his Censure" (391). Thus Langbaine praises the Duchess as the *only* woman who is *not* a plagiarist, revealing his assumption that women necessarily plagiarize when they write. Further, Langbaine takes the opportunity to demonstrate his own "good breeding" by his appreciation of this aristocratic playwright.

Langbaine was not alone in representing female authorship as necessarily plagiaristic. *The Triumphs of Female Wit, in Some Pindarick Odes; Or, the Emulation* (1683) brings together many elements of seventeenth-century debates over women's writing and capacity to own literary property. In the preface "to the Masculine Sex," "a Young Lady" uses metaphors of appropriation, expecting to find "my Appearance in behalf of injur'd Females, condemned not only as immodest and unfashionable, but as unnatural and unreasonable also; it being the common experienc'd Policy of Usurpers in Wit or Government, to overthrow the Justness of a Claimer's Title with Aspersions of Incapacity or Weakness." In *The Emulation* itself, the Young Lady similarly represents women's authorship as directly appropriative from masculine writing, but nevertheless seductive in its aims:

> But we are peaceful and will not repine,
> They still may keep their Bays as well as Wine.
> We've now no *Amazonian* Hearts,
> They need not therefore guard their *Magazine* of *Arts.*
> We will not on their treasure seize,
> A part of it sufficiently will please:
> We'll only so much Knowledge have
> As may assist us to enslave
> Those Passions which we find
> Too potent for the Mind.
> 'Tis o're them only we desire to reign,
> And we no nobler, braver Conquest wish to gain.[56]

The Young Lady nevertheless goes on to plead for women's access to learning as a strategy for increasing virtue.

Yet Mr. H., who responds in the same pamphlet, sees an urgent need for men to guard their "magazine of arts." In fact, he represents female authorship as necessarily plagiaristic:

> Stand valiant she, a Parley I desire;
> Whence had you this Poetick Fire?
> I fear, *Prometheus*-like, y'have stole
> A Spark design'd to form a manly Soul.
> Forbear, bold Nymph, thus to aspire,
> You needs must know, ingenious Dame,
> 'Twas from *Jove*'s Brain alone *Minerva* came. (7)

Later in the poem, Mr. H returns again to a representation of women's writing and poetic inspiration as stolen from men:

[56] *The Triumphs of Female Wit, in Some Pindarick Odes; Or, the Emulation* (London, 1683), 3. Future references are cited in the text.

'Tis not that Men insult or would enslave
Your Sex, that they engross *Apollo*'s mines;
For those whom you have rob'd of all their Store,
Than thus to envy them their toil and pains,
To gain some part of what they had before.
No, let 'em digg and delve, what need you care,
'Tis too hard labour for the fair.
And when the dross is purg'd and gone,
'Tis not for our selves alone
That we such tedious labour take,
Next to our selves, 'tis for your sake.
To our fair Sex we willingly commit
Our Golden Wisdom and our Silver Wit. (8)

Mr. H promises the male willingness to continue the hard labor of poetry with only the hope that the ladies will accept their efforts as a gift rather than steal text for themselves.

Women writers were themselves acutely aware of their limited entitlement to literary property and their gendered vulnerability to charges of plagiarism.[57] In a letter to Mr. Burnet (1704), Catherine Trotter defends Lady Masham against such an accusation. Trotter insists that Burnet criticized Lady Masham because he did not believe a woman could write so well: "I wonder you should suspect any other hand than her own in it. It is not to be doubted, that women are as capable of penetrating into the grounds of things, and reasoning justly, as men are, who certainly have no advantage of us, but in their opportunities of knowledge."[58] After demonstrating Lady Masham's access to this knowledge, Trotter remarks on women's particular vulnerability to the charge of plagiarism: "I see no reason to suspect a woman of [Lady Masham's] character would pretend to write any thing, that was not entirely her own. I pray be more equitable to her sex, than the generality of yours are; who, when any thing is written by a woman, that they cannot deny their

---

[57] See Janet Todd, *The Sign of Angellica: Women, Writing, Fiction, 1660–1800* (New York: Columbia University Press, 1989), intro. and chap. 1. For related challenges faced by women writers and their strategies for overcoming them, see Hobby, *Virtue of Necessity*. For a fine study of misogyny in general during this period, see Felicity A. Nussbaum, *The Brink of All We Hate: English Satires on Women, 1660–1750* (Lexington: University of Kentucky Press, 1984).

[58] *The Works of Mrs. Catherine* [Trotter] *Cockburn, Theological, Moral, Dramatic, and Poetical*, ed. Thomas Birch, 2 vols. (London, 1751), 2:190. Burnet is probably George.

approbation to, are sure to rob us of that glory of it, by concluding 'tis not her own; or at least, that she had some assistance, which has been said in many instances to my knowledge unjustly."[59] In Trotter's reconfiguration, the men become the thieves, stealing glory from women by denying them ownership of literary property. Similar charges of plagiarism so distressed Anne Killigrew that she devoted an entire poem to refuting them. Having taken the risk to publish, she laments that "Like *Esops* Painted Jay I seem'd to all,/Adorn'd in Plumes, I not my own could call." Killigrew nevertheless insists that

> Th'Envious Age, only to Me alone,
> Will not allow, what I do write, my Own,
> But let 'em Rage, and 'gainst a Maide Conspire,
> Do Deathless Numbers from my Tuneful Lyre
> Do ever flo; so *Phebus* I by thee
> Divinely Inspired and possest may be;
> I willingly accept *Cassandras* Fate,
> To speak the Truth, although believ'd too late.[60]

Killigrew refuses the charge of plagiarism, but embraces the position of Cassandra, the woman whose wise words fall uselessly on disbelieving ears. The charge must have been frequent, for Dryden seems to refer to such a reputation in his elegy: "Such Noble Vigour did her Verse adorn,/That it seem'd borrow'd, where 'twas only born."[61]

The stigma against women's publishing, while differing from the problem of adaptation and appropriation, nevertheless reveals the greater threat in women's *public* ownership of literary property.[62] Perhaps

[59] Ibid.

[60] Anne Killigrew, "*Upon the saying that my VERSES were made by another*," in *Poems* (London, 1686), 44.

[61] John Dryden, "To the Pious Memory of the Accomplisht Young Lady Mrs. Anne Killigrew," in Killigrew, *Poems.*

[62] Feminist scholars have explored this issue extensively. See, for example, Todd, *The Sign of Angellica*; Patricia Parker, *Literary Fat Ladies: Rhetoric, Gender, Property* (London: Methuen, 1987); Ruth Perry, *The Celebrated Mary Astell: An Early English Feminist* (Chicago: University of Chicago Press, 1986); Angeline Goreau, *Reconstructing Aphra*; Lamb, *Gender and Authorship in the Sidney Circle.* Other women who explain or apologize for their forays into print include, for example, Rachael Speght (*Mortalities Memorandum*), the duchess of Newcastle (many of her prefaces), and Lady Mary Wroth (*Urania*). Parker writes extensively and powerfully about the prohibitions against women as speakers in the Renaissance. Similar suspicions persist in the late

most famously, Katherine Philips in her *Letters from Orinda to Poliarchus* vehemently denies that she ever intended any of her writing for the press. The association of literary modesty with sexual modesty for women accumulated such force that women's apologies for print become more the rule (that is, after not publishing at all) than the exception. Print-shyness, in fact, becomes for William Walsh a key argument against "Misogynes." This defender of women points out that the world has only come to know the writings of a few ladies whose works have fallen accidentally to the public. The dearth of women writers thus evidences virtue rather than lack of wit, for women's "Modesty too often hinders 'em from making their Vertues known; That they are not of those eternal Scriblers who are continually plagueing the World with their Works; and that it is not the Vanity of Getting a Name, which several of the greatest men of the World have own'd to be the Cause of their writing, that is the Cause of the Womens."[63] One of this defender's highest praises of women consists in his gratitude that most of them spare the world from their writing. Although Philips vehemently protests the entrance of her private poems into the public sphere of print, she also wrote once for the stage. Again, however, Philips guards against potential accusations of usurpation by positioning herself as a translator who remains purely faithful in the service of the original play. "I cannot but be supriz'd," she writes of other translators, "at the great Liberty they have taken in adding, omitting and altering the Original as they please themselves: This I take to be a Liberty not pardonable in Translators, and unbecoming the Modesty of that Attempt."[64] As a playwright, Philips finds safety in the modest position of translator, a simultaneous claiming and disclaiming of authorship.

Authority

The proliferation of charges of and defenses against plagiarism suggests the extent to which property had become significant in literary authority.

---

seventeenth century. See, for example, the anonymous *Poor Robin's True Character of a Scold: Or, the Shrews Looking-Glass* (London, 1678) and *Psittacorum Regio. The Land of Parrots: or, the She-lands. By one of the late most reputed wits* (London, 1668).

[63] [William Walsh], *A Dialogue Concerning Women, Being a Defence of the Sex. Written to Eugenia* (London, 1691), 97–98.

[64] Katherine Philips, *Letters from Orinda to Poliarchus* (London, 1705), 179; letter dated September 17, 1663.

Playwrights who self-consciously adapted works from the past, in fact, commonly relied on tropes of Lockean appropriation to underscore the legitimacy of their projects. The very efforts of these writers to justify their adaptations attest to the ambiguous status of literary property at this time: they cannot simply, like their Elizabethan precursors, freely borrow from the past, but nor do they hesitate to appropriate.[65] Commonly, dramatists represent earlier and foreign plays as the raw material that the new writer must refine into a finished product. Adapters of Shakespeare in particular found this trope attractive, contributing to and benefiting from the representation of Shakespeare's plays as, in Michael Dobson's words, "virtually unmediated expressions of Nature."[66] John Crowne, for example, compares Shakespeare to produce:

> To day we bring old gather'd Herbs, 'tis true,
> But such as in sweet *Shakespears* Garden grew
> And all his Plants immortal you esteem,
> Your Mouthes are never out of taste with him.[67]

Crowne represents his own efforts as the transformation of nature into art. Although Shakespeare is "generally very delightful, he is not so always ... Paradise was never more pleasant than some parts of [Shakespeare's writing], nor *Ireland* and *Greenland* colder, and more uninhabitable then others. And I have undertaken to cultivate on the most barren Places in it. The Trees are all Shrubs, and Men Pigmies, nothing has any Spirit, or shape ... I have been more bold." Flecknoe describes Shakespeare most simply: "'Twas a fine Garden, but it wanted weeding."[68] Yet Flecknoe also represents his revision of Molière as a horticultural project: "I have not only done like one who makes a posie out of divers flowers in which he has nothing of his own, (besides the collection, and ordering of them) but like the *Bee*, have extracted the spirit of them into a certain

---

[65] See my "(Re)Writing Lear: Literary Property and Dramatic Authorship," in *Early Modern Conceptions of Property,* ed. John Brewer and Susan Staves (London: Routledge, 1995), 323–338.

[66] Dobson, *The Making of the National Poet,* 31–32.

[67] John Crown[e], *Henry the Sixth, The First Part. With the Murder of Humphrey Duke of Glocester* (London, 1681), prologue.

[68] Richard Flecknoe, *A Short Discourse on the English Stage* (1664), facsimile, intro. Peter Davison (New York: Johnson Reprint Corp., 1972), 3–4.

Quintessence of mine own."[69] Edward Ravenscroft emphasizes the crudity of Shakespeare's plays to call attention to the extent of his efforts and thus his foreclosure on Shakespearean property. Of Shakespeare's *Titus Andronicus,* Ravenscroft writes, " 'Tis the most incorrect and undigested piece in all his Works; It seems rather a heap of Rubbish then a Structure. —However as if some great Building had been design'd, in the removal we found many Large and Square Stones both usefull and Ornamental to the Fabrick, as now Modell'd: Compare the Old Play with this, you'll find that none in all that Authors Works ever receiv'd greater Alterations or Additions. . . . The Success answer'd the Labour."[70] A poem praising Dryden's operatic adaptation of *Paradise Lost* represents the laureate's achievement as the refinement of a different kind of property:

> He [Milton] first beheld the beauteous rustick Maid,
> And to a place of strength the prize convey'd;
> You took her thence, to Court this Virgin brought
> Drest her with gemms, new weav'd her hardspun thought
> And softest language, sweetest manners taught,
> Till from a Comet she a Star did rise,
> Not to affright, but please our wondring eyes.[71]

Just as the virginal fields of Shakespeare and Fletcher await enclosure and cultivation, so the maid immortalized by Milton serves as raw material awaiting courtly education. The woman and the text remain interchangeable in their potential for appropriation and refinement.

John Dryden, as David Bruce Kramer has argued, conceived of appropriation itself as a masculine, often sexual act.[72] While a model of Lockean

---

[69] Richard Flecknoe, *The Damoiselles a La Mode. A Comedy* (London, 1667). According to the preface, this play was printed before it was acted.

[70] Edward Ravenscroft, *Titus Andronicus, or the Rape of Lavinia. Acted at the Theatre Royall, A Tragedy. Alter'd from Mr. Shakespeares Works* (London, 1687). Quotation from a preface "To the Reader." The fact that Ravenscroft's message about literary property is addressed to a reader rather than an audience suggests that print made this issue more pressing.

[71] Nat[haniel] Lee, "To Mr. DRYDEN on his POEM of PARADICE." Preface to *The State of Innocence and Fall of Man: An Opera Written in Heroique Verse by Mr. Dryden* (London, 1677).

[72] David Bruce Kramer, *The Imperial Dryden: The Poetics of Appropriation in Seventeenth-Century England* (Athens: University of Georgia Press, 1994). Kramer connects this appropriative masculinity to Dryden's imperialism: "In Dryden, the imperial urge is always gendered, always male" (94).

appropriation (the addition of labor to nature) becomes prominent in the discourse of literary authority, a classical patriarchal trope of authorship as a form of masculine inheritance not only persists from earlier periods, but also becomes particularly powerful for some drama-tists at the same time that classical patriarchy itself was losing much of its political force. The figure of inheritance permeates Dryden's work.[73] *MacFlecknoe* provides the best example in the nondramatic poetry: Dry-den attacks his rival by placing him in a genealogical line of illegitimate poets, insinuating that Shadwell's claim to filiation with Ben Jonson more legitimately belongs to Dryden himself. Father Flecknoe declares his own kinship with Shadwell: "Thou art my blood, where *Johnson* has no part;/ What share have we in Nature or in Art?" When Flecknoe falls through a trap door at the end of the poem, "The Mantle fell to the young Prophet's part,/ With double portion of his Father's Art."[74] Shadwell, according to Dryden, rightly belongs to a poetic family of plagiarists: "When did his [Jonson's] Muse from *Fletcher* scenes purloin,/ As thou whole *Eth'ridg* dost transfuse to thine?" Those in Shadwell's clan can make no claim to the legitimate ownership of literary property.

Absalom and Achitophel demonstrates that Dryden was concerned about the problem of legitimate succession for kings as well as for poets. The force of "Absalom," Christopher Ricks argues, "lies in the congruity between [its] political principles and its literary principles and practice, since the legitimate use of literary allusion . . . is itself a matter of a principled literary succession, an inheritance neither grudgingly with-held . . . nor irresponsibly squandered."[75] Ricks further attributes Dry-den's concern with literary succession to his personal dependence on and support of Charles II. As in these two poems, many of Dryden's claims to authority as a dramatist also support Tory politics by locating legitimacy in proper succession. Further, his positioning of Jonson (and elsewhere Shakespeare) as an ancestor from whom he inherits resonates

---

[73] Christopher Ricks, "Allusion: The Poet as Heir," in *Studies in the Eighteenth Century III*, ed. R. F. Brissenden and J. C. Eade (Toronto: University of Toronto Press, 1976), 209–240. See also Alan Roper, *Dryden's Poetic Kingdoms* (London: Routledge and Kegan Paul, 1965); David Bywaters, *Dryden in Revolutionary England* (Berkeley: University of California Press, 1991); Kramer, *The Imperial Dryden*.

[74] *The Works of John Dryden*, ed. Edward Niles Hooker, H. T. Swedenberg, Jr., et. al., 20 vols (Berkeley: University of California Press, 1955–1990), 2:59. All quotations from *MacFlecknoe* are from this edition.

[75] Ricks, "Allusion," 219.

with the desire to create an unbroken line of succession from the pre-commonwealth world and mend the historical rupture of the years between.

Nevertheless, the trope of poetic genealogy attracted broader interest than Dryden's particular vision of kingship, association with the court, or Tory politics, and thus articulated masculine authority itself. "The Tory-Poets: a Satyr" (1682), attributed to Thomas Shadwell, invokes a similar trope of genealogy yet wishes for poetry "Free from those painted Cares, that do attend a Court."[76] If Ben Jonson could witness what passes for poetry these days, Shadwell contends, he would "try to lash the Ideots into Sence" (5:285). Just as Dryden represents Shadwell as an illegitimate successor, so the anti-Tory poet disinherits Dryden:

> *Spencers* old bones about do toss and turn
> With Indignation kicks his rusty Urn.
> When by great *Cowley*'s Tomb the Ladies walk
> And of the modern Poesie do talk,
> His stately Urn doth bow its drooping Head,
> And modest blushes ore the Marble spread,
> As if asham'd of his Posterity,
> As base, degenerate, sottish Progeny. (5:285–286)

Not only have these Tory poets disgraced literary ancestors, but they have found in *women* their most sympathetic audience. Shadwell attacks Dryden's claim to succession in the same breath that he attacks him as a plagiarist:

> Thou call'st thy self, and Fools call thee, in Rime,
> The goodly *Prince of Poets*, of thy time;
> And Sov'raign power thou dost usurp, *John Bayes*
> And from all *Poets* thou a Text does raise.
> Thou plunder'st all, t'advance thy mighty Name,
> Look'st big, and triumph'st with thy borrow'd fame.
> But art (while swelling thus thou think'st th'art Chief)
> *A servile Imitator and a Thief.*[77]

[76] *The Complete Works of Thomas Shadwell*, ed. Montague Summers, 5 vols. (London: Fortune Press, 1927), 5:287. Future references are from this edition and are cited in the text.

[77] "The Medal of Johns Bayes" (1682), in *Complete Works of Thomas Shadwell*, 5:254.

Dryden places Shadwell in succession to Flecknoe because, like his Tory
rival, Shadwell *claimed* a position as heir to Jonson. In prefacing *The
Sullen Lovers,* Shadwell announces that he had "endeavour'd to represent
variety of Humours . . . which was the practice of *Ben Johnson,* whom I
think all Dramatick *Poets* ought to imitate, though none are like to come
near" (1:11); elsewhere he insists that "I had rather be Author of one
Scene of Comedy, like some of *Ben. Johnson's,* then of all the best Plays
of this kind that have been, or ever shall be written."[78] So while the
model of succession might have supported Tory politics for Dryden, it
also articulated a more broadly based claim to masculine literary authority that depended upon a patriarchal conception of property rather than
a specific allegiance to the Stuart monarchy. Dryden, in fact, could be
quite precise about poetic families: "Milton was the poetical son of
Spencer, and Mr. Waller of Fairfax; for we have our lineal descents
and clans, as well as other families."[79] Whereas *MacFlecknoe* describes
inheritance through dullness, this comment suggests a positive male
parthenogenetic reproduction of poets.

In the trope of poetic genealogy, the privilege of ownership adheres
to the male body, and Dryden calls attention several times to the physical
inferiority of his rival. He comments early in *MacFlecknoe* that Shadwell's
"goodly Fabrick fills the eyes," which stands "Thoughtless as Monarch
Oakes, that shade the plain/ And, spread in solemn state, supinely reign"
(2:54). In claiming kinship to Ben Jonson, Shadwell should not "let thy
mountain belly make pretence/ Of likeness; thine's a tympany of sense./
A tun of Man in thy Large build is writ,/ But sure thou'rt but a Kilderkin

---

[78] Ibid., 1:11; preface to *Psyche,* 2:279.

[79] Preface to *The Fables,* in *Dryden: Poetry, Drama, and Prose,* ed. David Zesmer (New
York: Bantam Books, 1967), 450. Dryden's investment in the trope of poetic genealogy
is more extensive in his work than is possible or necessary to record here. See also,
for example, his poem "To Congreve," in which he elects Congreve as his heir. Upon
Dryden's death, Dr. Kenrick evaluated contemporary poets on the basis of who could
qualify as Dryden's heir:

> *Apollo,* who from High beheld their Jars,
> And all the tuneful Tribe at Civil Wars,
> Upon a Ray of his own Light slid down,
> To find amongst the Crowd some wond'rous *One,*
> Who might the sacred Wreath deserve to wear,
> And justly stand departed *Dryden's* Heir.

"New Session of Poets. Occassion'd by the Death of Mr. JOHN DRYDEN," in *The
Grove. Or, A Collection of Original Poets and Translations* (London, 1721), 130.

of wit" (2:59). The representation of Shadwell's texts as "Martyrs of Pies, and Reliques of the Bum" as well as the repetition of "Sh––," as in "loads of *Sh*–– almost choakt the way" (2:56–57), associates Shadwell with the "grotesque" authorial body used to distinguish writers of high culture from writers of popular culture.[80] But Dryden and Shadwell struggle over a *gendered* authorial body: it is from Shadwell's "Loyns" that "recorded *Psyche* sprung" (2:57).

While Dryden associates Shadwell with an inferior form of masculinity, Shadwell excludes his detractors from masculinity altogether. In his dedication to the duke of Newcastle in *The Virtuoso*, he reports that the play has no enemies "but some Women, and some Men of Feminine understanding, who like slight Plays onely, that represent a little tattle sort of Conversation, like their own; but true Humour is not like or understood by them."[81] "The Tory-Poets" attacks Dryden for plagiarism and writing for women in the same moment, implying that one follows from the other:

> Read *Dry––ns* plays, and read *Corneille's* too,
> You'l swear the *Frenchman* speaks good *English* now,
> 'Mongst borrowed Sense some airy flashes drop,
> To please the feeble Female and the Fop,
> So soft and gentle flourishes do move,
> The weak admiring Maid, and fire Love. (5:28)

This poem, in fact, systematically focuses on the insufficiency of other men's bodies: Dryden's "shapeless Body hangs an hundred ways/ The Poet looks just like a heap of Plays" (5:279). Dryden and William Davenant here share filiation and a diseased body: " 'Twas wit in *D'Avenant* too to lose his Nose,/ If so, then *Bays* is D'Avenants wisest Son,/ After so many claps to keep his on" (5:258). Otway's "very looks would drive the Fiends away" (5:283), and his association with Aphra Behn supplies mutual implication:

---

[80] Stallybrass and White, *Politics and Poetics*, chap. 2.

[81] It is clear that Shadwell is thinking of Dryden here, since he goes on to write that "the same people, to my comfort, damn all *Mr. Johnson's* Plays." Dryden, of course, did not damn all of Jonson's plays, but Shadwell frequently attacked Dryden for criticizing Jonson. *Complete Works of Thomas Shadwell*, 3:102.

Such stupid humours now the Gallants seize
Women and Bóys may write and yet may please.
Poetess *Afra* though she's damn'd to day
To morrow will put up another Play;
And *Ot--y* must be Pimp to set her off. (5:284)

These attacks on the diseased, ugly, and insufficiently manly bodies of the rival poets locate them, as Dryden does Shadwell, outside of legitimate masculinity in order to exclude them from legitimate authorship. By attacking these "feminized" bodies for weakness and corruption, for the desire to please women, and for contracting diseases *from* women, "The Tory-Poets" constructs the fully masculine classical (as opposed to grotesque) body as the only one authorized to own literary property.

Poetic genealogy served as a significant strategy of legitimation in general, but it became particularly useful in the justification of appropriation.[82] While Dryden represents Jonson as the father in *MacFlecknoe,* he gives this place to Shakespeare in his adaptations. In the prologue to Dryden's *Troilus and Cressida,* Betterton appears "Representing the Ghost of *Shakespear*" and delivers this challenge:

Now, where are the Successours to my name?
What bring they to fill out a Poets fame?
Weak, short-liv'd issues of a feeble Age;
Scarce living to be Christen'd on the Stage![83]

The birth metaphor of the "short-liv'd issue" underscores the genealogy trope's inscribed fantasy of male parthenogenetic creation. Dryden simi-

---

[82] I will mention only a few examples, but see also the dedication to Dryden's *Amphitryon*; his apology preceding *The State of Innocence* (in which he declares the license to use tropes and figures the "Birth-right which is deriv'd to us from our great Fore-fathers"); Robert Howard's epilogue to *The Committee*; John Crowne's epistle to the reader in his 1675 *Plays*; Crowne's prologue to his *Misery of Civil-War* (1680); William Mountfort's prologue to *The Injur'd Lovers* (1688); prologue to Edward Ravenscroft, *The Canterbury Guests* (1695); prologue to Thomas Scott, *The Unhappy Kindness* (1697); prologue to Edmund Waller's *Maid's Tragedy* (1690). The homage to Shakespeare and Jonson had become such a cliché that Charles Johnson could joke in the prologue to *The Country Lasses* (1735) about how often a prologue "gravely tell[s] you what you knew before,/How Ben and Shakespear wrote in Days of Yore."

[83] *Works of Dryden,* 13:249.

larly locates himself as Shakespeare's heir in his preface to *All for Love*; here the position demands triumph over his brother poets: "The death of *Antony* and *Cleopatra*, is a Subject which has been treated by the greatest Wits of our Nation, after *Shakespeare*; and by all so variously, that their example has given me the confidence to try my self in this Bowe of *Ulysses* amongst the Crowd of Sutors; and, withal, to take my own measures, in aiming at the Mark."[84] The property in question—the Shakespearean text and/as the desired woman—can be claimed only by Ulysses himself or his son. Sir William Davenant, the first adapter of Shakespeare in the Restoration, literalized the trope of poetic genealogy. According to John Aubrey, "Sir William would sometimes, when he was pleasant over a glass of wine with his most intimate friends . . . say, that it seemed to him that he writt with the very spirit that did Shakespeare, and seemed contented enough to be thought his Son. He would tell them the story as above [that Shakespeare commonly lodged in the Davenant household when visiting Oxford], in which way his mother had a very light report, whereby she was called a Whore."[85] Davenant exercised his filial rights by adapting Shakespearean plays. He revised a *Macbeth* that became the primary acting version until David Garrick. He also combined *Measure for Measure* and *Much Ado about Nothing* in *The Law against Lovers* (1662), keeping *Measure*'s basic plot but adding the witty Beatrice and Benedick.[86] Davenant, however, distinguishes his own rewriting from the plagiarism of less masculine authors:

> And some (a duce take 'em!) pretend
> They come but to speak with a friend;
> Then wickedly rob us of a whole Play
> By stealing five times an Act in a day.
> Oh little *England*! speak, it is not pity,
> That Gallants ev'n here, and thy chief City,
> Should under great Peruques have heads so small,

---

[84] Ibid., 10.

[85] *Aubrey's Brief Lives*, ed. Oliver Lawson Dick (London: Secker and Warburg, 1949), 85.

[86] See Dobson, *The Making of the National Poet*, chap. 1, esp. 37–38. In spite of his habit of rewriting, Davenant in his prefect to his heroic poem *Gondibert* argues that "whilst wee imitate others, wee can no more excell them, then he that sailes by others Mappes can make a new discovery." Sir William Davenant, *Gondibert*, ed. David F. Gladish (Oxford: Clarendon Press, 1971), 7.

As they must steal wit, or have none at all?
Others are bolder, and never cry, shall I?
    For they make our Guards quail,
    And 'twixt Curtain and Rail,
Oft combing their hair, they walk in Fop-Ally.[87]

"Effeminate" men can only plagiarize. Davenant's detractors, however, attack *him* in the same genealogical terms by insisting that the adaptations displeased his literary ancestors. In Richard Flecknoe's vituperative pamphlet, Sir William upon his death finds in Elyzium "never a Poet there, Antient nor Modern, whom in some sort or other he had not disoblig'd by his discommendations, as Homer, Virgil, Tasso, Spencer, and especially Ben. Johnson . . . Nay even Shakespear, whom he thought to have found his greatest Friend, was a much offended with him as any of the rest, for so spoiling and mangling of his Plays."[88]

John Dryden achieved tremendous literary authority by constructing, like his friend Davenant, a poetic genealogy based on masculine lineal descent. At the same time, however, Dryden became the object of considerable attack as a plagiarist. In Gerard Langbaine's *Account*, Dryden endures the most relentless assault. Although Langbaine recognizes Dryden as "A Person whose Writings have made him remarkable to all sorts of Men" (130), this compliment also implies that Dryden wrote to please the pit and the gallery as well as the boxes. According to Langbaine, Dryden built his career on the violation of literary property. In comedy, Dryden is "for the most part beholding to French Romances and Plays, not only for his Plots, but even a great part of his Language: tho' at the same time, he has the confidence to prevaricate, if not flatly deny the Accusation" (130). "Nor are his characters," Langbaine later adds, "less borrow'd in his Tragedies" (132). Langbaine would not have "medled in this Affair" (133), however, if Dryden had stolen only from foreign writers. The greater violation lies in transgressions against his own countrymen. Dryden is "not content with Conquests abroad, like another *Julius Caesar*, turning his Arms upon his own Country; and as if the proscription of his Contemporaries Reputation, were not sufficient to satiate his implacable thirst after Fame, endeavouring to demolish the

---

[87] Epilogue to *The Man's the Master*, in *The Works of Sr William Davenant, Kt,* 2 vols. (London, 1673), 2:383.
[88] Flecknoe, "Sir William Davenant's Voyage to the Other World," 8–9.

Statues and Monuments of his Ancestors, the Works of those his Illustrious Predecessors, *Shakespeare*, *Fletcher*, and *Johnson*: I was resolv'd to endeavour the rescue and preservation of those excellent Trophies of Wit ... to put a stop to his Spoils upon his own Countrymen. Therefore I present my self a Champion in the Dead Poets Cause" (133). Langbaine defends these playwrights not only against Dryden's plundering, but also against his criticism. Shakespeare, unlike Dryden, owns the "original" works he wrote: when listing Dryden's disrespectful attacks on Shakespeare, Langbaine singles out Dryden's comment that " 'Most of *Shakespear's* Plays, I mean the Stories of them, are to be found in the *Heccatomouthi*' " (135). Langbaine counters that "but two" of Shakespeare's plays come from that volume of stories (461) and repeats the Restoration commonplace of Shakespeare's innocence and ignorance—"Honest *Shakespear* was not in those days acquainted with those great Wits, *Scudery*, *Calprenede*, *Scarron*, *Corneille*, &c. He was as much a Stranger to French as Latine ... and yet an humble Story of *Dorastus* and *Fawnia*, serv'd him for *A Winter's Tale*, as well as *The Grand Cyrus*, or *The Captive Queen*, could furnish out a Laureate for a *Conquest of Granada*" (142). Thus, Shakespeare and Dryden both appropriated, but Shakespeare remains honest, humble, and original for the same gesture that renders Dryden dishonest and hubristic. "Honest" for Langbaine often means above the marketplace; he represents Shakespeare as alternately too rustic and too learned to descend to it. By contrast, "All ingenious Men, that know how [Dryden] has dealt with *Shakespear*, will count him ungrateful; who by furbishing up an Old Play, witness *The Tempest*, and *Troilus and Cressida*, has got more on the third Day, than its probable, ever *Horace* receiv'd from his Patron for any One Poem in all his life" (141). But Langbaine does not, as argued earlier, object to adapting Shakespeare per se. After attacking Dryden for "despis[ing]" *Measure for Measure* and *Much Ado about Nothing*, he counters that those plays "were believ'd by Sr. *William Davenant* ... to have Wit enough in them to make one good Play" (142). Davenant's adaptation honors Shakespeare, whereas Dryden's constitutes the ingratitude of the profiteer.

While the poet's genuine habit of intertextuality and the critic's personal animosity may account for some of Langbaine's representation of Dryden as a plagiarist, it cannot account for Dryden's self-proclaimed position as the most attacked writer of his time. Dryden occupied, as James Anderson Winn has demonstrated, a highly unstable social and professional position.[89] Born into a Puritan family, Dryden constantly endured the insults of the court wits who formed the social group to which he aspired and with whom he occasionally collaborated. Dryden, as Dustin Griffin points out, negotiated with booksellers and aristocrats, "derived some income from patrons, some from family property, some from his royal salary, and some from a royal grant to his aristocratic wife." But if Dryden saw "no inconsistency in combining the two roles of gentleman author and professional," his rivals took a different view.[90] From Langbaine's perspective, Dryden resembles "Vulgar Painters, who can tolerably copy after a good Original, but have either not judgment, or will not take the pains themselves to design any thing of value" (151). Sir Charles Sedley attacks Dryden in similar terms, apparently for obscenity but certainly also for his failure to be able to participate in upper-class pranks and repartee:

> Dryden in vain tried this nice way of wit,
> For he to be a tearing blade thought fit.
> But when he would be sharp, he still was blunt:
> To frisk his frolic fancy, he'd cry, "Cunt!"[91]

Sedley, who not only wrote obscene verses but also performed public acts of obscenity, ridicules Dryden's attempts to fit into the court culture by imitating its sexually explicit discourse.

Sedley and Langbaine inscribe, with varying degrees of subtlety, Dryden's exclusion from the right to appropriate, while others more explicitly attack Dryden for hiring out his pen:

> Tempted by Gold, he lets his Satyr fly,
> And swears that all within its Tallons dye;
> He Huffs, and Struts, and Cocks an hundred ways,
> And damns the Whiggs 'cause they damn his Plays.[92]

[89] James Anderson Winn, *John Dryden and His World* (New Haven: Yale University Press, 1987).

[90] Dustin Griffin, "The Beginnings of Modern Authorship: Milton and Dryden," *Milton Quarterly* 24 (March 1990): 2, 4. See also James Eli Adams, "The Economies of Authorship: Imagination and Trade in Johnson's Dryden," *Studies in English Literature 1500–1900* 30 (Summer 1990): 467–486.

[91] Sir Charles Sedley, quoted by Winn, *John Dryden*, 225.

[92] "Tory-Poets," *Complete Works of Thomas Shadwell*, 5:281.

This parody of a strutting and huffing Dryden, of a man who pretends to a higher rank than he occupies, appears in frequent anti-Dryden attacks and has to do, as it clearly does for Langbaine, with Dryden's attempts to straddle the positions of professional and courtly authorship. Buckingham creates such a character in Bayes of *The Rehearsal*, as does Shadwell in his character Drybob. The dramatis personae describes Drybob as "A Fantastick Coxcomb, that makes it his business to speak fine things and wit as he thinks; and alwayes takes notice, or makes others take notice of any thing he thinks well said."[93]

The case of *Sir Martin Mar-all*, a collaboration between John Dryden and the duke of Newcastle, shows Dryden's consciousness of this problem. Although Dryden later claimed *Sir Martin* as one of his own, for years he let Newcastle take full credit for it. Herringman entered the play into the *Stationer's Register* on 24 June 1668 as "A Comedy written by the Duke of Newe Castle."[94] Pepys understood it as "a play made by my Lord Duke of Newcastle, but, as everybody says, corrected by Dryden."[95] Kirkman's 1671 catalog lists the play anonymously. Years later, though, Downes gave most of the credit to Dryden: "Sir *Martin Marral*, The Duke of *New-Castle*, giving Mr. *Dryden* a bare Translation of it, out of a Comedy of the Famous *French* Poet *Monseur Moliero*: He Adapted the Part purposely for the Mouth of Mr. *Nokes*, and curiously Polishing the whole."[96] As John Loftis points out, only after waiting fifteen years past Newcastle's death did Dryden claim the play for himself by placing his name on the title page; before that, it "was generally not regarded as his literary property."[97] Loftis supports this position by noting that the Duke's Company, led by Davenant (a close friend of the duke's), performed the play, and not the King's Company, with which Dryden had close and eventually contractual relations. Clearly for Dryden, the hope of friendship and patronage from the duke of Newcastle had more value—personally, socially, and economically—than any property in *Sir Martin Mar-all.*

Dryden's endless self-positioning in prefaces to adaptations also illustrates his consciousness of the instability of his capacity to appropriate—

[93] *The Humorists,* ibid., 1:191.

[94] *Works of Dryden,* 9:354.

[95] Ibid., 352.

[96] John Downes, *Roscius Anglicanus* (1708 reprint), (Los Angeles: William Andrews Clark Memorial Library, Augustan Reprint Society, no. 134, 1969), 28.

[97] *Works of Dryden,* 9:355.

and indeed the instability of the borders dividing texts.[98] On the one hand, he had sufficient confidence to rewrite Shakespeare and Chaucer; on the other hand, he rarely produced such an (inter)text without extensive theorizing of the problem of rewriting. In his preface to *Troilus and Cressida*, a self-conscious adaptation of Shakespeare's play, he argues that since Athenians held Aeschylus "in the same veneration . . . as Shakespear is by us," "his Countrymen ordain'd an equal reward to those Poets who could alter his Plays to be Acted on the Theater, with those whose productions were wholly new, and of their own. The case is not the same in *England*; though the difficulties of altering are greater, and our reverence for *Shakespear* much more just, then that of the *Grecians* for *Aeschylus*."[99] Dryden insists on the artistic seriousness of adaptation through the authority of Shakespeare himself. Further, "The Original story," he repeats from Chaucer, "was Written by one *Lollius* a *Lombard*, in *Latin* verse, and Translated by *Chaucer* into *English.* "[100] In the context of a heightened professional property consciousness, Dryden looks back to an earlier form of intertextuality in which repetition located the writer in a tradition rather than opening him to charges of plagiarism or triviality.

Even in the same preface, however, Dryden represents rewriting inconsistently. First, by quoting Longinus he characterizes adaptation as classical imitation, entangling the new author in anxieties of influence: "We ought not to regard a good imitation as a theft; but as a beautiful Idea of him who undertakes to imitate, by forming himself on the invention and the work of another man; for he enters into the lists like a new wrestler, to dispute the prize with the former Champion."[101] But in spite of the effort to represent his *Troilus* as the high-culture exercise of a gentleman-poet, Dryden's professionalism eventually intrudes. By the end of the preface, he offers a rather mechanical division of his literary property from Shakespeare's: "The beginning Scenes of the fourth Act are either added, or chang'd wholly by me; the middle of it is *Shakespear* alter'd, and mingled with my own, three or four of the last Scenes are altogether new. And the whole Fifth Act, both the plot and the Writing

---

[98] For a more extensive discussion of Dryden's strategies of appropriation, see Kramer's important work in *The Imperial Dryden*.

[99] *Works of Dryden*, 13:225.

[100] Ibid.

[101] Ibid., 228.

are my own Additions."[102] Even Langbaine falls into inconsistencies over literary ownership. While he expresses outrage that Dryden earned money, as quoted above, "by furbishing up an Old Play [*Troilus and Cressida*]" (141), in his more detailed account he uncharacteristically offers Dryden a significant compliment: "[*Troilus and Cressida*] was likewise first written by *Shakespear*, and revis'd by Mr. *Dryden*, to which he added several new Scenes, and even cultivated and improv'd what he borrow'd from the Original. The last Scene in the third Act is a Masterpiece, and whether it be copied from *Shakespeare*, *Fletcher*, or *Euripides*, or all of them, I think it justly deserves Commendation" (173). Even in Langbaine, Dryden becomes at once a plagiarist and the creator of a new masterpiece, an unscrupulous literary profiteer writing to indulge the masses and a commendable dramatic poet. If Davenant and Newcastle (William, and to a lesser extent Margaret) inhabit the position of owner and (re)write without plagiarizing, but D'Urfey and Behn transgress at every turn, then where does Dryden, who behaved as both a professional and an amateur, fall?

Ultimately, Dryden negotiated his position with a fair amount of success, at least part of which must be attributed to his consciousness of cultural meanings of literary appropriation. If Dryden appears so much more aggressive in his usurpation of literary property than his courtly contemporaries, it was because he did not inhabit a position in which ownership could be assured. Dryden attempted, as he admiringly remarks of Ben Jonson, "to invade his sources like a monarch," an attempt that brought to him material profit, vehement attacks, and the honor of the laureateship.[103] As his prologue to a revival of *Albumazar* (which he believed provided a source for Jonson's *Alchemist*) demonstrates, Dryden worried about the instability of literary property and recognized a variety of positions of entitlement:

But *Ben* made nobly his, what he did mould,
What was anothere's Lead, becomes his Gold;
Like an unrighteous Conquerer he raigns,
Yet rules that well, which he unjustly gains.
But this our age such Authors does afford,
As make whole Playes, and yet scarce write one word:

[102] Ibid., 228–229.
[103] Ibid., 17:57.

56

Who in this Anarchy of witt, rob all,
And what's their Plunder, their Possession call;
Who like bold Padders scorn by night to prey,
But Rob by Sun-shine, in the face of day;
Nay scarce the common Ceremony use,
Of stand, Sir, and deliver up your Muse;
But knock the Poet down; and, with a grace,
Mount *Pegasus* before the owners Face.[104]

Dryden baldly distinguishes here between acts of appropriation by literary conquerors who take their place in an elite genealogy, and literary commoners who plunder on the highways. Dryden spent his career struggling to locate himself as one of the former.

[104] Ibid., 1:141.

"Authoress of a Whole World":
The Duchess of Newcastle
and Imaginary Property

A Garden of One's Own: The Economy of Originality

Margaret Cavendish, the duchess of Newcastle, did not achieve the reputation of being a great playwright; she did, however, achieve the reputation of being a notorious plagiarist. Some contemporaries alleged that her scientific writing simply repeated Hobbes and Descartes, and that she had "pluckt Feathers out of the Universities."[1] The physician Walter Charleton understood this charge as sufficiently serious to write in her defense that "among those, who have perused your Writings, I meet with a sort of Infidels, who refuse to believe, that you have always preserved your self so free from the Contagion of Books, and Book-men."[2] The charges of plagiarism against Cavendish must have been frequent, particularly disturbing, or both, for she defends herself vehemently. In *Nature's Pictures Drawn by Fancies Pencil*, Cavendish responds that "if they will not believe my Books are my own, let them search the Author or Authoress: but I am very confident that they will do like Drake, who went so far about, until he came to the place he first set out at."[3] She goes so far as

[1] Margaret Cavendish, *The Life of the Thrice Noble, High, and Puissant Prince William Cavendishe* (1667; London, 1675), dedication. Quoted by Sara Heller Mendelson, *The Mental World of Stuart Women: Three Studies* (Brighton: Harvester Press, 1987), 38.

[2] Walter Charleton, *Letters and Poems in Honour of the Incomparable Princess, Margaret, Dutchess of Newcastle* (London, 1676), 146. Several of the letters in this collection defend Cavendish's originality against apparent charges of plagiarism.

[3] Cavendish, *Nature's Pictures Drawn by Fancies Pencil to the Life* (London, 1665), 367.

to cite her physical lack of access to assistance and witnesses to her originality: "As for my being the true and onley Authoress of them [my works], . . . my attending servants are witness that I have had none but my own Thoughts, Fancies, and Speculations to assist me; and as soon as I have set them down, I send them to those that are to transcribe them, and fit them for the Press; whereof since there have been several, and amongst them such as only could write a good hand, but neither understood Orthography, nor had any Learning."[4] But whatever her detractors believed, the Duchess herself understood the attacks on her literary property as gendered: "Nor do I so much wonder at it, since I, a Woman, cannot be exempt from the malice and aspersions of spiteful tongues, which they cast upon my poor Writings, some denying me to be the true Authoress of them; . . . those Books I put out first, to the judgment of this censorious Age, were accounted not to be written by a Woman, but that some body else had writ and publish'd them in my Name."[5] In her praises of originality, accusations against others for plagiarism, and defenses of her own authorship threaded throughout her writing, Cavendish reveals an understanding of differing social capacities to possess writing. In the face of unequal access to literary culture, the duchess insists upon her own originality, supported by a combination of class privilege and gendered modesty, as a strategy for owning literary property, which in turn provides a strategy for constructing full social subjectivity.

Cavendish represents her own authorship with ambivalence and contradiction, characterizing herself as both humbly insignificant and unique in her literary greatness.[6] Prefacing her 1662 *Plays Written by the*

---

[4] Cavendish, *Life of William Cavendishe*, 2d ed., dedication.

[5] Cavendish writes this in the dedication to her *Life of William Cavendishe*. Her husband, she reports, "was moved to prefix an Epistle before one of [the duchess's books] in my vindication, wherein you assure the world upon your Honour, That what was written and printed in my name, was my own." She refers here to "An Epistle to justify the Lady Newcastle, and truth against falsehood, laying those false, and malicious aspersions of her, that she was not author of her books," prefixed to her *Philosophical and Physical Opinions* (London, 1655). The same volume further supports the possibility that Cavendish faced more accusations of plagiarism than have been preserved, since she reports that various people became convinced that she did not write her works because she could not recite her own verses.

[6] See Mary Beth Rose, "Gender, Genre, and History: Seventeenth-Century Women and the Art of Autobiography," *Women in the Middle Ages and the Renaissance: Literary and Historical Perspectives*, ed. Mary Beth Rose (Syracuse: Syracuse University Press,

Thrice Noble, Illustrious and Excellent Princess, the Lady Marchioness of New-castle, the duchess includes a poem that expresses more modesty than the volume's title:

> But Noble Readers, do not think my Playes,
> Are such as have been writ in former daies;
> As *Johnson, Shakespear, Beaumont, Fletcher* writ;
> Mine want their Learning, Reading, Language, Wit:
> The Latin phrases I could never tell,
> But *Johnson* could, which made him write so well.
> Greek, Latin Poets, I could never read,
> Nor their Historians, but our English Speed;
> I could not steal their Wit, nor Plots out take;
> All my Playes Plots, my own poor brain did make:
> From *Plutarchs* story I ne'r took a Plot,
> Nor from Romances, nor from Don Quixot,
> As others have, for to assist their Wit,
> But I upon my own Foundation writ.[7]

This poem simultaneously insists on its author's inadequacy and significance, for if her plays cannot demonstrate the skill that comes from a classical education, they nevertheless remain free of influence and repetition. Thus Cavendish takes what she understands as one of the greatest disadvantages facing women writers—lack of access to education[8]—and turns it into an authorial strategy that assures the readers of the uniqueness of the text. Her originality remains, however, evidence of both a lack of and proof of her importance.

Cavendish's writing reveals a sharp awareness of her exteriority to

---

1986), 245–278. Rose explores the contradictory self-representations in Cavendish's autobiography.

[7] Cavendish, *Playes Written by the Thrice Noble, Illustrious and Excellent Princess, the Lady Marchioness of Newcastle* (London, 1662), 4.

[8] In the preface to *The World's Olio. Written by the Right Honourable, the Lady Margaret Newcastle* (London, 1655), Cavendish argues that "our Sex make great complaints, that men from their first Creation usurped a Supremacy to themselves, although we were made equal by Nature, which Tyrannical Government they have kept ever since . . . in Nature we have as clear an understanding as Men, if we were bred in Schools to mature our Brains, and to mature our Understanding, that we might bring forth the Fruits of Knowledge."

an elite masculine literary tradition, and she repeatedly insists on her originality as a necessary compensation for her ignorance of this tradition.[9] That her contradictions become particularly pronounced in her attempts to describe *herself* suggests a relationship between these inconsistencies and her attempt to define her social subjectivity. In the autobiography, as Mary Beth Rose has observed, Cavendish asserts her self-worth as vehemently as she denies it, characterizing herself as both shy and gregarious; serious and frivolous; plain and fashionable.[10] The contradiction between the need to be noticed and her self-reported modesty appears throughout her work: "All I desire," she writes in the preface to her *Poems and Phancies*, "is *Fame*, and *Fame* is nothing but a *great Noise*, and *noise* lives most in a *Multitude*; wherefore I wish my *Book* may set a worke every *Tongue*."[11] In spite of this passion for fame and a delight in drawing specular attention to her unique clothing that she designed herself, Cavendish nevertheless insists that she would "willingly exclude myself, so as never to see the face of any creature but my Lord as long as I live, inclosing myself like an anchorite, wearing a frieze gown, tied with a cord about my waist."[12]

But if her gender excludes, her rank entitles and enables a career as a poet, scientist and dramatist. At the very least, William's money supported her expensive publishing career.[13] Beyond providing simply the resources for access to a public voice, Margaret's upwardly mobile mar-

[9] Bathsua Makin echoes Cavendish's authorial self-construction: "The present Duchess of New Castle, by her own Genius, rather than any timely Instruction, overtops many grave Gown-Men." *An Essay to Revive the Antient Education of Gentlewomen*, intro. Paula L. Barbour (1673; reprint, Los Angeles: William Andrews Clark Memorial Library, Augustan Reprint Society no. 202, 1980), 10.

[10] Rose, "Gender, Genre, and History."

[11] Cavendish, "To All Noble and Worthy Ladies," letter prefacing *Poems and Phancies Written by the Thrice Noble, Illustrious, and Excellent Princess, the Lady Marchioness of Newcastle. Second Impression* (London, 1664). (First published in 1653 as *Poems and Fancies*.)

[12] Cavendish, *The True Relation of My Birth, Breeding, and Life,* published in *Nature's Pictures Drawn by Fancies Pencil to the Life* (London, 1656). Quoted by Rose, "Gender, Genre, and History," 252. In Cavendish's autobiography, she boasts of the pleasure she took in designing her clothes; further, contemporary comments suggest that she succeeded in drawing attention to her appearance.

[13] Mendelson believes that the duchess's publishing career cost the couple a great deal, noting that Walter Charleton mentions the "great summs of money" the duchess bestowed on her own book. *The Mental World of Stuart Women*, 39.

riage to William enabled her to understand herself as at least potentially an owner of literary property. Throughout her writing, Cavendish stakes out a claim to her own literary authority on the basis of her originality, which enables her to circumvent competing with men who consider writing "their *Prerogatives*; for they hold *Books* as their *Crowne*, and the *Sword* as their *Scepter*, by which they rule, and governe."[14] Shakespeare, Jonson, Beaumont, and Fletcher may all compose dramatic works that reveal the extent of their reading, but her works offer the reader new and unfamiliar stories. Thus originality provides a form of ownership to which she would otherwise not have access.

By eliding the claim of originality with a claim of singularity, Cavendish can also insist on her own importance without necessarily extending this possibility of authorship to women in general. Statements of self-proclaimed difference from other women, as well as contradictorily powerful "feminist" statements, appear throughout her writing. In one of her *Sociable Letters*, for example, she provides a long apology for writing and comically describes her attempts to undertake household tasks, such as spinning, candle making, and baking. She performed these so ineptly, she writes in this letter and in an epistle that prefaces the volume, that her bungled attempts ended up wasting more resources than they produced. Her endearing description, however, exploits humility to insist on class privilege: she decides to farm out these tasks to other women. Similarly, another letter describes a fantasy in which "Nature sent the Muses to Invite all the Poets to a Banquet of Wit."[15] Upon arrival at this splendid event, "I was extremely out of Countenance, as being all Men, and never a Woman but my self." Yet the sight of "my Lord one of the Chief Guests amongst them" gives her confidence "insomuch as I went to him, and stood close by him." Cavendish not only represents herself as unique among and superior to other women, but she also erases the existence from history of all other women writers. The comfort that the duke provides here can be read as another expression of privilege, for just as Margaret achieves her aristocratic and land-owning status through William, so she also represents the achievement of her authorial and literary property-owning status as enabled by her husband.

Yet Cavendish elsewhere suggests that valuing originality could argue

[14] Cavendish, preface, "To All Noble, and Worthy Ladies," *Poems and Phancies*.

[15] Cavendish, *CCXI Sociable Letters, Written by the Thrice Noble, Illustrious, and Excellent Princess, the Lady Marchioness of Newcastle* (London, 1664), no. 199.

for the possibility of all women's authorship.[16] Originality had certainly not accumulated the central critical value that it would in the eighteenth century: Dryden ridiculed Settle for his flights of fancy and Swift preferred the bee-like ancients who gathered material to produce sweetness and light to the spidery moderns who produced from the materials of their own bodies. But for some women writers, originality offered an otherwise unimaginable source of authority. The duchess used precisely the same image as Swift to prefer the spider: "A true Poet," she insists, "is like a Spider that spins all out of her own bowels."[17] The figure of the poet as original spinner commonly stands for *women's* authorship in Cavendish. *"True it is,"* she admits,

> Spinning with the Fingers is more proper to our Sexe, than Studying or Writing Poetry, which is the Spinning with the braine: but I having no skill in the Art of the first . . . made me delight in the latter; since all braines work naturally, and incessantly, in some kinde or other; which made me endeavour to Spin a Garment of Memory, to lapp up my Name, that it might Grow to after Ages: I cannot say the Web is strong, fine, or evenly Spun, for it is a Course peice; yet I had rather my Name should go meanly clad, then dye with cold: but if the Sute be trimmed with your Favour, shee may make such a Shew, and appeare so lovely, as to wed to a Vulgar Fame.[18]

[16] The duchess expresses similar ambivalence about women's intellectual capacity. In the preface to *The World's Olio*, she defends women's natural equality. Later in the same passage, however, she argues that *"Men have great Reason not to let us in to their Governments, for there is great difference betwixt the Masculine Brain and the Feminine."* For further thoughts on Cavendish's feminism, see Catherine Gallagher, "Embracing the Absolute: The Politics of the Female Subject in Seventeenth-Century England," *Genders* 1 (Spring 1988): 24–39; Dolores Paloma, "Margaret Cavendish: Defining the Female Self," *Women's Studies* 7 (1980): 55–66; Linda R. Payne, "Dramatic Dreamscape: Women's Dreams and Utopian Vision in the Works of Margaret Cavendish, Duchess of Newcastle," in *Curtain Calls: British and American Women and the Theater, 1660–1820*, ed. Mary Anne Schofield and Cecilia Macheski (Athens: Ohio University Press, 1991), 18–33; Sophie Tomlinson, "'My Brain the Stage': Margaret Cavendish and the Fantasy of Female Performance," and Kate Lilley, "Blazing Worlds: Seventeenth-Century Women's Utopian Writing," in *Women, Texts, and Histories, 1575–1760*, ed. Clare Brant and Diane Purkiss (London: Routledge Press, 1992), 102–133, 134–163.
[17] Cavendish, *The World's Olio*, 6.
[18] Cavendish, dedication to *Poems and Phancies*. See Sylvia Bowerbank, "The Spider's Delight: Margaret Cavendish and the 'Female Imagination,'" *English Literary Renaissance* 14 (Autumn 1984): 392–408. Bowerbank demonstrates the importance of

In the context of traditional histories of criticism that locate the emergence of originality as an aesthetic value in the mid-eighteenth century,[19] Cavendish's passion for original composition has appeared idiosyncratic to critics, as the eccentricity of a misplaced romantic poet born in the wrong century. But given the emerging relationship between authorship and ownership, the duchess's stake in originality can be understood as a gendered alternative to imitation as well as a privileged assertion of the capacity to possess. Sensing herself as excluded from the tropes of both poetic genealogy *and* Lockean appropriation, Cavendish asserts the value of original composition approximately 100 years before Edward Young. Cavendish's significance lies not so much in originality itself—her plays, for example, clearly echo Shakespeare's—as it does in her *claim* to it as a strategy of entitlement.

For Cavendish, originality becomes the best way for a woman and an aristocratic amateur to stake a claim in the ownership of literary property; the claim to originality allows her to negotiate the dominant tropes of both appropriation and poetic genealogy. In "The Mine of Wit," for example, the duchess inverts one of the clichés of appropriation—the transformation of natural, raw material into refined product—and transforms it into a trope for originality:

> Fancies are Min'rals, and the Mine the Head,
> Some Gold, some Silver, Iron, Tin, some Lead;
> The Furnace which 'tis Melted in is great,
> And Motion quick doth give a Glowing heat;
> The Mouth's the Gutter, where Oar runs along,
> The Hammer, which the Barrs do beat, the Tongue;
> The Ear's the Forge, to Shape and Form it out,
> And several Merchants send it all about;

---

silkworms, spiders, and spinning as images for literary creativity throughout Cavendish's works, considering these images a "defense of free fancy or subjective expression" and calling Cavendish "a pioneer of such an approach." Nevertheless, she contends that it is "also useful . . . to see Cavendish's place in literary history as a cautionary tale for those of us who would suggest that craftsmanship and order are masculine, and artlessness and chaos are feminine" (407).

[19] See, for example, Ian Watt, *The Rise of the Novel: Studies in Defoe, Richardson, and Fielding* (Berkeley: University of California Press, 1957), chap. 1. Watt argues that originality first becomes a critical value with the rise of the eighteenth-century novel.

And as the Metall's worth, the Price is set,
Scholars, which are the Buyers, most do get;
On Gold and Silver, which are Fancies fine,
Are Poets Stamp'd, as Masters of that Coin.[20]

Cavendish takes a familiar metaphor for literary production, but then locates a distinctly different origin of wit: instead of finding the unpolished jewels in the texts of Shakespeare or Fletcher, the duchess insists that those jewels must originate in the head itself. The head, in fact, becomes in this poem a self-sufficient poetry machine, melting, hammering, and forging in an entirely self-enclosed system. Thus she does not credit, as do Dryden and others, a more advanced age of British civilization with offering the labor of refinement to the raw material of the past. In fact, those who find these jewels of fancy outside of their own minds, she implies, do not have the same kind of property in them. Publishers, or perhaps teachers (the merchants of wit), circulate these fine fancies for the consumption of scholars; the learned, however, do not qualify as owners of literary property. Judging from the poem prefacing her 1662 *Playes* (quoted above), in which Cavendish characterizes herself as an ignorant (or self-sufficient) poet as opposed to learned poets like Ben Jonson, "scholars" in this poem can be taken to include poets steeped in the traditional education accessible to men. In this gendered division, gentleman scholar-poets acquire these pieces of gold and silver through education, but always discover the likeness of the original poet stamped on them. No matter how long literary property circulates, then, it continues to bear the likeness of its origin, of the head that originally provided the mine and the forge. As she states more explicitly in *The World's Olio*, the learned may possess, but do not own, these golden fancies: "Now may some say, they are become his own, since he bought them, it is true they are so to keep them, or make use of them, or to sell, and traffick with them, by imparting them to pettie Maerchants, which are young students and Scholars, but otherwise they are no more his, then when they were in the Authors head."[21]

In "Of Poets and their Theft," in fact, the duchess attacks literary imitation as a property violation:

[20] Cavendish, *Poems and Phancies*, 188.
[21] Cavendish, *World's Olio*, 6.

As *Birds,* to hatch their *Young* do, sit in *Spring,*
Some Ages severall *Broods* of *Poets* bring,
Which to the *World* in *Verse* do sweetly Sing;

Their *Notes,* great Nature set, not *Art,*
So *Fancies,* in the *Braine* that *Nature* wrought,
Are *best*; what *Imitation* makes, are naught.[22]

Nature produces poets, but those who imitate merely convey fancies from one place to another:

To *Messengers* Rewards of *Thanks* are due,
For their great *Paines,* telling their *Message* true;
But not the *Honour* to *Invention new.*

Many there are, that *Sutes* will make to weare,
Of severall *Patches,* stole, both here, and there;
That to the *World* they *Gallants* may appeare:

And the *Poore Vulgar,* which but little know,
Do *Reverence all,* that makes a *Glistring Shew*;
Examines not, the *fame,* how they came to.[23]

Like Langbaine's plagiarists, Cavendish's imitators dress themselves in the clothing of others, dishonestly raising their social capital in a way imperceptible to those who have none to begin with.

"Of Poets and their Theft" and another poem, "Upon the Same Subject," show how far Cavendish would sometimes go, for they ultimately refuse to recognize any distinction between plagiarism and imitation. The conversation between two gentlemen in *The Comical Hash* most explicitly collapses this distinction. In discussing Monsieur Theft's book of poems, these men conclude that Theft "hath only new placed the words, as they do Anagrams of names." The second gentleman at first defends imitation as different from copying, but soon refutes his own distinction: "An Imitator is but an Artificer, when as the Original Author is a Creator . . . but there are or have been but few Poets that have such powers and parts to make a perfect Creature, which is a perfect work."[24]

---

[22] Cavendish, *Poems and Phancies,* 152.
[23] Ibid.
[24] Cavendish, *Playes Written by the Marchioness of Newcastle,* 561.

Even though most of them fail, some poets nevertheless "are like Chymists, that strive and labour to make as Nature makes." Even for Edward Young, the imitation of nature constitutes originality; for Cavendish, however, the poet must go so far as to *make* nature. In "Upon the Same Subject," she expounds on this criticism of other writers:

Some will a Line or two from *Horace* take,
And pick his Fancies, which their own they make;
And some of *Homer, Virgil, Ovid* sweet,
Will steal, and make them in their Books to meet,
Yet make them not in their right Shapes appear.
But like as Spirits in dark Shades to err:
Thus as Magicians Spirit-troublers they're,
And may the Name of Poet-Juglers bear,
Which th' Ignorant by Sorcery delude,
Shewing false Glasses to the Multitude,
And with a small and undiscerned Hair,
Do pull great *Truth* out of her place she were:
These should by th' Poets Laws be Hang'd, and so
Into the Hell of Condemnation go.[25]

These thieves of writing becomes metaphorical magicians, using sorcery to delude; they deserve hanging and condemnation to hell. While the duchess here condemns imitation generally, she may also intend specific references to precursing playwrights. Ben Jonson took a line or two from Horace, and Shakespeare repeated Homer, Virgil, and Ovid. This poem thus collapses distinctions between Jonsonian imitation, Shakespearean intertextuality, and plagiarism.

Even Shakespeare, for whom the duchess expresses great admiration, falls short of true originality. Shakespeare's ability to create such a variety of characters, however, confirms for Cavendish the authenticity of his writing. "One would think," she comments, "he had been Transformed into every one of those Persons he hath Described."[26] Creating characters means comprehending various social positions, from fools and watchmen to Caesar and Antony. She even claims Shakespeare, as would Aphra

[25] Cavendish, *Poems and Phancies,* 153.
[26] Cavendish, *Sociable Letters,* no. 123.

Behn, as something of an honorary woman writer: "One would think that he had been Metamorphosed from a Man to a Woman, for who could Describe *Cleopatra* Better than he hath done."[27] Like Behn, Cavendish deploys Shakespeare's reputation as the unlearned poet of nature who understood human souls rather than books as a source of women's literary authority in dramatic writing. Nevertheless, "*Shakespear*'s Wit and Eloquence was General, for, and upon all Subjects, he rather wanted Subjects for his Wit and Eloquence to Work on, for which he was Forced to take some of his Plots out of History."[28] Shakespeare thus lacks the kind of originality that Cavendish claims for her own work. Her contemporaries who follow Shakespeare, however, have even greater debts to pay. Shakespeare had so much wit that "those, who Writ after him, were Forced to Borrow of him, or rather to Steal from him; I could mention Divers Places, that others of our Famous Poets have Borrow'd, or Stoln, but lest I should Discover the Persons, I will not Mention the Places, or Parts."[29]

Cavendish differs from the men of her class in her incapacity to share in their literary property; through originality, however, she can foil this economy by defining the subject position of ownership through purely internal and inherent, rather than inherited and acquired, qualities. Yet her construction of authorship nevertheless depends upon a class location that justifies such self-valuation. Valuing originality has no democratizing effect: it is both a form of and, at least for the duchess, an expression of ownership. She articulates her position as always already an owner in the same language her contemporaries use to articulate appropriation. As opposed to others, who steal plots "for to assist their wit,"

> But I upon my own Foundation writ;
> Like those that have a little patch of Land,
> Even so much whereon a house may stand:
> The Owner builds a house, though of no shew,
> A Cottage warm and clean, though thach'd and low;
> Vitruvius Art and Skill he doth not take,
> For to design, and so his house to make;

[27] Ibid.
[28] Ibid.
[29] Ibid.

Nor Carpenters, nor Masons doth not hire,

. . .

He steals nor borrows not of any Neighbor,
But lives contentedly of his own labour.[30]

While Restoration adapters describe how they build upon the foundations of earlier plays, Cavendish represents herself as not only owning (through invention) the original piece of property, but also as borrowing none of the materials for her house of drama. She also constructs an alternative poetic genealogy: "Just so, I hope, the works that I have writ/ Which are the building of my natural wit;/ My own Inheritance, as Nature's child." As the child of nature rather than the offspring of precursing poets, wit constitutes her inheritance and inherent value. Literary property does not need to be appropriated, for it originates within.

Cavendish further insisted on property in her writing though publication. In the seventeenth century, publication remained, as Elaine Hobby has demonstrated, a sign of immodesty for women, who nevertheless found a "repertoire of devices to make their writing a 'modest' act."[31] Although exile and revolution shaped conditions in Cavendish's life that may have destabilized some notions of propriety, she nevertheless expresses serious concern for the risks of publication: "It is most certain, That those that perform Publick Actions, expose themselves to Publick Censures; and so do Writers, live they never so privately and retir'd, as soon as they commit their Works to the Press."[32] In her preface to *Poems and Phancies*, she addresses her apology specifically to those of her own class and gender, asking "All Noble, and Worthy Ladies" to "Condemne me not as a *dishonour* of your *Sex*, for Setting forth this *Work*; for it is *harmlesse* and *free* from all *dishonesty*." Further, in *The World's Olio* she notes that "a woman by striving to make her wit known, by making much discourse, loses her reputation, for wit is copious, and busies its self in

---

[30] Cavendish, preface to *Playes Written by the Marchioness of Newcastle*, 5.

[31] Elaine Hobby, *Virtue of Necessity: English Women's Writing, 1649–88* (Ann Arbor: University of Michigan Press, 1988), 9. Hobby's fine survey of the variety of forms that women's writing takes during this time shows the range of strategies that different women discovered for negotiating their position in relation to authorship.

[32] Cavendish, preface to *Plays, Never Before Printed. Written by the Thrice Noble, Illustrious, and Excellent Princesse, the Duchess of Newcastle* (London, 1668).

all things . . . in women the greatest wisdom, if not wit, is to be sparing of their discourse."[33]

Publication emerges in her writing as worth this risk, however, for its ability to secure ownership. In her play *Youth's Glory and Death's Banquet*, Lady Sanspareille, who becomes a philosopher and orator, insists that "*I* will publish to the world in print [any inventions or fancies] before *I* make them common by discourse."[34] While the dominant culture signified women's public speaking and publication as violations of chastity, Lady Sanspareille insists that such practices *protect* a lady's honor, while private exchanges threaten it by offering opportunities for intimacy.[35] Still, Lady Sanspareille ultimately subordinates the protection of chastity to a more important benefit of print: the protection of property. She tells her father:

> *I* would never speak but in publick, for if nature, and education, have given me wit, *I* would not willingly bury it in private discourses; besides, private hearers are secret Thieves, and boldly steal, having no witnesses, to betray, or reveal the truth, or divuldge their thefts; and so they will adorn their discourses with my wit, which they steal from me. . . . I will never speak of any considerable matter, or subject, or of any new conception, but I will have them ready writ to print them, so soon as my discourse of them is past, or else print them before I discourse of them; and afterwards explain them by my tongue, as well as by my pen, least they should mistake the sence of my workes, through Ignorance; for those subjects that are only discourst off, in speech, flyes away in words; which vanisheth as smoak, or shadows, and the memory or remembrance of the Author, or Oratour, melts away as oyle, leaving no sign in present life, or else moulders as dust, leaving no Monument to after posterity, to be known or remembred by; when writeing or printing, fixes it to everlasting time, to the publick view of the World.[36]

According to Cavendish, women not only endure more accusations of plagiarism, but also remain more vulnerable to being plagiarized *from*, since their literary property so commonly remains private.

Although the Duchess expends a great deal of energy establishing

---

[33] Cavendish, *The World's Olio*, 23.

[34] Cavendish, *Playes Written by the Marchioness of Newcastle*, 131.

[35] See also Hobby, *Virtue of Necessity*, 9, 81–84.

[36] Cavendish, *Playes Written by the Marchioness of Newcastle*, 131–132.

and defending her literary property, she nevertheless also represents herself as without any capacity to own. In one extraordinary poem that concludes *Poems and Phancies*, she not only makes this incapacity explicit but also contradicts everything she has written about her own originality:

> A Poet I am neither Born nor Bred,
> But to a Witty Poet Married,
> Whose Brain is Fresh, and Pleasant, as the Spring,
> Where Fancies grow, and where the Muses sing;
> There oft I lean my Head, and List'ning hark,
> T'observe his Words, and all his Fancies mark;
> And from that Garden Flow'rs of Fancies take,
> Whereof a Posie up in Verse I make;
> Thus I, that have no Garden of my own,
> There gather Flowers, that are newly Blown.[37]

In the dedication of *The World's Olio* to William, she similarly declares of her writing that "if there be any Wit, or anything worthy of Commendation, they are the Crumms I gathered from your Discourse." Further, in a closing note in her 1662 *Playes*, she appears to retract her claim to the avoidance of all imitation: "I take as much delight as Painters, which draw men, and other creatures; So I, to draw my fancies opinions and conceptions upon white Paper, with Pen and Ink, words beeing the figures of thoughts, and letters of words; but writing is but the figuring of the figure, and Writers are but Copyers." Elsewhere she calls writers copiers, but only to distinguish inferior imitators from original composers like herself. Even more striking, however, is her willingness to attribute all creativity to William and none to her own brain. But if we understand authorship as property, the tension between Cavendish's claims to originality and to having "no Garden" of her own do not contradict each other as much as initial appearances might indicate. All property for the former Margaret Lucas belongs to her through the privilege of her marriage to William. In her efforts to represent her singularity—or, as I have argued, her aristocratic privilege—she becomes both an owner and not an owner, both the duchess of Newcastle and "humble Margaret," both a richly capacious mine of original wit and a mere collector of flowers grown on William's land.

[37] Cavendish, *Poems and Phancies*, 298–299.

The complexities and contradictions of Cavendish's authorial self-construction articulate an intricate personal and historical situation in which she found herself both privileged and disempowered. Born the youngest daughter to a wealthy family, the future duchess only achieved her high aristocratic status upon her marriage at twenty-two to the fifty-one-year-old duke of Newcastle.[38] She met William while maid of honor in the exiled court of Henrietta Maria, having fled her home first to Oxford and then to France during the civil war. Parliamentary forces seized her family's home, dismembered her mother's exhumed body, and executed her brother Charles.[39] During the Commonwealth, she and William continued to live abroad, mostly on whatever credit they could raise. In spite of her prestigious marriage, then, Margaret Cavendish enjoyed neither her ancestral nor her marital estates for much of her life, living in the isolation and uncertainty of exile. With William declared a traitor by Parliament, Margaret, like many royalist wives, returned to England to petition for her husband's property. War and exile allowed these women the unusual opportunity to negotiate for property, but in her autobiography she distances herself from any potential regendering of property relations. In spite of the purpose of her trip, she insists that she "did not stand as a beggar at the Parliament doore, nor stood I ever at the doore, as I do know, or can remember, I am sure, not as a Petitioner, neither did I haunt the Committees."[40] Upon learning of the sale of William's land, she "whisperingly spoke to my brother to conduct me out of that ungentlemanly place, so without speaking to them one word good or bad."[41] Cavendish underscores her self-representation as modestly unwilling to beg for property by contrasting her behavior to a new trend in women negotiators: "The Customes of England being changed as well as the Laws, where Women become

---

[38] Biographies of Margaret Cavendish, the duchess of Newcastle, include most recently Sara Heller Mendelson, *The Mental World of Stuart Women,* and Kathleen Jones, *A Glorious Fame: The Life of Margaret Cavendish, Duchess of Newcastle, 1623–1673* (London: Bloomsbury, 1988). See also Thomas Longueville, *The First Duke and Duchess of Newcastle-upon-Tyne* (London: Longmans, Green, 1910), and Douglas Grant, *Margaret the First: A Biography of Margaret Cavendish, Duchess of Newcastle, 1623–1673* (Toronto: University of Toronto Press, 1957). The duchess offers her own account of her and William's lives in her biography of her husband and her autobiography, *A True Relation of My Birth, Breeding and Life.*

[39] Jones, *A Glorious Fame,* 68–70.

[40] Cavendish, *A True Relation,* 379.

[41] Ibid., 380.

Pleaders, Atturneys, Petitioners and the like, running about with their severall Causes, complaining of their severall grievances, exclaiming against their severall enemies, bragging of their severall favours they receive from the powerfull, thus Trafficking with idle words bringing in false reports, and vain discourse; for the truth is, our Sex doth nothing but justle for the Preheminence of words, I mean not for speaking well, but speaking much."[42] The duchess attacks other women for activities that she herself clearly finds empowering and pleasurable, such as commenting on the political situation, negotiating property, and endlessly trafficking in words. She represents herself both as an owner and as one who is exterior to property relations: she undertakes the task of pleading for William's property but insists that she does not transgress traditionally gendered positions.

The duchess's relationship to literary property, then, articulates the instability of her relationship to property itself in the context an increasingly anachronistic Filmerian patriarchal absolutism. At times she locates herself fully as an aristocratic owner: not only did she return to England to petition for William's land, but she also apparently took quite an active role in running the Newcastle estates upon their permanent return. She helped to engineer, in fact, harsh but profitable policies of enclosure and rackrenting, the extremity of which prompted the Newcastle children to rebel against her. They believed that she not only exploited the tenants, but also wheedled property for herself out of William.[43] But as her autobiography evidences, Cavendish could just as easily construct herself as modestly unable to own. In at least one instance, she even functioned *as* property. When Charles II took the throne, William grew eager to return to England as soon as possible. He and Margaret, however, had accumulated such a great deal of debt from living on credit that the duke left his wife behind in pawn for his charges.[44] Thus Margaret could function as a negotiator for property and even as the Newcastle voice of ownership at the same time she could serve as a symbol for William's property itself.

Her name itself raises the same problem. Cavendish's title and literary

---

[42] Ibid.

[43] See Mendelson, *The Mental World of Stuart Women*, 42; Jones, *A Glorious Fame*, 170. Jones defends Cavendish against these charges.

[44] Jones, *A Glorious Fame*, 135; Longueville, *The First Duke*, 208; Mendelson, *The Mental World of Stuart Women*, 41.

entitlement remained for her inseparable, shaping her authorship as profoundly as did her gender. On the other hand, the name "Newcastle" fails to distinguish her from any other of William's wives, past or future, leaving her with no unique identity. She confronts this problem at the end of her autobiography: the very advantage that enabled her particular form of authorship—the marriage to William—threatens to condemn her to complete anonymity: [45]

> I verily believe some censuring Readers will scornfully say, why hath this Ladie writ her own Life? since none cares to know whose daughter she was, or whose wife she is, or how she was bred, or what fortunes she had, or how she lived, or what humour or disposition she was of? . . . neither did I intend this piece for to delight, but to divulge, not to please the fancy, but to tell the truth, lest after-Ages should mistake, in not knowing I was daughter to one Master *Lucas* of *St. Johns* neer *Colchester* in *Essex*, second Wife to the Lord Marquis of *Newcastle*, for my Lord having had two Wives, I might easily have been mistake, especially if I should dye, and my Lord Marry again. [46]

The importance of imaginary property to Cavendish had less to do with the literary marketplace than with her own struggle to establish full social subjectivity through an amateur writing career. Her particular form of conservatism—what Catherine Gallagher calls her "Tory absolutism"[47]—resembles a Hobbesian belief in authority and stable property relations as being at the heart of all social order and even at the heart of the definition of self. Ownership of language constitutes full subject-

---

[45] Catherine Gallagher, by contrast, sees a consistency in Cavendish's writing between her "protofeminism" and her royalism. "In [Cavendish's] proclamations of what she calls her 'singularity,' she insists that she is an autotelic, self-sufficient being, not a secondary creature, a satellite orbiting a dominant male planet, but a self-centered orb, eccentric because outside of anyone else's circle. In describing and justifying this absolute singularity, Cavendish repeatedly invokes the model of the absolute monarch. . . . However, much in Cavendish's texts suggests that the absolutist desire, the desire to be the sovereign monarch, itself derives from a certain female disability: not from her inability to be a monarch but her inability to be a full *subject* of the monarch. Of the two available positions, subject and monarch, monarch is the only one Cavendish can imagine a woman occupying." "Embracing the Absolute," 26–27.

[46] *A True Relation*, 390–391.

[47] See Gallagher, "Embracing the Absolute."

hood, for in speech lies both power and pleasure: it exists, Hobbes argues, "to make known to others our wills" and "to please and delight our selves, and others, by playing with our words, for pleasure or ornament, innocently."[48] Both Hobbes and Cavendish write to reconstruct property relations in the context of radical disruption. But the same historical circumstances that provided the conditions for Cavendish's authorship— exile and isolation during the civil war and Commonwealth[49]—also threatened to undermine the absolutist organization of property on which that authorship depended. Further, the condition that enabled her publication and public notice—her marriage to the duke of New- castle—threatened her self-construction as an author. For Cavendish, the capacity to own literary property offers the possibility of full social subjectivity and even a public self that becomes, in her circumstances, both utterly inappropriate and absolutely necessary.

(Im)material Worlds and Female Appropriation: The Plays

Just as the duchess represents her own social subjectivity with ambiva- lence, so she articulates conflicting positions on the relationship between women and property, literary and otherwise, throughout her writings. While in one poem she represents herself as the only woman poet at the Muse's banquet, elsewhere she configures imaginative writing as a feminine capacity and strength. She requests special consideration from her own sex, promising her poetry's innocence in spite of its vanity: "For that is so *naturall* to our *Sex*, as it were *unnaturall*, not to be so. Besides, *Poetry*, which is Built upon *Fancy*, Women may claime, as a *worke* be- longing most properly to themselves."[50] She takes the qualities of vanity and active imagination, signified in her culture as evidence of women's triviality, and reconstructs from them a position from which women can claim authority.[51]

[48] Thomas Hobbes, *Leviathan*, ed. Richard Tuck (Cambridge: Cambridge University Press, 1991), 25.
[49] Mendelson suggests that the proliferation of women's writing during the com- monwealth may have given Cavendish the courage to publish. *The Mental World of Stuart Women*, 29.
[50] Cavendish, "To All Noble and Worthy Ladies," letter prefacing *Poems and Phancies*.
[51] See Ian Maclean, *The Renaissance Notion of Woman: A Study in the Fortunes of Scholasticism and Medical Science in European Intellectual Life* (Cambridge: Cambridge University Press, 1980).

The extent to which sheer ambivalence informs such contradictions should not be underestimated. Still, Cavendish may have silently assumed limitations by rank in her conception of "women." Although Sara Heller Mendelson concludes that gender "entailed certain common experiences which transcended class differences," she nevertheless points out that "some writers have questioned whether seventeenth-century women formed a group in any meaningful sense of the word."[52] Thus when Cavendish makes generalizations about "women," it remains unclear whom she intends to include. An aristocratic ideology of property, in which ownership falls to a "worthy" elite, provides the conditions for the ability to imagine certain women in positions of full social subjectivity to which gender would otherwise prevent access.[53] Cavendish's plays, which were probably never performed on the public stage, attempt to imagine ways in which the elite woman could inhabit the position of author and owner.

Marriage and sexuality occupy a prominent place in Cavendish's dramatic compositions because they stand as the greatest barriers to elite women's property and independence. Yet the duchess goes further than attempting to renegotiate marriage alone; her plays and her *New Blazing World* try to reimagine structures of gender and desire. Women commonly fall in love with women in her plays: in *Matrimonial Trouble, The Sociable Companions,* and *Loves Adventures,* cross-dressed women find themselves the objects of female desire. Following Valerie Traub, I will call those relationships "homoerotic," "in order to differentiate between, on the one hand, the early modern legal and medical discourses of sodomy and tribadism and, on the other hand, the modern identificatory classifications of 'lesbian,' 'gay,' and 'homosexual.' "[54] Traub observes that female homoerotic desire appears commonly on the early modern stage, but it only provokes what Judith Butler calls "gender trouble" when it threatens reproduction. Cavendish, it seems to me, exploits what Traub terms the "(in)significance" of " 'femme-femme' " love in order to make some gender trouble, both for its own sake and as an imaginative way to reconfigure the property relations so profoundly intertwined with

[52] Mendelson, *The Mental World of Stuart Women,* 6, 5.

[53] See Gallagher, "Embracing the Absolute."

[54] Valerie Traub, "The (In)significance of 'Lesbian' Desire in Early Modern England," in *Erotic Politics: Desire on the Renaissance Stage,* ed. Susan Zimmerman (New York: Routledge, 1992), 156. See also her "Psychomorphology of the Clitoris," *GLQ: A Journal of Gay and Lesbian Studies* 2 (1995): 81–113.

reproduction. While the three plays mentioned above use the trope of mistaken homoerotic desire conventionally (the audience always knows the character's gender), other plays make more serious gender trouble by deliberately withholding the character's "true" gender identity.

Judith Butler has powerfully argued that we must understand desire not as a force naturally emerging from biological sex, but rather as a social construction shaped by gender differences that uphold a heterosexual matrix.[55] Butler's argument, I believe, offers insight into why Cavendish, in plays that quite clearly insist on full social subjectivity for elite women, imagines so many situations of alternative desire (of which homoeroticism is only one). The duchess seeks to disrupt a system within her elite experience in which the opposition between masculine and feminine (in the service of the heterosexual matrix) creates an opposition between the subject positions of owner and non-owner. Her plays explore alternative forms of eroticism for their own sake and as part of a strategy that provides the conditions for reimagining these property relations. Like Butler, Cavendish uncovers the potential to reimagine subject positions through a recognition of gender as performance.[56] While the duchess's writing *about* writing endlessly struggles to define grounds for owning literary property, mostly in the form of claims to originality, her plays imagine alternative economies of desire in which aristocratic women become owners of themselves, their words, and even sometimes of estates.

Youth's Glory and Death's Banquet (Parts I and II) represents marriage as irreconcilable with authorship for its heroine.[57] In the primary of two plots, Lady Sanspareille asks her parents for permission never to marry and instead to read, write, study, and lecture. She succeeds tremendously at this project, even gaining the notice of Queen Attention. The men

[55] Judith Butler, *Gender Trouble: Feminism and the Subversion of Identity* (New York: Routledge, 1990).

[56] On this point, see Sophie Tomlinson's excellent essay, "'My Brain the Stage': Margaret Cavendish and the Fantasy of Female Performance." Tomlinson points out that "one of the most striking features of Cavendish's plays is their use of performance as a metaphor of possibility for women" (137). She argues that while aristocratic female performance was seen as self-expression, professional performance signified inauthenticity.

[57] Linda R. Payne sees this play as a warning. Cavendish's dream world, she argues, "is populated by women who seek to live their lives without restraint and others who warn them that to do so means failure or death." "Dramatic Dreamscape," 31.

who attend her lectures all want to marry her, but Lady Sanspareille rejects them with philosophical arguments against marriage. The suitors press more and more insistently. Instead of resolving this situation with marriage, however, Cavendish has the lady grow ill and die. Sanspareille's father, consumed by grief, delivers her funeral oration and dies as well. A subplot provides more bodies for Death to feast on: Lady Incontinent runs away with Lord de l'Amour, leaving a husband who was "rich, and used [her] well" to live instead as a "Wanton."[58] Lord de l'Amour must marry Lady Innocent, but he promises Lady Incontinent that she will nevertheless rule his household. But Lord de l'Amour gradually falls in love with Lady Innocent; Lady Incontinent, fearing for her position in the household, accuses her rival of theft and wanton conversation, bribing the maid Falshood to give false testimony. Lady Innocent kills herself in despair. Lady Incontinent, however, kills herself as well when she finds out that Falshood planned to betray her; the maid herself falls dead upon her confession. Lord de l'Amour has the bodies of Falshood and Incontinent thrown to the beasts, then kills himself at the tomb of Lady Innocent. Oddly, these two plots never intersect; nevertheless, they tell parallel and frustrated stories of women's attempts to find happiness, property, and social subjectivity outside of marriage.

Lady Sanspareille offers the performance of female intellectual authority: philosophers come from all over to hear her speak and gaze upon her beauty. Her authorship, however, depends upon the disruption of traditional economies of property and desire. She resists, for example, her mother's desire to make her "a good housewife"(123) and studies science and literature with her father instead.[59] "Let me tell you, Wife," argues Father Love, "that is the reason all women are fools; for women breeding up women, one fool breeding up another, and as long as that custom lasts there is no hopes of amendment" (123). For Lady Sanspareille to become a philosopher, she must disrupt the family's genealogy, inhabit the traditionally masculine position of heir, and avoid the feminine tasks of housekeeping and reproduction. "Do you love me as well," she asks her father, "as you think you could your Grand-

---

[58] Cavendish, *Playes Written by the Marchioness of Newcastle*, 125. Future references are cited in the text.

[59] In much of her writing, Cavendish similarly avoids a feminist political position without giving up the possibility of women's authorship and accomplishment by claiming an exceptional status for herself or for one character.

children?" (130). When he answers positively, she carefully presents her request: "Would you not think me strangely unnatural, and unworthy of your love, to wish or desire you to break the line of your Posterity, and bury succession in my grave?" By creating a father who answers that he would "rather live in thy fame, than live or dye in an infamous and foolish succession" (131), Cavendish imagines a paternal authority that values the daughter's individual potential for accomplishment over her capacity to bear children. Lady Sanspareille's authorship in this play depends upon shifting the family's genealogy from one in which she provides a link between a patriarch and his male succession to one in which she becomes the only and final heir.[60]

Lady Sanspareille's authorship, then, depends upon her position as heir rather than (reproductive) wife. As her mother exemplifies, a wife does not appear to be able to lead an intellectual life. Her mother, in fact, dismisses Sanspareille's desire to speak as the equivalent of becoming a "Stage-player" (126). (Sanspareille, however, defends the legitimacy of drama.) As the owning subject in the marriage, the man, Lady Sanspare-ille fears, would take control over her writing and speaking. Even if she found a husband who allowed her time for contemplation, he might "not approve of my works, were they never so worthy, and by no perswasion, or reason allow of there publishing; as if it were unlawfull, or against nature, for Women to have wit" (131).

Lady Sanspareille remains chaste in order to preserve her literary property; she finds an alternative eroticism, however, in spectacle and scholarship itself. As she earns a wider reputation, men come from afar to hear her philosophy and gaze on her beauty. Lady Sanspareille, reversing traditional arguments, rejects all private audiences and partici-pates in every imaginable public one: "She can plead cases at the Bar, decide causes in the Court of Judicature, make Orations on publick Theaters; act parts, and speak speeches on the Stage, argue in the Schooles, preach in the Pulpits, either in Theology, Philosophy, moral and natural, and also phisick and Metaphysick" (158). As noted, speaking in public protects not only her literary property but also her body as

---

[60] Father Love offers her the choice of any desire, but she chooses the life of a scholar: "What doth your ambition aim at? If it be honour, I have an Estate will buy thee an honourable Husband; if it be riches, I will be saving, and live thriftily, if it be gallantry, or bravery, I will maintain thee at the hight of my fortune, wear Frieze my self, and adorn thee in Diamond, Silver and Gold" (129).

sexual property, for it avoids the temptation of a private discussion. Lecturing, however, proves as erotic as it is chaste: the entire male audience falls under the twin spells of her wit and beauty. In her final philosophical discourse of the play, Sanspareille appears before her admiring male audience dressed as a bride "and her audience," the stage direction reads, "which are all Lovers; these stand gazing upon her" (158). In this erotically charged context, she delivers a speech on the inconveniences of marriage. As Lady Sanspareille increasingly feels pressure to marry from both these suitors and her mother, she reconstitutes public lecturing as her own erotic alternative to private marriage: "I c[a]nnot be wife to you all," she declares, "wherefore since I cannot be every mans wife, I will dye every mans Maid" (161). Like her writing, her authorial body can be shared by all men but owned by none.

The inexplicable death of Lady Sanspareille has been read as Cavendish's inability to imagine her heroine's future.[61] Alternatively, though, it could be read as resistance to the marital closure that the plot appears to require. The lady's scholarly life reconfigures desire and thus challenges received subject positions; her death comes abruptly, but carries an emotional force that originates from a sense of the impossibility of this desired alternative. It is as if fame itself—her sharing of herself with so many lovers—necessitates death as an escape from marriage. "The people do flock about the house to see her," Father Love remarks, "as I think they will pull it upon my head if she shews not her self to them" (166). Earlier, in fact, a Gentleman has suggested that "the Lady Sanspareilles wit, is as if it would over-power her brain" (145). Death closes in on Sanspareille at the moment that the plot demands marriage.

The interspersed scenes from the subplot further suggest that the duchess's abrupt and pessimistic ending nevertheless seeks an alternative to the institution of marriage and women's vulnerability within it. The heterosexual relations and deceptions in this plot represent marriage not merely as unappealing, but as so corrupting that it seems to infect Sanspareille, even though the plots never meet. Lady Sanspareille grows ill the moment that Lady Incontinent accuses Lady Innocent of stealing her necklace; she loses her pulse right after a scene showing Lady Innocent weeping on the ground, lamenting that "the spring of grief doth send forth streams of tears to wash off my disgrace, and the foul spots which slandring tongues have stain'd, or rather stain'd my reputation;

[61] See Payne, "Dramatic Dreamscape," 29.

... but my dead reputation is imbalm'd with salt tears, bitter groans, shrowded in sorrows, and intomb'd in misery" (166). The fragility of Lady Innocent's reputation within a corrupt patriarchal institution resonates through the main plot, in which the heroine does not shrink from fame. But while Sanspareille tries to construct a position *outside* of patriarchal relations by disrupting the family genealogy and choosing the love of many over the love of one, Lady Incontinent and Lord de l'Amour accept this system but cheat within it. Lord de l'Amour wants to keep Lady Incontinent as his lover, but will not alter property relations or defy his "Fathers commands so terrifying, and my vows so binding" (125). "Would you have me cut off the line of my Posterity," he demands of Lady Incontinent, "by never marrying?" (125). Lady Sanspareille puts the same question to her father with all seriousness; for Lord de l'Amour, however, ending his line represents an unthinkable possibility. Lady Innocent's loss of her reputation over a presumed desire for illegitimate ownership (stealing a necklace) plunges her into melancholy and suicide. Although the plots never meet, the slander against Lady Innocent for theft reveals the precariousness of Lady Sanspareille's literary appropriation. Both women struggle to establish an appropriate relationship to property: Lady Sanspareille through the self-ownership that her rejection of marriage permits, Lady Innocent through passive acquiescence to an unhappy marriage. Neither survives.

Bell in Campo similarly represents a world in which property confirms social and political subjecthood, yet offers more optimism than *Youth's Glory and Death's Banquet*. The heroine finds alternative pleasure in a community of warrior women; her pleasure in women, however, increases the happiness of her marriage. This play compares the responses of three women to civil war: Madam Jantil, a traditionally virtuous wife and later widow; Madam Passionate, who becomes a foolish and profligate widow, and Lady Victoria, who refuses to stay behind and instead leads a female army to triumph. Lady Victoria offers a hopeful alternative to Lady Sanspareille, for she integrates heroism, social subjectivity, marriage, and survival; when she wins the war, she demands and receives new property rights for the warrior women. Still, the performance of heroic deeds demands at least temporary separation from men, for "men are apt to corrupt the noble minds of women, and to alter their gallant, worthy, and wise resolutions" (593). Women can achieve self-determination only in the absence of men; since men "have ... Authority over [the women], as Husbands, Fathers, Brothers, or the like, they are apt to fright them with threats into a slavish obedience" (593). When war breaks out, Lady Victoria begs her husband for permission to accompany him, for compared to the misery of his absence, "Long marches will be but as a breathing walk, the hard ground feel as a Feather-bed, and the starry Sky a spangled Canopy" (581). After much argument, the Lord General consents; Seigneur Valeroso, however, will not allow Madam Jantil to attend. She shows slightly less courage, obeying more readily than Lady Victoria and even suggesting that her husband stay home. Madam Passionate merely weeps at the news of war and demands of her husband, "Why should you go to the Wars now you are in years, and not so fit for action as those that are young?" (586).

Lady Victoria earns the right to attend her husband in war by playing off one patriarchal value against another. She declares her passion for her husband, but reminds him to

> consider and reckon all the married women you have heard or read of, that were absented from their Husbands, although upon just and necessary occasions, but had some Ink of aspersions flung upon them, although their wives were old, illfavoured, decrepid and diseased women, or were they as pure as light, or as innocent as Heaven; and wheresoever this Ink of aspersion is thrown, it sticks so fast, that the spots are never rubb'd out, should it fall on Saints, they must wear the marks as a Badge of misfortunes, and what man had not better be thought or called an uxorious Husband, than to be despised and laught at, as being but thought a Cuckhold? (581)

Even the virtuous Penelope, Victoria cleverly argues, "parled and received Amorous Treaties . . . questionless there were Amorous Glances shot from loving Eyes of either party" (581). While she represents her desire to attend the wars as the protection of patriarchal sexual property, her creation a female army self-consciously renegotiates patriarchal authority. If women can prove themselves courageous on the battlefield, she reasons, "Men might change their opinions, insomuch as to believe we are fit to be Copartners in their Governments, and to help rule the World, where now we are kept as Slaves forced to obey; wherefore let us makes our selves free, either by force, merit, or love" (588–589).

Cavendish's Lady Victoria uses female heroism to challenge women's subordination in a way that many representations of warrior women do not. As Simon Shepherd has argued, this popular trope tends to expose the insufficient masculinity and heroism of men rather than posing any challenge to patriarchy.[62] Like other literary Amazons, Lady Victoria succeeds where men fail: having lost the first battle, the men find themselves once again overwhelmed by the enemy when the women's army rescues them: "[The women] did not only rout this Army of Faction, killing and wounding many, and set their own Countrymen at liberty, and recovered their losses, and gained many spoils, and took numbers of Prisoners of their Enemies with Bag and Baggage, but they pursued those that fled into their Trenches" (611).[63] Instead of showing gratitude for their lives, though, some of the men only experience their rescue as humiliation, feeling "doubly or trebly overcome, twice by their Enemy, and then by the gallant actions of the Females which out-did them" (612). The Lord General attempts to reconcile the two armies by representing the relations between them as an imaginary courtship:

> The General told them he made no question but that most men knew by experience that women were won by gentle perswasions and fair promises, and not by rigid actions or angry frowns, besides said he, all noble natures strive to assist the weakest in all lawfull actions, and that he was no gallant man that submits not to a woman in all things that are honourable, and when he doth dissent it must be in a Courtly manner, and a Complemental behavior and expression, for that women were Creatures made by nature, for men to love and admire, to protect and defend, to cherish and maintain, to seek and to sue to, and especially such women which have out-done all their Sex . . . 'tis fit to these women above all others we should yield our selves Prisoners, not only in love but in Arms. (612)

The Lord General's symbolics of courtship nostalgically recall the court of Queen Elizabeth, in which men could offer humble obedience to the monarch without disturbing patriarchal relations by similarly representing their obedience as courtly love.[64] The women themselves, however, find symbolic courtship an unsatisfactory reward and demand material

[62] Simon Shephard, *Amazons and Warrior Women: Varieties of Feminism in Seventeenth-Century Drama* (New York: St. Martin's Press, 1981).

[63] The "Army of Faction" appears to be a thinly veiled version of the Puritans.

[64] See Louis A. Montrose, "*A Midsummmer Night's Dream* and the Shaping Fantasies of Elizabethan Culture: Gender, Power, Form," in *Rewriting the Renaissance: The Discourses of Sexual Difference in Early Modern Europe,* ed. Margaret W. Ferguson, Maureen Quilligan, and Nancy J. Vickers (Chicago: University of Chicago Press, 1986): 65–87.

prizes. Upon receiving a letter of apology for their ingratitude in which the men declare themselves "*taken Captives by your Beauties*" and "*bound as your Slaves by your valours,*" the women "fall into a great laughter" (616). The women laugh in their triumph, but they also laugh *at* this letter in which the men place them all on a pedestal with no concrete concessions. In the final act, however, the king offers more substantial rewards. Thanks to Lady Victoria, women will now "keep the purse," order the servants, "buy in what Provisions they will," claim as their own "all the Jewels, Plate, and household Furniture, and shall "hereafter in this Kingdome be Mistriss in their own houses and Families" (631). Women now also get to go "abroad when they will" to plays, balls, and other public events, wear whatever they want and eat "when they will, and of what they will, and as much as they will, and as often as they will." The aristocratic women earn greater access to family resources, and the lower ranking women get to claim one level of status above women who did not serve in the army. If the men's army rewards the women with clichés about their enslavement to beauty, the king himself rewards them for heroic action with new forms of domestic authority and consumer pleasures.[65]

In another kind of play, the subplot might simply tell a comparative moral tale between two widows, one loyal and modest, the other lustful and profligate. Yet the true point of comparison in *Bell* lies between women who cannot imagine themselves in the subject position of possessor and women who can. While Lady Victoria leads her army to triumph, Madam Jantil and Madam Passionate stay home and lament the battlefield deaths of their husbands. Madam Jantil barely eats, spending her days and nights in prayer, sadness, and contemplation. Madam Passionate, on the other hand, throws parties, drinks spirits, and invites

---

[65] As usual in Cavendish's work, property rights for women have different meanings for women in different classes. Lady Victoria's social revolution takes as its goal the redistribution of property into the hands of elite women as well as elite men. Her army strictly maintains a hierarchy of class. In order to acquire arms, the army attacks the garrison town to which the men sent them for safety. "We shall easily Master the Pesants," Lady Victoria imperiously declares, "who are for the most part naked and defenceless . . . by which means we may plunder all their Horses, and victual our selves out of their Granaries" (594). As Lady Victoria predicts, though, many of the town women "did so approve of their gallant actions" that they joined the army that plundered their town. The women of the town in this play do not see themselves as having the same kind of stake in the property the Amazons pirated.

young men to visit her. Cavendish identifies ethical differences between the two responses, but neither lady copes productively with the responsibilities and power of widowhood; their ultimately similar fates deconstruct the ethical polarities. Just as Madam Passionate wept when her husband left, so she becomes hysterical upon first hearing of his death and repeatedly faints. Soon, however, she begins to eat and drink heartily, taking pleasure in the visits of gold-digging young men. (For both Madam Passionate and the Amazons, Cavendish associates self-determination with the freedom to choose one's food.) Passionate rejects the attentions of Monsieur la Gravity, who vows "affection, respect, and tender regard," resolving this time to marry "to please my fancy" (622). Meanwhile, Monsieur Comerade counsels the young and handsome Monsieur Compagnion to pursue Passionate, for even if she lives long, "You will have her Estate to please your self withall, which Estate will buy you fine Horses, great Coaches, maintain Servants and great Retinues to follow you" (623). Giving in to the "young Tooth in her old head," Lady Passionate marries this man—a mistake, for once she re-enters a marriage she loses all the property rights that she had enjoyed after her husband's death. Along with her property, she loses pleasure, choice food, and her very sense of self: "O unfortunate woman that I am, I was rich, and lived in plenty, none to control me, I was Mistress of my self, Estate and Family, all my Servants obeyed me ... devising delightfull sports to entertain my time, making delicious meats to please my palat ..." (626). Now the servants scoff at her orders, bowing to the greater authority of her husband and "following those that command the purse." Monsieur Compagnion secures all her property as his first conjugal act: as Madam Passionate complains, he "seized on all my goods, then let Leases for many lives out of my Lands, for which he had great fines, and now he cuts down all my Woods, and fells all my Lands of Interitance, which I foolishly and fondly delivered by deed of gift, the first day I married, devesting my self of all power" (626). Once she enters into this marriage, Madam Passionate can no longer even claim the privilege of her rank: her new husband brings his whores into their house and kicks Madam Passionate out of bed, inviting her maid to replace her. Husbands retain the ability to treat servants like ladies, and ladies like servants.[66]

Madam Jantil behaves far more virtuously than Madam Passionate,

[66] The scandal of an upper-class man marrying a maid or a lower-class woman is a theme throughout Cavendish's writing.

but nevertheless also ends up bereft of all property and unable to go on living. Upon learning of her husband's death, she rejects all worldly pleasures and spends her time praying and planning his monument. She ritually bids farewell to all possession as well, appearing first on stage "attired in a Garment of rich Cloth of gold girt loosly about her, and a Mantle of Crimson Velvet lined with powdered Ermins over that ... upon her Head a rich Crown of Jewels, as also Pendant Jewels in her Ear, and on her Wrists costly Bracelets" (613). She recites some verses to the tomb of her husband and lays aside all her jewels and her rich clothes, donning a "pure white light silk loose Garment, girt about her with a white silk Cord, and then puts on a thin black Veil over it" (614). "Thus," she declares, "all these Worldly vanities I wave,/ And bury them all in my Husband's grave." She later gives away her entire estate and even her life: in an equally ritualistic scene, a secretary reads Jantil's generous will, which enumerates all her material divestments. Jantil then joins her husband in death. But while Jantil dies peacefully and Passionate faces the end of her life in misery, both experience widowhood as the loss of all property and pleasure, with death as the only escape. Unlike Lady Victoria, neither of these ladies can inhabit the position of owner or negotiate an alternative to loss and death.

Bell in Campo, then, offers three alternatives for female social subjectivity that ultimately differ by access to pleasure and property. Passionate, like the triumphant Amazons, eats and drinks what she wants, but loses all property, luxury, and selfhood upon the indulgence of heterosexual desire. Madam Jantil presents a more complex alternative: she makes no parallel error, but unlike Lady Victoria, cannot imagine life without her husband. The duchess compares these alternatives in terms of property: in one scene Jantil enumerates all the possessions she gives away, and in the next a herald itemizes the new rights that Lady Victoria has gained for women, many involving the control of household funds. The two widows keep men, dead or alive, central to their identities; Lady Victoria, by contrast, creates an alternative female empire in which men remain only ambivalently admitted allies. The result, however, is not a denial of sexuality, but rather an attempt to imagine desire outside of patriarchal gender and property polarities. Lady Victoria returns to her husband only when patriarchy as previously organized no longer stands. And in this play, the temporary deconstruction of gender polarity leads ultimately to greater conjugal love, for the Lord General "seems to be very proud of his Lady, . . . he looks upon her with a most pleased Eye"

(633). Victoria, however, must first explore an alternative to the limits of traditional gender divisions. Her reward includes greater control of household resources, authorship, and public recognition, for the king commands that "poets shall strive to set forth your praise" and that "all your gallant acts shall be recorded in story, and put in the chief Library of the Kingdome" (632). Victoria herself "shall alwayes wear a Lawrel Garland."

Cavendish's heroines must reimagine the possibilities of desire in order the achieve the gender disruption that would permit them full social subjectivity and the capacity to own writing, estates, clothes, and food. In *Youth's Glory and Death's Banquet* and in *Bell in Campo,* this reimagination takes the form of temporarily rejecting monogamous heterosexuality in favor of, respectively, the erotics of speaking to lots of men and a community of warrior women. In two other plays—*The Presence* and *The Convent of Pleasure*—the duchess explores female homoerotic desire as both an articulation of pleasurable possibilities and a strategy for making gender trouble. This is not to argue that Cavendish constructs homosexuality as a category, a social phenomenon that, as Foucault and others have argued, was not institutionalized until the eighteenth century.[67] But the inscription of women's erotic desire for other women, like Lady Sanspareille's marriage to all men and Lady Victoria's Amazon army, permits the disruption of bipolar gender oppositions that regulate reproduction, ownership, and authorship. The performativity of gender captured the duchess's imagination and shaped her dramatic writing. She may even have seen or hoped to see these plays performed by the women at court. As Sophie Tomlinson points out, Cavendish lived for a time in a court culture in which women fully—and sometimes even *exclusively*—participated as performers.[68] Further, as Tomlinson argues, Cavendish may cast professional actresses as signifiers of inauthenticity, but nevertheless represents amateur women's performance as a mode of self-expression and "self-enhancement."[69]

Cavendish's fascination with the disruptive potential of the performativity of gender found expression outside her writing, too; several

---

[67] See Michel Foucault, *History of Sexuality, Vol. 1,* trans. Robert Hurley (New York: Vintage Books, 1980); see also Kristina Straub, *Sexual Suspects: Eighteenth-Century Players and Sexual Ideology* (Princeton: Princeton University Press, 1992).

[68] Tomlinson, "'My Brain the Stage,'" 138–139.

[69] Ibid., 141.

contemporaries report the duchess's fondness for wearing men's attire and sometimes even a combination of men's and women's clothes. Biographer Sara Heller Mendelson quotes a ballad composed by John Evelyn about Cavendish:

> her head-geare was so pritty
> I ne'er saw anything so witty
>   Tho I was halfe a feard
> God blesse us when I first did see her
> She look'd so like a cavaliere
>   But she had no beard.

In 1665 Sir Charles Lyttleton saw the duchess "dressed in a vest, and instead of courtesies, made legs and bows to the ground with her hand and head."[70] Cavendish declares in her autobiography that she took the greatest delight in inventing her own fashions. She reports being captivated by a foreign woman who "was the Best Female Actor that ever I saw; and for Acting a Man's Part, she did it so Naturally as if she had been of that Sex, and yet she was of a Neat, Slender Shape; but being in her Dublet and Breeches, and a Sword hanging by her side, one would have believed she never had worn a Petticoat, and had been more used to Handle a Sword than a Distaff; and when she Danced in a Masculine Habit, she would Caper Higher, and Oftener than any of the Men, although they were great Masters in the Art of Dancing, and when she Danced after the Fashion of her own Sex, she Danced Justly, Evenly, Smoothly, And Gracefully."[71] It is not cross-dressing alone that fascinates the duchess, but the actress's skillful capacity to slip into different gender identities. Indeed, Sara Heller Mendelson describes Cavendish's own gender identity as "constant improvisation."[72] Homoerotic desire even becomes a trope for women's writing itself. Lady Sanspareille, for example, describes composition as an erotic encounter with the Muses in *Youth's Glory and Death's Banquet*: "The Muses the Handmaids to Nature, doth as all other Maidens, loves the Courtship of the Masculine Sex, which is the cause, or reason they seldome visit their own Sex, but passes time in their Company, and Conversation of men; by some men, they

---

[70] Mendelson, *The Mental World of Stuart Women*, 46.

[71] Cavendish, *Sociable Letters*, no. 195.

[72] Mendelson, *The Mental World of Stuart Women*, 57.

are only admired, and loved, by others, they are sued to, and enjoyed, which happy Suters, are Poets" (149). Sanspareille later wishes to return to these ladies on her deathbed:

I in the Muses Arms desire to Dye,
For I was bred up in their Company:
And my request's to them, when I am dead,
I may amongst them be remembered. (169)

"The Purchase of Poets," in which a group of poets travels to Parnassus to compete for the hand of Fame in marriage, similarly represents writing as an erotic encounter with female muses.[73] Cavendish embraces rather than diminishes this trope's eroticism without adopting a masculine voice.[74]

The main plot of *The Presence*, which has been read as an autobiographical account of Margaret Lucas's own adventures at court, tells the story of Lady Bashful's discomfort with the more worldly maids of honor and her marriage to Lord Loyalty, who has much in common with the duke of Newcastle. The secondary plot, however, provides greater interest for our purposes. The Princess falls in love by imagining her perfect mate and interviewing all the men in the kingdom to see if any of them fit her platonic ideal. Scandal arises, however, when she unambivalently selects a humble sailor. Her outraged father condemns the sailor to death for the audacity to love the Princess, and after impassioned protestations of love by both characters (through a Fool who acts as a go-between), the sailor mounts the scaffold. But before the hanging can take place, a "grave Man" steps forward and announces to the crowd that "this Person which is here ready to die for Love, (yet not for the Love you imagine) is no wayes capable of Marrying your Princess; for this Person is not only a Woman, but a Princess her self; being Daughter to the Emperor of *Persia*."[75] The Princess, it appears, had been in love with another woman! When one of the maids asks the Princess if her "Melancholy passion of Love" has passed with the new knowledge of its object's sex, the Princess answers that "My Melancholy is past, but not

[73] Cavendish, *Poems and Phancies,* 66–67.
[74] In "To Poets," for example, Cavendish begs her colleagues not to dismiss her work simply on the grounds that women do not usually compose verse. *Poems and Phancies,* 148–150.
[75] Cavendish, *Plays, Never Before Printed,* 80. Future references are cited in the text.

my Love; for that will live so long as I shall live, and will remain pure in my Soul, when my body is dead and turn'd to dust" (84). Thus her feelings have changed little with this new gender information. The important difference to the community, however, emerges as property rather than sexuality, for the revelation of the sailor's femaleness actually *excuses* desire. The sailor's exposure as female renders her unthreatening and innocent, for she cannot, as the grave man tells the crowd, *marry* the Princess. In itself, the homoerotic love disturbs no one in the play; the sailor cannot violate class boundaries because she cannot inhabit the position of patriarchal husband to the Princess, and thus the next emperor and owner of the royal estate.[76] After introducing the possibility of such a great violation of status, the play's homoerotic configuration of desire, which dispels the status disparity of the lovers, poses little threat by comparison.

The play "explains" this strange desire between women when the audience finds out that the Fool had actually managed to switch the jailed sailor with his twin sister to prevent the hanging. Nevertheless, this literal explanation does not dispel the play's homoerotic suggestion, for the Princess herself maintains that individuals, rather than sexual difference, inspire desire. Further, the ragged edges of this play leave open ambiguities surrounding sexuality and property division. The Fool initially attempts to convince the jailor to release the sailor by insisting that authority actually follows a matriarchal lineage: "The Princess must be Empress, because that Dignity comes by her Mother; and the Emperor is but Emperor during life, and so upon Courtesie; and when the Princess is Empress, she will be sure to hang you . . . and ruine all your Posterity" (73). Although this ploy fails, it suggests an alternative control of property and authority, confirms the power of the Princess, and may even have had something to do with the Fool's ability to switch the twins. Unlike in Shakespearean gender disguise, the audience has no more information than the Princess and must, at least momentarily, believe in her love and desire for another woman. *The Presence*, then, leaves open the possibility of an economically autonomous princess who falls in love with another woman. With the dignity of her office inherited from her mother and her love partner a woman, no man would stand between the princess and her authority, property, and power.

[76] See Traub, "The (In)significance of 'Lesbian' Desire in Early Modern England." Traub, as noted earlier, emphasizes the related issue of reproduction.

The Presence thus continues to reassert homoerotic desire in spite of the plot resolution of two marriages, not only as an erotic possibility but also as an alternative configuration of gender and social subjectivity. When the Princess insists on her platonic love for the disembodied being of this person, the Fool challenges her: "Lady, you speak extravagantly, talking of Chast Love, when as never Lover was Chast, for they commit Adultery either in Mind or Body" (86). Through the Fool, Cavendish explores the eroticism of platonic love. Further, the Princess does not cross these boundaries alone, for upon the revelation of the sailor's female sex, her father the Emperor falls in love with the person he was about to hang. (Unsurprisingly, the twins turn out to be the children of a foreign king; the Princess and her father each marry one of them.) The sailor might be differently signified, but the twins still resemble each other, as the Fool puts it, "as a Pea to a Pea" (87). In the courtier plot, the sailor's gender instability sparks thoughts about new pleasures and gender possibilities:

> SPEND[-ALL]. Why, the *Sailer* that was a Man, and the Man that was proved a Lady, and the Lady a Princess, is now proved no Lady, but is a Man again, and a *Sailer*.
> MOTH[ER] OF THE MAIDS. How so?
> SPEND. How so? why even as the Man that could change himself into a Wolf, and from a Wolf into a Man again; so the *Sailer* has the art to make himself a Man, or Woman when he pleases.
> MODE. I would he could teach all the Court this art.
> MOTH. The gods forbid; for if all you Gentlemen should be Women, what would my pritty birds do for Courtly Servants.
> SPEND. Why, they might convert themselves into Men, and then there would be a better agreement amongst us; for when we are Women, we shall be kinder to them, when they are Men, then they are to us now they are Women.
> MODE. But what would your old Lady do, if you were a Woman? [Spend-all is about to marry a rich old woman for her money.]
> SPEND. Faith, as well as she doth now.
> MODE. But let us leave our talking, and go to the *Sailer*, to learn this Art. (84–85)

The sailor's trick of sexual metamorphosis encourages the proliferation of sexuality, for men inhabiting the female position would offer more acts of sexual kindness than women now offer, and women inhabiting the male position would surely oblige. Further, Spend-all insists that he would offer his future wife equal sexual pleasure as a man or a woman. On one level, this comment jokes that he plans to offer her no pleasure either way, but it also suggests that his lovemaking *as a woman* would bring as much pleasure as his lovemaking as a man. The sexual ambiguity of the sailor/prince/princess, then, may end in two traditional heterosexual unions, but suggests a range of possibilities of desire.

The Convent of Pleasure, however, offers the most disruptive vision of gender, property, and desire in Cavendish's drama. While women become warriors in her *Bell in Campo* in order to negotiate with the men for control over family resources, Lady Happy of *The Convent of Pleasure* establishes women's property as an entirely separate place. She contends, in fact, that women can best experience pleasure on real estate owned by women. *The Convent of Pleasure* opens with two men discussing the death of Lord *Fortunate*, who "left his Daughter, the Lady *Happy*, very rich, having no other Daughter but her" (1). The other man immediately notes that all young men will now spend their money in attempts to attract her attention. Cavendish, then, establishes marriage from the opening as a way for men to take over women's property: before learning anything about Lady Happy, the gentleman predicts the way he and his friends will invest in their own adornment in order to gain her estate. Lady Happy, however, rejects not just marriage in particular but all imaginable forms of heterosexuality for their inability to produce sufficient female pleasure. When Madam Mediator insists that Lady Happy marry, she responds,

> Put the case I should Marry the best of Men, if any best there be; yet would a Marry'd life have more crosses and sorrows then pleasure, freedom, or hapiness: nay Marriage to those that are virtuous is a greater restraint then a Monastery. Or, should I take delight in Admirers? they might gaze on my Beauty, and praise my Wit, and I received nothing from their eyes, nor lips; for Words vanish as soon as spoken, and Sights are not substantial. Besides, I should lose more of my Reputation by their Visits, then gain by their Praises. Or, should I quit Reputation and turn Courtizan, there would be more lost in my Health, then gained by my Lovers, I should find more pain than Pleasure . . . since there is so much folly, vanity and falshood in Men, why should Women trouble and vex themselves for their sake; for retiredness bars the life from nothing else but Men. (3–4)

In this speech, Lady Happy explores every permutation of heterosexuality she can imagine—marriage, courtship and flirtation, the free accumulation of lovers—and rejects each not for moral reasons, but for their lack of pleasure. Further, she distinguishes emphatically between the traditional convent, in which people inflict pain on themselves to please gods,[77] and her convent, in which women pursue pleasure.

Pleasure and property become truly possible for Lady Happy only in a world without men. The goal of her convent becomes the creation of an all-female economy as the only way to experience the range of sensual pleasures fully. This economy demands not the erasure of gender but the reorganization of subject positions along different lines. Thus she finds "Women-Physicians, Surgeons and Apothecaries," taking the job of "Lady-Prioress" herself (11). The convent further employs women "in all Places in their Gardens; and for Brewing, Baking, and making all sorts of things . . . some keep their Swine" (20). The convent creates its own economy in which women perform all the jobs, yet it offers pleasure only to the elite guests of Lady Happy. Cavendish recognizes—and even celebrates—the ways in which her imagined female pleasure and self-ownership depend upon the sacrifice of other women's pleasure. On any piece of property, she assumes, live the owners and the owned; Cavendish experiments with the possibility of a world that reserves both social positions for women alone, eliminating traditionally conceived gender as a significant distinction within the convent. She vows to take with her "many Noble Persons of my own Sex, as my Estate will plentifully maintain, such whose Births are greater then their Fortunes" (7).

Rather than imagining equality, then, the duchess reorganizes subject positions along purely class and proprietary lines; she imagines women as able to inhabit all of them. The ladies of the convent thus take the place of the gentlemen who opened the play, for they, not the gentlemen, gain access to property through affective and erotic ties to Lady Happy. In a world with no male presence, subject positions become restructured as pleasure seekers and pleasure providers, elite women who experience the multiple delights of the convent and laboring women who provide

[77] Lady Happy further defends her convent by wondering what kind of gods would take pleasure from the suffering of their worshippers. The duchess clearly uses this plot to attack Puritan rejections of sensual pleasure as well as the traditional Catholic convent.

those conditions for pleasure. The women who tend the swine provide pleasure from their labor, not from any erotic delight that their bodies potentially offer. The courtiers who hope to infiltrate the convent, in fact, figure out the irrelevance of traditional gender bipolarities. When Monsieur Take-pleasure suggests that the men "resolve to put our selves in Womens apparel" in order to sneak into the convent, Monsieur Adviser points out that "We shall never frame our Eyes and Mouths to such coy, dissembling looks, and pritty simpering Mopes and Smiles, as they do" (19–20). Courtly then concludes that "we will go as strong lusty Country-Wenches, that desire to serve them in Inferiour Places, and Offices, as Cook-maids, Landry-maids, Dairy-maids, and the like." Male laboring bodies can replace female laboring bodies without a noticeable difference: in this play, they inhabit the same subject position, for they potentially provide pleasure (through labor) to elite women. As dairy maids they would relinquish any phallic authority and become indistinguishable from "female" dairy maids. These men cannot, however, replace the erotic pleasure that Happy's friends provide; in fact, all erotic pleasure in *The Convent* originates in elite women's bodies. In a rare moment of sympathy, Adviser suggests that if he had the money, he would encloister himself in the same luxurious conditions. Take-pleasure, however, would not go "unless you had Women in your *Convent*" (19). Although Adviser suggests that "since Women can quit the pleasure of Men, we Men may well quit the trouble of Women," he nevertheless plots how to get into the convent. Elite women, then, remain the source of all erotic pleasure for both women and men.

The crisis in *The Convent* arises when the internal delineation of subject positions, based on a division between elite and laboring bodies with pleasure circulating only among the former, meets the external delineation, based on heterosexual binary gender positions. Without men, the convent becomes a playground for erotic pleasure reminiscent of the multiplicity of Julia Kristeva's "semiotic"—but it is available only to select women.[78] When Lady Happy describes her boredom with heterosexuality, she notes that she receives nothing from the way admirers "gaze on [her] Beauty" (3). In the convent of (nonphallic) pleasure, however, she provides "a great Looking-Glass in each Chamber, that we

---

[78] See Julia Kristeva, "The Semiotic and the Symbolic," in *Revolution in Poetic Language*, trans. Margaret Waller (New York: Columbia University Press, 1984), 19–106.

may view our selves and take pleasure in our own Beauties, whilst they
are fresh and young" (14). The position as the object of a male heterosexual gaze provides no pleasure, but the dual position of both object and
subject of female gazes offers tremendous pleasure. Thus the convent
also provides "Change of Garments . . . of the newest fashions for every
Season, and rich Trimming; so as we may be accoutred properly" (15).
The convent also furnishes elaborately decorated rooms and impeccably
tended lush gardens made possible through the semi-invisible labor of
lower-class women. Only aristocratic women are fully subjects, in the
sense that their bodies alone provide and experience the homo- and
autoerotic pleasures of the convent.

The homoerotic pleasures of the convent find both their central
expression and their crisis with the arrival of "a Princely brave Woman
truly, of a Masculine Presence" (16) with whom Lady Happy falls in love.
The Prince/ss enters the play as a masculine woman and leaves as a
feminine man. Even though this character becomes signified as masculine by the end, she functions as the feminine love object of Lady Happy
for most of the play. The audience shares Lady Happy's ignorance of
this person's "true" gender. Sophie Tomlinson, in fact, astutely notes
that the duchess withholds the dramatis personae until the end, thus
enhancing the suspense for the reader; further, Tomlinson persuasively
argues that Cavendish intended this role to be played by a woman.[79] The
Prince/ss fits comfortably into the erotic economy of the convent, in
which ladies regularly "do accoustre Themselves in Masculine-Habits,
and act Lovers-parts" (22). The Prince/ss thus instantly recognizes the
rules of the convent, in which gender is understood as performance.
Further, within the convent, the performance of "masculinity"—even by
a man—offers no threat and perhaps no difference from this performance by a woman. By giving up phallic authority, the Prince/ss gains
access to otherwise unavailable pleasures.[80]

In spite of the fluidity of delight and desire within the convent, the
erotic feelings Lady Happy experiences for the Prince/ss cause her concern: "My Name is *Happy*," she laments, "and so was my Condition,

[79] Tomlinson, "'My Brain the Stage,'" 157.
[80] "When the penis itself becomes simply a means of pleasure," writes Luce Irigaray,
". . . *the phallus loses its power*. Pleasure, so it is said, should be left to women, those
creatures so unfit for the seriousness of symbolic rules." "When the Goods Get
Together," trans. Claudia Reeder, in *New French Feminisms: An Anthology*, ed. Elaine
Marks and Isabelle de Courtivron (New York: Schocken Books, 1981), 108.

before I saw this Princess; but now I am like to be the most unhappy Maid alive: But why may not I love a Woman with the same affection I could a Man? No, no, Nature is Nature, and still will be/The same she was from all Eternity" (32). Nevertheless she *does* fall in love with the Prince/ss, who she, as well as the audience, understands as a woman. While this makes a tremendous difference given the division of subject positions outside the convent, her love for the Prince/ss remains appropriate given the circulation of desire within the convent. In the convent, nature is *not* nature but, like everything else, a performance. Lady Happy and her friends, for example, perform pastoral versions of nature by dressing up and acting out the parts of shepherds and shepherdesses. Further, the convent itself embraces and constructs nature with its carefully tended interior gardens. The love between Lady Happy and the Prince/ss, especially in their performance of a "marriage" to each other while dressed as shepherd and shepherdess, represents not only female homoeroticism, but also a threatening reconfiguration of positionality in which elite women become owning and pleasure-seeking subjects.

For the women in the convent, alternative configurations of desire offer alternative constructions of gender. The courtiers who protest the convent, however, resist this alternative and thus cannot comprehend the possibility of women's pleasure without them. When Madam Mediator tells them that Lady Happy has "above twenty Ladies with her, yet she hath a numerous Company of Female Servants, so as there is no occasion for Men," Take-pleasure responds: "If there be so many Women, there will be the more use for Men ... you say, The Lady *Happy* is become a Votress to Nature; and if she be a Votress to Nature, she must be a Mistress to Men" (12). Take-pleasure can comprehend pleasure only in heterosexual terms and imagines no other possibility. While the courtiers do not object to the pleasures within the convent, they become outraged by an arrangement that renders Lady Happy's fortune inaccessible to them. Cavendish explores this relationship between property and identity in a comic exchange between Take-pleasure and his servant Dick:

TAKEPL. Dost thou think I shall get the Lady *Happy*?
DICK. Not if it be her fortune to continue in that name.
TAKEPL. Why?
DICK. Because if she Marry your Worship she must change her Name;
    for the Wife takes the Name of her Husband, and quits her own.
TAKEPL. Faith, *Dick*, if I had her wealth I should be *Happy*.

DICK. It would be according as your Worship would use it; but, on my conscience, you would be more happy with the Ladie's Wealth, then the Lady would be with your Worship. (9)

Upon her marriage to Monsieur Take-pleasure (who, perhaps, would take all her pleasure), Lady Happy would literally no longer be Happy. All her Happy-ness would belong to her husband. Dick concludes that "Women are always unhappy in their thoughts, both before and after Marriage" (9); Cavendish, however, allows Lady Happy to be Happy by placing her, not before nor after, but outside of marriage.

In the context of Lady Happy's effort to control her own pleasure and property, men pose the double (and sometimes indistinguishable) threats of penetration (of bodies and convent walls) and appropriation. The women of the convent perform these possibilities in a series of skits presented to Lady Happy and the Prince/ss. Penetration risks pregnancy: in one skit, a woman writhes in the agony of childbirth while other women complain of wayward and ungrateful sons and daughters. The woman and her child both die. In another skit, a lady flees to a nunnery for fear that a certain married gentleman will rape her. The women understand gender as performance within the convent, but the physical threat of masculine penetration from without, these skits remind them, remains. Upon penetration, female bodies lose their fluidity and access to alternative pleasure. Further, they lose their distinction from each other: the skits show women from both elite and laboring classes in similar situations and concludes, uncharacteristically for this play and for the duchess in general, in an elision between them: "Marriage is a Curse we find,/ Especially to Women kind:/ From the Cobler's Wife we see,/ To Ladies, they unhappie be"(30). For Cavendish, women share little across the ranks; they do, however, share vulnerability to the threats of rape and pregnancy.

The threat of penetration becomes potentially appropriative for elite women: the courtiers wish to tear down the convent walls to marry (and thus control the wealth of) the ladies within, and the Prince/ss penetrates the convent for the same reason. The courtiers provide a cruder parallel to the success of the Prince/ss: they consider using physical force, but decide that the walls are too thick and only consider entering, like the Prince/ss, as women. Other gentlemen see the convent as impenetrable, resolving "to get Wives, before they are Incloister'd" (31). The end of play, then, in which Lady Happy marries the Prince/ss (now revealed as a man), offers at one level a conventional resolution in which Lady Happy's initial experiences of multiple pleasures give way to proper heterosexual closure. The revelation of the "true" sex of the Prince/ss could even be read as rewriting their erotic attachment as heterosexual all along, leaving gendered divisions undisrupted. Cavendish certainly makes this conventional reading available, but does not leave it as the only possibility.

The play represents the final marriage with ambivalence. In his parallel to the violent, antifeminist courtiers and by the fact of his invasive deception, the Prince performs a metaphorical rape in his penetration of the convent and the resulting marriage, which gives him control over Happy's land and reproductive capacity. Further, marriage itself had been represented as a dismal choice throughout the play: any woman with the opportunity joins the convent in preference to it, and once within they perform skits about its misery. As Monsieur Take-pleasure and his servant pun, upon marriage Lady Happy will necessarily no longer be Happy. The Prince takes over her property at the end, for he, not the former Lady Happy, decides on the fate of the convent. Finally, the play ends with some pessimistic comments on marriage by the fool Mimick. After the wedding dance, Lady Happy "as now Princess" asks Mimick to leave his Lady and go with her:

> MIMICK. I am a Married Man, and have Married my Ladies Maid *Nan*, and she will keep me at home do what I can; but you've now a *Mimick* of your own, for the *Prince* has imitated a Woman.
> L. HAPPY. What you Rogue, do you call me a Fool?
> MIMICK. Not I, please your Highness, unless all Women be Fools.
> PRINC. Is your Wife a Fool?
> MIMICK. Man and Wife, 'tis said, makes but one Fool. (51)

Mimick and his wife make one fool because marriage subsumes Nan under his identity, which is a fool. But the Prince and his wife make one fool as well: he literally shares the fool's identity as a mimic, and Lady Happy, the fool implies, has been fooled into marriage through his mimickry. Yet she acts no more foolishly than all women.

Even a reading in which *The Convent* questions the conventional satisfaction of closure by marriage, however, assumes the stable and bipolar gender identities of Lady Happy and the Prince/ss. In spite of its apparent final conventionality, *The Convent of Pleasure* also makes available an alternative reading that would question the extent to which gender has been restabilized. To what extent do any "men" actually penetrate the convent? The courtiers plan to penetrate disguised as laboring women and thus inhabiting the position of those who create the conditions for pleasure. Within the gender economy of the convent, this would locate them as non-erotic laborers; their differences from female non-erotic laborers become irrelevant. The Prince/ss, by contrast, provides erotic pleasure to Lady Happy, but within the convent this pleasure remain indistinguishable from that provided by a female body. In one scene, the entire convent pairs off into shepherds and shepherdesses, with Happy and the Prince/ss gendered in the same way as all the rest of the couples. In fact, the Prince/ss performs masculinity in a way that differs from any of the other ladies' performance of masculinity only when the Embassador arrives to request the Prince/ss's return. This reminder of his/her position as ruler *of a place outside the convent* alone transforms the gender performance of the Prince/ss; only at that point does the Prince/ss become dangerous, a potentially violent penetrator of a woman's body and property. He/she says, "But since I am discover'd, go from me to the Councellors of this State, and inform them of my being here, as also the reason, and that I ask their leave I may marry this Lady; otherwise, tell them I will have her by force of Arms" (47).

Madam Mediator had already proclaimed the "true" gender of the Prince/ss in an earlier scene, but it made no difference. Mediator had interrupted a party in which Lady Happy and the Prince/ss were dancing as partners, the latter dressed as a man. Bursting into a room filled with such partnerships, she cries, "O Ladies, Ladies! you're all betrayed, undone, undone; for there is a man disguised in the *Convent*, search and you'l find it" (45). Clearly the duchess, with the use of the neuter pronoun, chooses to leave the gender identity of the Prince/ss undefined.[81] The Prince/ss makes no moves to alter his/her gender performance:

> PRINC. You may make the search, Madam *Mediator*; but you will quit me, I am sure.
> M. MEDIAT. By my faith but I will not, for you are most to be suspected.
> PRINC. But you say, the Man is disguised like a Woman, and I am accoustred like a Man. (46)

---

[81] See Tomlinson, "'My Brain the Stage,'" 156–158.

The performance of masculinity offers no indication of maleness: it does not evidence phallic authority or the fact of penetration. Masculine dress, the Prince/ss declares, in fact *removes* him/her from suspicion! This scene of refusal to recognize an essential masculinity undermines any security in heterosexual closure. Lady Happy's love for the Prince/ss at the end, in fact, can be read as a continuation of her earlier homoerotic passion rather than a confirmation of heterosexuality. Heterosexuality, in fact, becomes feasible for Lady Happy only upon meeting a "man" who can participate in a feminine erotic economy.

The Convent of (nonphallic) *Pleasure* leaves open two possible readings of the final marriage that we might call the Fool's reading and the Happy reading. Mimick the Fool implies, as discussed above, that the Prince tricks Lady Happy into marriage. In the Fool's reading, the Prince does not differ from the courtiers except in his greater skills of appropriation. When Mimick asks the Prince to divide the convent between married men (who are madmen) and fools, he acknowledges that this female property has now fallen under the control of the Prince. In the Fool's reading, the former Lady Happy is no longer Happy but rather a fool, for she fell in love with the Prince/ss as a woman and does not recognize his masculinity, which has less to do with the body than with the capacity to possess. In the Fool's reading, their dance as a married couple thus mimics the (homo)eroticism of their dance as shepherd and shepherdess; Lady Happy herself becomes Mimick the Fool, for her marriage and move out of the convent can only mimic the pleasure she experiences within the boundaries of women's property.

Yet the ending also allows a "Happy" reading that suggests the possibility of pleasure in marriage by imagining a way for it to remain as one of the multiple pleasures available in the convent. Given that only elite women generate eroticism in this play, the lady can continue to be Happy by continuing to understand her relationship with the Prince/ss as "homoerotic"—or, more precisely, as not defined by bipolar gender oppositions—for neither the feminine nor masculine gender constructions, as the rest of the play demonstrates, originate in the body. In her reading, the gender of the Prince/ss has not necessarily changed. When the couple dances after their wedding as husband and wife, they repeat and recall earlier scenes in which they performed as shepherd and shepherdess, Neptune and Sea-Goddess, masculine and feminine dancing partners. When Madame Mediator interrupts a dance to announce that one of the masculine partners really is a man, all the couples jump apart except Happy and the Prince/ss. The Fool might read this as the triumph of patriarchy and heterosexuality; Happy, by contrast, might allow us to read it as a refutation of the dependence of desire upon bipolar gender oppositions and thus as a refusal of those oppositional categories themselves.

Finally, what remains only ambiguously possible in *The Convent of Pleasure*—women's property and pleasure—becomes more substantially realized in Cavendish's fictional narrative, *The Description of a New World, Called the Blazing World*, added to the end of her *Observations upon Experimental Philosophy* (1666).[82] *Blazing World* further demonstrates the dependence on property, written and real, in Cavendish's authorial identity; as in her other works, she articulates this relationship in aristocratic rather than professional terms. Writing from a gender position that would deny her access to property and living in a historical situation that radically destabilized property, however, the duchess in her *Blazing World* imagines her own capacity fully to inhabit the position of owner through a deconstruction of materiality itself. If *The Convent* suggests the possibility of female pleasure on a separate estate, *Blazing World* finds the greatest hope in confirming an identity between real, intellectual, and imaginary property. Professionals achieve this by realizing textual property and configuring it as their estate; the duchess, alternatively, textualizes real property and configures it as discourse.

Blazing World tells the story of a lady who accidentally discovers another world attached to the North Pole in which creatures take the form of worm-men, bird-men, bear-men, and fish-men. The apparently human-formed emperor of this world falls in love with the lady, makes her the empress, and gives her complete dominion. Whereas *The Convent* ends, in the Fool's pessimistic reading, with an act of penetration, *Blazing World* begins with an averted penetration, for the lady finds herself at the North Pole because a foreign merchant had stolen her away in a boat. Before he can enjoy his prize, however, Heaven, "frowning at his Theft," raises a tempest that blows the boat to the North Pole where the

[82] See Lilley, "Women's Utopian Writing." Lilley points out the utopian qualities of this text, "its meta-concern with the relations between power, gender and discourse" and also the "attractions of utopian writing for women as an area of unrestricted fancy, through which perceived wants can be aesthetically supplied." *Blazing World*, she argues, "is a text which revels in design, ornament, rhetorical description and amplification, a material and linguistic opulence which is self-consciously extravagant and excessive, even parodic" (120).

men all die of cold, but the lady, "by the light of her beauty, the heat of her youth, and protection of the gods," remains alive.[83] *Blazing World* writes women's property as paradox: on the one hand, the duchess describes the astonishing wealth and delightful ostentation of this world, from entire ships made of gold to the empress's cap made of pearl; on the other hand, she conceives this wealth as ultimately immaterial, for within the fiction of the narrative, travelers between the worlds cannot transport the wealth of the blazing world beyond its borders.

The blazing world offers an immaterial world most literally in its entire status as literary rather than real property: it remains self-consciously a narrative and an imaginary alternative to owning material property. In her epilogue, Cavendish concludes that "By this poetic description, you may perceive, that my ambition is not only to be Empress, but Authoress of a whole world; and that the worlds I have made, both the Blazing and the other Philosophical World, mentioned in the first part of this description, are framed and composed of the most pure, that is, the rational parts of matter, which are the part of my mind" (224). Cavendish self-consciously signifies her literary world as the immaterial one, in opposition and preference to the world of real property: "in the formation of those worlds, I take more delight and glory, than ever Alexander or Caesar did in conquering this terrestrial world" (224). Just as the blazing world occupies an ambiguous status as different from but also comparable to conquered territory, so the characters within the narrative itself slip in and out of materiality. In the blazing world, the Empress converses with material creatures as well as "immaterial spirits"; she eventually calls to her world the soul of the Duchess of Newcastle. She and the Duchess travel between the worlds in both material and immaterial form.

The dematerialization of land and bodies provides the conditions for the gender disruption of homoerotic pleasure in *Blazing World*. The immaterial spirits offer to the Empress a scribe to help her write her own cabala, giving her the choice of all souls living or dead. The spirits understand this act of transport as the traveling soul's gesture of love, for "according to Plato's doctrine, there is a conversation of souls, and the souls of lovers live in the bodies of their beloved" (181). The Empress

---

[83] Cavendish, *The Description of a New World Called the Blazing World* [1666] *and Other Writings*, ed. Kate Lilley (New York: New York University Press, 1992), 125. Future references are from this edition and are cited in the text.

first wants "some ancient famous Writer," but the spirits insist that the men she mentions "were so wedded to their own opinions, that they would never have the patience to be Scribes" (181). Then she requests a famous modern writer, but the spirits similarly declare that "they would scorn to be scribes to a woman." Finally, they offer her the soul of the Duchess of Newcastle: the immaterial spirits reject male platonic lovers for the Empress and instead bring her the soul of a woman whom she embraces and salutes "with a Spiritual kiss" (181). These two souls become true platonic lovers—at one point they even return to England and together inhabit the body of the Duke of Newcastle. The narrative both affirms and denies the difference between material and immaterial love: "husbands have reason to be jealous of platonick lovers," the spirits warn, "for they are very dangerous, as being not onely very intimate and close, but subtle and insinuating" (181). The Duchess and the Empress, we later learn, "became platonick lovers, although they were both Females" (183).

In *Blazing World*, women achieve both ownership and pleasure through this construction and deconstruction of the difference between the material and the immaterial. The Empress becomes the ruler of a world of extraordinary wealth, but wealth that can have no proprietary consequences in her original world. (It can, however, have political consequences, for the Empress leads a battle that defeats the rebellious faction of a civil war in her homeland in a thinly veiled fantasy of rescuing the Stuart monarchy.) Homoerotic pleasure has the same textual instability. On the one hand, the spirits warn of the danger of platonic love, signaling the encounter between the Duchess and the Empress as a sexual one. On the other hand, the immateriality of the traveling souls of the Duchess and the Empress allows them to become lovers and, in a reversal of the gender positions, to penetrate a male body. Through alternative configurations of desire, Cavendish suggests alternative gender positions; these alternative gender positions in turn suggest possibilities of pleasure, ownership, and writing. Homoeroticism, like all eroticism, nevertheless remains the privilege of aristocratic women for Cavendish; her gender trouble insistently (almost *over*insistently) recognizes only elite women as potential sexual and social subjects. Thus her writing confirms a conservative social order even as it protests the limitations of this order and seeks ways to reconfigure it.

Blazing World ends with a contemplation of authorship in which the issues of pleasure, ownership, and writing converge. "By this poetical description," the Duchess concludes (as quoted above), "you may perceive, that my ambition is not only to be Empress, but Authoress of a whole world; and that the Worlds I have made, both the Blazing and the other Philosophical World, mentioned in the first part of this description, are framed and composed of the most pure, that it, the rational part of matter, which are the parts of my mind" (224). Cavendish dissolves the division between the science that takes up the first four hundred pages of this volume and the science fiction appended to it, once again characterizing true authorship as not the imitation of nature, but the *creation* of nature. The blazing world, as the author's imaginary property, provides an alternative site of authorship. This becomes literally true within the narrative, for the Empress first calls the Duchess to the blazing world in order to help her write. Further, the Empress promises to build a theater in the blazing world to produce the Duchess's plays. According to the Duchess, critics in London insist on unreasonable rules, and playwrights, as the Empress observes as her soul flies through London, merely recycle old plots. For the Empress, the plagiarists are the men who write for the public stage as opposed (implicitly) to her platonic friend. The blazing world provides a *location*, both literally and figuratively, for a different kind of authorship. Authorship signifies and remains a position of ownership for Cavendish, not in the proprietary sense that concerns professionals, but in a Hobbesian sense of property as both an extension and realization of the self and at the same time as something deeply and bitterly contested. Others might make their own worlds, but "let them have a care, not to prove unjust usurpers, and to rob me of mine: for, concerning the Philosophical World, I am Empress of it my self; and as for the Blazing World, it having an Empress already, who rules it with great Wisdom and Conduct, which Empress is my dear Platonic Friend" (225). Like Hobbes, Cavendish represents a world perennially embattled over ownership. Unlike Hobbes, however, Cavendish finds that the social contract fails to offer sufficient real or literary space to women, and thus it similarly fails to offer a sufficiently powerful form of social subjectivity. Originality, or the creation of new worlds rather than the conquest of extant ones, provides an alternative space and an alternative economy of authorship for elite women, potentially free from penetration and appropriation by men.

THREE

Aphra Behn and the Hostility of Influence

It is difficult to imagine a dramatic career less like the duchess of Newcastle's than that of Aphra Behn. Cavendish wrote as an elite amateur, fashioning her plays for a courtly audience; Behn earned her living as a professional, associating (like Dryden) with other professionals, performers, and amateurs who nevertheless understood the difference between her position and theirs. Cavendish hoped for social capital, while Behn sought economic capital; the duchess returned from exile to her husband's diminished but significant estate, while Behn returned from her Dutch spying mission to debtor's prison. Thus both these women negotiated a gendered system of literary property, but each invented, unsurprisingly, significantly different strategies for ownership and authorship. Cavendish clearly found empowerment in her aristocratic status; Behn's position offered no such possibility.

How, then, did Aphra Behn manage to position herself as an owner of literary property? One answer might be that she never truly did, for she endured the charge of plagiarism throughout her career. Although critics now generally agree that Behn repeated earlier texts no more than contemporaries who escaped the charge,[1] this reproach must have dogged her career, for she responds to it in *The Rover*'s postscript, in a preface to *Sir Patient Fancy*, in the dedication to *The Dutch Lover,* and in one of her published letters. She addresses accusations with varying degrees of concern. She answers the charge that she plagiarized her

---

[1] In regard to Behn's use of sources, Frederick M. Link, for example, argues that "Mrs. Behn is typical of her period in this practice as in many other respects" (91). *Aphra Behn* (New York: Twayne, 1968).

play *Lust's Dominion* with apparent nonchalance in a letter to Mrs. Price: "In your last, you inform'd me, that the World treated me as a *Plagiery*, and, I must confess, not with Injustice. ... whenever I take the Pains next to appear in Print, [I shall let the World know] of the mighty Theft I have been guilty of."[2] She proceeds to defend herself with the familiar claim to having "weeded and improv'd" the earlier play and eagerly hopes that the world will have the chance to compare them. The appropriation of an obscure, anonymous play troubles Behn little, although her sex, "wou'd not prevent my being pull'd to Pieces by the Criticks." Her letter articulates a fluid sense of dramatic property as well as a confidence in her Lockean ability to appropriate the raw material of the past.[3]

Yet Behn clearly recognized accusations of plagiarism as gendered, for in an epistle attached to *The Dutch Lover* (1673) she defends women's authorship and implies that often *men* fail to recognize the boundaries of literary property. With ironic modesty, Behn insists that her *Dutch Lover* aims for nothing above comedy, with no pretension to university subjects such as "Logic, etc. and several other things (that shall be nameless lest I misspell them)," citing her own "want of Letters."[4] If Cavendish at this point would claim originality and singularity, Behn insists on the capacity of women to participate in popular genres. In the world of playwrights, she comments, "I dare say I know of none that write at such a formidable rate, but that a woman may well hope to reach their greatest heights" (1:224). Like Cavendish, Behn enlists Shakespeare in the cause of women's writing: Shakespeare had no more education than a woman and "Plays have no great room for that which is men's great advantage over women, that is Learning" (1:224). This epistle makes the contradictory point of diminishing the genre *and* insisting on the "the dignity of Playes" (1:221) as part of a struggle for authorial legitimacy.

It is men, in fact, whom Behn exposes as the ones who fail to respect literary propriety. The learned Jonson not only failed to write as skillfully

---

[2] Aphra Behn to Mrs. Price, *Familiar Letters*, ed. Thomas Brown (London, 1718), 31–32.

[3] Although, as Angeline Goreau notes, Behn "was well aware that she was being singled out for punishment." *Reconstructing Aphra: A Social Biography of Aphra Behn* (New York: Dial Press, 1980), 210.

[4] *The Works of Aphra Behn*, ed. Montague Summers, 6 vols. (New York: Benjamin Blom, 1967), 1:221–222. Future references are cited in the text.

as Shakespeare, but did not actually possess the learning he claimed; as
a result, his imitations bled into plagiarism. His learning sufficed only,
she argues, "to rob poor Salust of his best orations" (1:224). Thus Behn,
like Cavendish, challenges the distinction between imitation and plagiarism. Similarly, Behn responds to a "phlegmatick, white, ill-favour'd,
wretched Fop" who dismisses any woman's play as "woful" by questioning
the fop's ownership of *his* words: "Now how this come about I am not
sure, but I suppose he brought it piping hot from some who had with
him the reputation of a villanous Wit: for Creatures of his size of sense
talk without all imagination, such scraps as they pick up from other
folks. I would not for a world be taken arguing with such a propertie as
this. . . ." (1:223–224). Finally, the play itself failed on stage as a result
of another male abuse of literary property, for the Dutch Lover himself
"spoke but little of what I intended for him, but supplied it with a great
deal of idle stuff, which I was wholly unacquainted with until I had
heard it first from him" (1:225). Thus Behn represents the relationship
between literary ownership and authorship as both less important and
more important than her contemporaries have recognized. On the one
hand, dramatic writing belongs to an unenclosed, unlearned field. On
the other hand, Behn takes possessive individualism to its extreme conclusion by refusing the distinction between Ben Jonson's reworking of
ancient texts and her own reworking of earlier plays.

Her most vehement defense against a charge of plagiarism appears
in a postscript to *The Rover*, which suggests something special about this
case. A "very malicious or very ignorant" report that *The Rover* was "*Thomaso* altered," she reports, "made the booksellers fear some trouble from
the proprietor of that admirable play." Behn claims that she only stole
the "sign of Angellica" and that the "plot and business (not to boast
on't) is my own." She argues for Angellica as a kind of a footnote,
citing her debt but also calling attention to her difference. Yet Behn
incorporated more of *Thomaso; or, The Wanderer* than she acknowledges,[5]
and unlike in the case of *Lust's Dominion*, she lashes out at what she
understands as the gendered distribution of literary property: "Though
had this succeeded ill, I should have had no need of imploring that

---

[5] See Jones DeRitter, "The Gypsy, *The Rover*, and the Wanderer: Aphra Behn's
Revision of Thomas Killigrew," *Restoration* 10 (Fall 1986): 82–92; and Janet Todd,
The Sign of Angellica: Women, Writing and Fiction, 1660–1800 (New York: Columbia
University Press, 1989), intro.

justice from the critics, who are naturally so kind to any that pretend to usurp their dominion, especially our sex: they would doubtless have given me the whole honor on't. Therefore I will only say in English what the famous Vergil does in Latin: I make verses, and others have the fame."[6] Her irony reverses the charge: critics accuse her of being a plagiarist because she is a woman, and others feel free to plagiarize *from her* for the same reason. This postscript raises not only the general problem of a woman's capacity to own a text, but also the specific problem of *The Rover*'s intertextuality with *Thomaso*. Behn deflects this relationship by pointing out *The Rover*'s multiplicity of intertexts, such as Brome's *Play of the Novella*. At the same time, the "sign of Angellica" self-consciously positions *The Rover* as an engagement with Killigrew's play. Because of the particular attention Behn pays to this accusation, I will later return to this case.

Both the attackers and defenders of Behn reveal the association of her supposed plagiarism with gender. In an ambivalent gesture of praise, one poet defends Astrea against plagiarism by echoing her own strategy of claiming, in the tradition of Cavendish, that her (feminine) ignorance necessarily produces original writing. This poem characterizes her accusers as charging that a man wrote her plays and poems:

> Rest in peace, ye blessed Spirits, rest,
>   With Imperial bliss for ever blest:
> Upon your sacred Urn she scorns to tread,
> Or rob the Learned Monuments of the dead:
> Nor need her Muse a foreign aid implore
> In her own tunefull breast there's wonderous store. . .
> Curst be the balefull Tongue that dares abuse
> The rightfull off-spring of her Godlike Muse:
> And doubly Curst be he that thinks her Pen
> Can be instructed by the best of men.[7]

A similar gendering of plagiarism appears in Alexander Radcliffe's attack. In "News from Hell," the narrator finds seven male poet in Hades,

---

[6] Frederick M. Link notes that Behn refers to a story in which "the poet wrote a distich anonymously for which a hack writer took credit." *The Rover*, ed. Frederick M. Link (Lincoln: University of Nebraska Press, 1967), 130.

[7] "Upon these and other Excellent Works of the Incomparable Astraea," in Aphra Behn, *Poems on Several Occasions: With a Voyage to the Island of Love* (London, 1684).

damned for a range of offenses. Behn alone, however, has been damned
by the public for plagiarism:

> Amongst this Heptarchy of Wit,
> The censuring Age have thought it fit
> To damn a Woman, 'cause 'tis said,
> The Plays she vends she never made.
> But that a *Greys Inn* Lawyer does 'em,
> Who unto her was Friend in Bosom.[8]

While Radcliffe damns several male poets for a range of aesthetic inade-
quacies, Behn, he informs us, earned a reputation for passing off the
work of a lover (probably John Hoyle) as her own. The satirist parallels
Behn's sexual transgression to her proprietary transgression, hinting
that Behn traded her affections for plays, which she in turn sold to the
public. "News from Hell" recalls similar accusations against Cavendish
for receiving help from men, although the commodification of Behn's
writing contributes to the charge of sexual impropriety.[9] Behn's public
trafficking in literary property contributed to the suspicion that she did
not really own her plays.

In spite of these charges against her, Behn managed to build a professional career as a playwright and even to earn the respect of some of
her contemporaries. As recent feminist scholarship has brought to light,
Behn's authorial self-fashioning constantly needed to account for gender, whether through its exploitation, denial, or multiple identification.[10]

[8] Alexander Radcliffe, *The Ramble: An Anti-Heroic Poem* (London, 1682).

[9] The duchess did not escape this charge either, though, as evidenced by John
Stansby's poem: "Shame of her sex, Welbeck's illustrious whore,/The true man's
hate and grief, plague of the poor,/The great atheistical philosophraster,/That owns
no God, no devil, lord nor master." Quoted by Sara Heller Mendelson, *The Mental
World of Stuart Women: Three Studies* (Brighton: Harvester Press, 1987), 60.

[10] See Janet Todd, *The Sign of Angellica*; Jacqueline Pearson, *The Prostituted Muse:
Images of Women and Women Dramatists, 1642–1737* (New York: Harvester Wheatsheaf,
1988); Catherine Gallagher, *Nobody's Story: The Vanishing Acts of Women Writers in the
Marketplace, 1670–1820* (Berkeley: University of California Press, 1994); Deborah
C. Payne, "'And Poets Shall by Patron Princes Live': Aphra Behn and Patronage"
(105–119), Frances M. Kavenik, "Aphra Behn: The Playwright as 'Breeches Part,'"
(177–192), and Jessica Munns, "'I by a Double Right Thy Bounties Claim': Aphra
Behn and Sexual Space" (193–210), in *Curtain Calls: British and American Women and
the Theater, 1660–1820*, ed. Mary Anne Schofield and Cecilia Macheski (Athens: Ohio
University Press, 1991).

Cavendish's elite homoerotic vision provides an imagined alternative to the current economy; Behn, by contrast, participates fully in the public marketplace. In this chapter, I explore two different strategies of Behn's. In appropriating and rewriting Thomas Killigrew's *Thomaso; or, The Wanderer* as *The Rover*, Behn, I argue, implicitly insists that male bodies and literary property are equally as alienable as their female counterparts. In *Oroonoko*, though, Behn nostalgically idealizes a "precapitalist" gift economy. When Thomas Southerne rewrites her novel as a play, he reinscribes the position of owner as both English and masculine. In both of these cases of cross-gendered intertextuality, literary property relations emerge less as anxiety than as hostility.

Playwright and Plagiarist: The Rover

That Aphra Behn's writing for the public stage left her vulnerable to attacks on her sexual propriety has long been observed by feminist critics. Further, some have seen (especially in *The Rover*) the author's consciousness and even critique of such objectification and commodification of women's bodies.[11] Building on these important insights, I explore not only the commodification of text and self, but also the gendered possibilities of their ownership and alienability inscribed in Killigrew's *Thomaso* and Behn's *Rover*. In *The Rover*, Behn risked both charges of sexual impropriety because of her portrayal of prostitution, and charges of plagiarism because of her rewriting of Killigrew's play. "A Satyr on the Modern Translators" connects these sexual and literary transgressions:

> The Female Wit [Behn]; who next convicted stands,
> Not for abusing *Ovid*'s Verse but *Sand*'s:
> She might have learn'd from the ill-borrow'd Grace
> (Which little helps the ruin of her Face)

---

[11] See Catherine Gallagher, "Who Was That Masked Woman? The Prostitute and the Playwright in the Comedies of Aphra Behn," *Women's Studies* 15 (1988): 23–42 [this essay is incorporated into chap. 1 of *Nobody's Story*]; Goreau, *Reconstructing Aphra*; Elin Diamond, "*Gestus* and Signature in Aphra Behn's *The Rover*," *ELH* 56 (Fall 1989): 519–541; Cynthia Lowenthal, "Portraits and Spectators in the Late Restoration Playhouse: Delariviere Manley's *Royal Mischief*," *The Eighteenth Century: Theory and Interpretation* 35 (Spring 1994): 119–134.

That Wit, like Beauty, triumphs o'er the Heart,
When more of Nature's seen, and less of Art.
Nor strive in *Ovid*'s Letters to have shown,
As much of Skill, as Lewdness in her own:
Then let her from the next inconstant Lover,
Take a new Copy for a second Rover:
Describe the cunning of a jilting Whore,
From the ill Arts her self has us'd before;
Thus let her write, but paraphrase no more.[12]

Although this poem is in some ways typical of the attacks on Behn, it offers insight into the precise nature of her violation. The text equates her supposedly inept theft of a translation with equally inept applications of cosmetics that fail to disguise a ruined face. Further, it accuses her of simply reproducing her own lover in the character of the Rover, and reproducing herself in the character of the *jilting* whore—not, significantly, the sentimental and powerful Angellica Bianca, but the streetwalker Lucetta, who cheats her customer. Whereas Shakespeare commonly earns praise from presenting unadulterated nature, Behn here earns the poet's scorn for failing to transform nature by adding enough labor: she takes her work too directly from life. At the same time, she violates propriety by actually adding the labor of excessive beauty treatments to her face and to her verse. What exactly *is*, then, her transgression, and what connects copying from (and adulterating) Sandys to reproducing her own position as the jilting whore as a character on stage? What, in other words, connects plagiarism and prostitution?

The satirist's parallel makes the most sense when we recall Carole Pateman's argument about the gendering of the Lockean individual. Pateman contends that prostitution differs in structure from other kinds of employment because it most commonly assumes both the gender of the worker (female) and the gender of the client (male).[13] Prostitutes do not sell a service, she argues, but actually sell themselves: the prostitution

[12] Mr. P--r, "A Satyr on the Modern Translators," in *Money Masters all Things: Or, Satyrical Poems, Shewing the Power and Influence of Money* (London, 1698), 119.

[13] Carole Pateman, *The Sexual Contract* (Stanford: Stanford University Press, 1988), chap. 7. Pateman acknowledges that male prostitutes exist, but notes that while male heterosexual prostitutes are rare, male homosexual prostitutes are common. But "from the standpoint of contract, [male homosexual prostitutes] are no different from female prostitutes" (192).

111

contract consists not so much of the exchange of money for sex (a service), but of the temporary subordination of a woman to the demands of the client. Thus the prostitution contract institutionalizes a relationship of subordination. Behn's *Rover* offers a similar insight, for Blunt becomes Lucetta's cully out of the misguided conviction that Lucetta loves him. Lucetta, Blunt believes, wants nothing more than to subordinate herself to him—a mistake that earns him the ridicule of his friends. Lucetta, however, proves an untrustworthy maker of contracts (a *jilting* whore) because she helps her pimp steal Blunt's purse when no money has been demanded *and* she cheats Blunt out of the promised sexual experience. So although Lucetta offers to subordinate herself *gratis*, she does not even fulfill her sexual end of the bargain before her pimp robs Blunt.[14] Similarly, the author of "A Satyr on the Modern Translators" calls Behn not just a whore but a *jilting* whore: lacking self-ownership, Behn, like Lucetta, has no stake in legitimate contracts and therefore cannot be trusted. To stretch Pateman's argument a little further, though, *any* whore, it seems, who provides anything less than complete subordination is a jilting whore, for the client contracts for authority over the prostitute herself that sexual *services* alone do not satisfy.[15] Prostitutes, then, destabilize contractual relations for two reasons: first, as women they do not fully inhabit the position of "individual," and so their ability to make legitimate contracts remains in doubt; second, they are *necessarily* untrustworthy (jilting) makers of contracts because they rarely—if ever—fulfill their promise of total subordination. Behn earns the title of whore most obviously as one of the worst things one can say about a woman and by way of connecting, as Goreau and Gallagher have argued, a woman who sells the contents of her mind with one who sells her body. Yet the "Satyr" and *The Rover* reveal another meaning, for the title of whore comes to signify a position of compromised, since alienated, individuality and thus the incapacity to make trustworthy or even legitimate contracts. The charges of plagiarist and of jilting whore appear together not just because both attack Behn, but because they both attack her for a gendered form of illegitimate ownership.

[14] Lucetta is, however, willing to fulfill this part of her contract, but her pimp won't permit it.

[15] "When a man enters into the prostitution contract," Pateman asserts, "he is not interested in sexually indifferent, disembodied services; he contracts to buy sexual use of a *woman* for a given period. Why else are men willing to enter the market and pay for 'hand relief?'" (207).

While Behn's detractors commonly represent her in the simultaneously subordinated and not-subordinated-enough position of whore, her
advocates sometimes praise her in similar terms. "To Madam Behn, on
her Poems," for example, compares the relationship of poetess to the
masculine institution of literature with the relationship of Eve to Adam:

> When th'Almighty Powers th'Universe had fram'd,
> And Man as King, the lesser World was nam'd,
> The Glorious Consult soon his joys did bless,
> And sent him Woman his chief happiness.
> She by an after-birth Heaven did refine,
> And gave her Beauty with a Soul divine;
> She with delight was Natures chiefest pride,
> Dearer to Man than all the World beside;
> Her soft embraces charm'd his Manly Soul,
> And softer Words his Roughness did controul:
> So thou, great *Sappho*, with thy charming Verse,
> Dost here the Soul of Poetry rehearse. . . .[16]

The charges that Behn "too loosely writ" have become familiar. But this
poet represents Behn's writing as *necessarily* erotic, for Astrea charms the
reader with her poems in the same way that Eve charmed Adam with
her embraces.[17] Confronted with the task of praising a woman writer,
the poet (one H. Watson) repeats the story of woman's original subordination: God made "Man as King," then created Woman to give him
pleasure. Placing Behn in the position of Eve constructs her literary
pleasure giving as a function of her sexual subordination. Eroticization
of Behn, whether in the form of attack or praise, thus commonly performs the cultural work of constructing this woman writer in a way that
neutralizes the possibility of her becoming an owner of literary property.
For a male reader to comprehend the purchase of Behn's *Poems* as an
act of purchasing Behn herself more comfortably represents this author
as the object of exchange rather than as the owning subject who sold a
collection of poems for profit.[18]

[16] H. Watson, preface to Behn's *Poems*.

[17] In "Masked Woman," Catherine Gallagher writes extensively and insightfully
about Aphra Behn's eroticized authorial position.

[18] Those who praise her, like those who attack her, often elide her body and her text:

> How soft and fine your manly numbers flow,
> Soft as your Lips, and smooth as is your brow.

It should come as no surprise, then, if Behn exploits this desire and sometimes represents authorship as a way of giving sexual pleasure to men, especially in the early part of her career when she apparently had little or no access, as Deborah C. Payne points out, to the social capital of patronage.[19] But as Payne goes on to argue, this does not necessarily mean that Behn, as Catherine Gallagher has contended, "embraced the title of whore." Gallagher sees Behn as a writer who "embraced possessive individualism" but who nevertheless would have recognized that she "could only do so with a consciousness that she thus contradicted the notion of female identity on which legitimate property relations rested." Gallagher writes convincingly of Behn's recognition of the contradictions of her position; Payne demonstrates the ways in which Behn welcomed the opportunity to construct herself as a "patronized aesthete" as well as a "working professional" and quickly abandoned any "playwright as whore" representation as soon as she had the chance to recast herself.[20]

Behn's ambivalence toward, rather than embracing of, possessive individualism, is apparent in the prologue to *The Forc'd Marriage*.[21] As Gallagher points out, this prologue configures wit as a privileged weapon in a woman's arsenal of charms.[22] Beauty now goes for too cheap a rate, so smart women "Court a new Power that may the old supply,/To keep

---

Gentle as Air, bright as the Noon-days Sky,
Clear as your skin, and charming as your Eye.
No craggy Precipice the Prospect spoyles,
The Eye no tedious barren plain beguiles
But, like *Thessalian* Feilds [sic] your Volumes are,
Raptures and charms o'er all the soyl appear,
Astrea and her verses are *Tempe* everywhere.

"To Mrs. B. on her Poems," in Aphra Behn, *Lycidus* (London, 1688). Behn's numbers write her body onto the page. The purchase of her volume, this poem implies, provides access to the poet's physical beauty. This poem praises the aesthetic pleasure offered by Behn's body (of work), whereas other encomiastic verses celebrate erotic pleasure. This poem goes on to praise Behn as "more than Woman! more than man she is," echoing back what Jessica Munns identifies as the "double right" of both masculine and feminine parts that Behn claimed. See Munns, "Aphra Behn and Sexual Space."

[19] Payne, "Aphra Behn and Patronage."

[20] Ibid., 116–117.

[21] Margaret W. Ferguson also demonstrates Behn's ambivalence toward the marketplace in her "Juggling the Categories of Race, Class, and Gender: Aphra Behn's *Oroonoko*," *Women's Studies* 19 (1991): 159–181.

[22] Gallagher, "Masked Woman," 24.

as well as gain the Victory./They'll join the force of Wit to Beauty now,/ And so maintain the Right they have in you."[23] "The woman's play of wit," Gallagher comments, "is a kind of afterplay specifically designed to prolong pleasure . . . and keep a woman . . . from being traded in for another woman." After noting that Behn frames her play "by the larger comedy of erotic exchange between a woman writer and a male audience, Gallagher asks a crucial question: "What kind of woman would stage her sexual desire as her primary motivation?"[24] The first part of the prologue does indeed suggest the author's alliance with the prostitute, but in the second part, which Gallagher reads as ironic, an actress intervenes and insists that she and the author scorn "the petty Spoils, and do prefer/The Glory not the Interest of the War."[25]

Encouraging a completely ironic reading, however, would have been impolitic for Behn, for the prologue (read unironically) flatteringly connects the author to the women spectators, asking, "Can any see that glorious sight and say [Woman pointing to the Ladies.]/A Woman shall not Victor prove to day?"[26] Women constituted a significant portion of the paying audience;[27] the first speaker may tease the ladies with a playful confusion of their sexuality with that of prostitutes, but the actress distinguishes pleasure seekers from prostitutes, whom she calls "picaroons." Prostitutes in this prologue are *necessarily* thieves (picaroons), for they do not fulfill their sexual contract: they do not offer the true and consistent subordination they appear to promise and thus can only make a deceptive contract. The author, on the other hand, like most of the female spectators, offers a better contract: she distinguishes herself (and the spectatrix) from the prostitute for the reliability of her offer to give them the dominant place in an unequal relationship. In this sense, Behn fashions herself as a long-term mistress or even a wife rather than as a prostitute. Offering to pleasure men in exchange for their devotion is not the same thing as prostitution, for it simultaneously pledges mutual constancy—a relationship generally outside of the prostitution contract—and creates the fantasy of a form of authorship that transcends financial exchange. Behn has it both ways here, allowing a (presumably)

[23] *Works of Aphra Behn*, 3:285.
[24] Gallagher, "Masked Woman," 25.
[25] *Works of Aphra Behn*, 3:286.
[26] Ibid.
[27] See David Roberts, *The Ladies: Female Patronage of Restoration Drama, 1660–1700* (Oxford: Clarendon Press, 1989).

male actor to represent her as a prostitute, and an actress to insist on her distinction from the prostitute. Finally, the kind of woman who can speak from a position of sexual experience, advocate sexual pleasure, and potentially offer a permanent and "honest" rather than picaroon relationship is actually a widow, not a prostitute. In this prologue, Behn both playfully confronts and denies her participation in the market, exploiting her own position as a widow to construct a place as both an owner of literary property and an alienable sexual self and at the same time above the sexual and textual marketplace.[28]

The position of widow can combine virtue with experience as well as offering the rare possibility of female self-ownership. As Gallagher and Goreau both argue, the married woman who sold the contents of her mind sold what did not belong to her. As a widow, though, Behn could inhabit both the masculine position of owner and household head and the position of sexually experienced woman,[29] positions she played against each other. For a widow, writing does not entail selling the

---

[28] Restoration playwrights assumed the sexual assertiveness of the widow, and Behn's play *The Widow Ranter* makes no exception. Behn's writing, especially her poetry, also exploits the widow's sexual experience and authority, distinguishing the widow's experience from that of a prostitute. Her erotic letters dramatize the insights of an experienced lover, expressing desire and demanding constancy rather than financial reward. In fact, the letters to Lysander express a combination of both virtue and experience—potentially consistent only for a widow. Further, while critics have brought attention to Behn's reputation as whore, they have paid less attention to a counter-discourse that insists on her virtue. The seventeenth-century biography of Behn by "One of the Fair Sex" insists on Astrea's irreproachable behavior in the face of rumors to the contrary. The unfavorable comparisons of Behn to Katherine Philips are well known; preceding Behn's *Poems*, however, one F. N. W. insists that Orinda lives again in Astrea, recommending Astrea's poetry to those "that would be truely wise/And vertues fair *Idea* prize." When Thomas Brown pairs a fictional Aphra Behn in an epistolary exchange with an actress, he chooses Mrs. Bracegirdle, "the famous Virgin Actress." Brown's joke in these fake letters, of course, is that Bracegridle only pretends to virginity; he posits the sexual activity and hypocrisy of both women. Nevertheless, the fact that he chose to parallel Behn to an actress so well known for her claims to virtue indicates a perception that Behn claimed a similar reputation. See Thomas Brown, *Works*, 4 vols., 9th ed. (London 1760), 2:250–257. The possibility of Behn's virtue coinciding with her experience fades quickly in the eighteenth century, but during the earlier period it could circulate alongside the rumors of scandal.

[29] Gallagher notes two possibilities: "As a woman, all of [Behn's] properties were at least the potential property of another; she could either reserve them and give herself whole in marriage, or she could barter them piecemeal, accepting self-division

property of a husband or a father, and a sexual encounter does not significantly alter her relation to the marriage market.[30] Seventeenth-century widows, in fact, could own property and often took over the businesses of their late husbands.[31]

In declaring *The Rover*'s relationship to *Thomaso*, Behn claims the "sign of Angellica" as a kind of footnote that should exonerate her from the charge of plagiarism, yet she slyly represents her intertextual contract with the figure of a prostitute. And in spite of Behn's praise for Killigrew, *The Rover* constitutes an attack not just on the gender politics of *Thomaso*, as Jones DeRitter has shown, but on the powerful Killigrew himself.[32] Killigrew and Behn had a long history of acquaintance; Goreau, in fact, believes that Killigrew knew Behn's mother.[33] But when Aphra Behn entered the world of professional theater, she sought and maintained a long-standing relationship with the Duke's Company, the company run by Sir William Davenant and the rival to Killigrew's King's Company. This choice has at times puzzled commentators,[34] for why would she have neglected to take advantage of this family connection? She clearly continued to maintain some kind of relationship with Killigrew, for she reports in the preface to *The Lucky Chance* that she had submitted the play for Killigrew's approval of its decency before bringing it to the stage.[35] Killigrew held a tremendously powerful position in the London

---

to achieve self-ownership and forfeiting the possibility of marriage." "Masked Woman," 27. The position of widow, it seems to me, offers another alternative.

[30] The reputation of being a whore, of course, would damage a widow; still, a sexual encounter for her would have a different social meaning than it would for a never-married woman losing her virginity.

[31] See Barbara J. Todd, "The Remarrying Widow: A Stereotype Reconsidered," in *Women in English Society, 1500–1800*, ed. Mary Prior (New York: Methuen, 1985), 45–92.

[32] See DeRitter, "The Gypsy." As DeRitter argues, Behn's Willmore is better seen as a satire on the rake than as an homage to this figure. Examining the explicit relationship between *The Rover* and *Thomaso* renders the satire most visible.

[33] Goreau, *Reconstructing Aphra*, 12.

[34] "Her association with the Duke's company is curious," writes Link, "since Thomas Killigrew was connected with the other and his is the name appearing in connection with her experiences in Antwerp." *Aphra Behn*, 22. Woodcock, as Link notes, speculates that she chose the Duke's Men because of Davenant's introduction of women actors. See George Woodcock, *The Incomparable Aphra* (London: Boardman, 1948), 49.

[35] *Works of Aphra Behn*, 3:185.

theater world and Behn had a stake in cultivating his approval. But she also may have had reason to resent him.

Killigrew, Behn's biographers agree, recommended Behn for her spying mission, and although she might have been initially grateful for the employment, the venture ended in disaster. In spite of some success in the actual espionage, Behn could neither complete her mission nor leave, for she could not pay her bills. She sent letters to Killigrew and others, complaining of her desperate plight and the threat of jail. She had pawned all her goods and William Scot, her collaborator, had already been thrown into debtor's prison.[36] Neither money nor letters arrived. Goreau concludes that Behn's requests for money infuriated Killigrew.[37] No doubt prompted by her poverty and the danger of living as a foreign spy, Behn privately borrowed 150 pounds from one Edward Butler and returned home. She promptly petitioned Charles II three times for her salary, "sadly complaining of two years' bitter suffering."[38] Still placing her hope in Killigrew, Behn insisted to the king that this man could testify to her hard work. She appended a heartbreaking plea to Killigrew:

Sr.

if you could guess at the affliction of my soule you would I am sure Pity me 'tis to morrow that I must submitt my self to a Prison the time being expird & though I indeaverd all day yesterday to get a ffew days more I can not because they say they see I am dallied wth all & so they say I shall be for ever: so I can not revoke my doome I have cryd myself dead & could find in my hart to break through all & get to ye king & never rise till he weare pleasd to pay this; but I am sick & weake & unfitt for yt; or a Prison; I shall go to morrow: . . . oh, god, who considers my misery & charge too, this is my reward to all my great promises, & my indeavers. Sr if I have not the money to night you must send me som thing to keepe me in Prison for I will not starve.[39]

Killigrew must not have responded, for Behn was taken to prison. Biographers have traditionally speculated that Killigrew finally pleaded her

[36] Ibid., 1:xxiv–xxv.
[37] Goreau, *Reconstructing Aphra*, 103.
[38] *Works of Aphra Behn*, 1:xxvi.
[39] Ibid., 1:xxvi–xxvii.

case and helped free her, but there is no evidence for this.[40] All the evidence, in fact, points to his exploitation of her vulnerability in that he gave her such a dangerous assignment and was deaf to her pleas for assistance. These specific circumstances, as well as the fact that either Behn never tried to produce her plays at the King's Company or Killigrew never accepted them, suggest the likelihood of tension in their relationship. Behn was, however, in no position to attack the powerful manager directly.[41] Instead, I would like to suggest, she appropriated and rewrote Killigrew's autobiographical play *Thomaso*, in order to comment on gender, property, and Killigrew himself.[42] She footnotes her hostility of influence with the sign of Angellica.

Killigrew's *Thomaso* tells the story of impoverished cavalier exile, but it also tells a story of elite masculine privilege. The play flaunts a social, and by autobiographical extension, authorial position to which Behn did not have access. Killigrew's fictionalized self-representation enjoys the complete sexual liberty of a rake abroad, an elite genealogy, and the assurance of royal support—perhaps a particular source for resentment, given Behn's experience with Charles II. Killigrew served Charles and James abroad during the Commonwealth, both in their households and as a diplomat. He returned at the Restoration to royal favor, a large income from a series of royal grants, and a patent to open a theater with the prime choice of actors and plays. Killigrew lived extravagantly, accumulating debt in spite of his salaries, but never seems to have faced the possibility of imprisonment.[43] In addition to his favor from Charles, Killigrew courted and married Charlotte de Hess, "a Dutch woman seventeen years his junior and an heiress to ten thousand pounds." Charles himself had written to Charlotte and encouraged her to accept the courtier.[44] The marriage took place late in 1654, at about the same time

---

[40] "It would be reassuring to discover," writes Goreau, "that Thomas Killigrew, guilty about his role in Aphra's imprisonment, had tried to redress the injury by accepting her play for production at his theater, but this was not the case." *Reconstructing Aphra*, 118.

[41] DeRitter, "The Gypsy," 82.

[42] Richard Flecknoe's satire on Killigrew, entitled *The Life of Thomaso the Wanderer*, demonstrates the extent to which contemporaries understood Killigrew's play as autobiographical.

[43] Alfred Harbage, *Thomas Killigrew, Cavalier Dramatist 1612–83* (1930; reprint, New York: Benjamin Blom, 1967), chaps. 3 and 4.

[44] Ibid., 105–106.

that Killigrew composed *Thomaso*. Whether or not Behn compared the advantages acquired by each of their Dutch spouses, both she and Killigrew address the marriage market in their plays. Further, Killigrew enjoyed a completely different relationship to the literary marketplace: he experienced the luxury of amateur authorship, writing his unstaged plays during exile and publishing them in 1664. Nevertheless, he participated in the London theater world as no less than its most powerful single individual.[45] So even if Behn harbored no resentment for his role in her imprisonment, she could not have failed to notice the difference between their relationships to property and propriety.

Killigrew's *Thomaso* boasts of rakish sexual adventure,[46] but the play also insists on an elite male privilege in ownership. As an exiled cavalier waiting with Charles II to come into his perceived birthright, Killigrew not only dramatizes Thomaso's prowess on his own behalf, but also inscribes in this character a wisdom, perception, and attractiveness on behalf of all those in a similar position. Killigrew's Thomaso remains in control throughout the play, attracting not just the attention of the wealthy and virtuous Serulina and the courtesan Angellica Bianca, but also the courtesans Saretta and Paulina. What distinguishes Thomaso most of all from other men, though, is his capacity to discern nuances of sexual property on sight: [47] he can instantly tell a virgin from a whore, a call girl from a hooker. The second scene of the play, in fact, finds Thomaso attempting to educate Edwardo (who becomes Blunt in *The Rover*) and Ferdinando on the differences among street whores, lady whores, and real ladies.

Edwardo proves a poor student. Like Behn's Blunt, Edwardo believes that the mulatto Lucetta has fallen in love with him. When he gleefully creeps into her bedroom to consummate their flirtation, he finds not Lucetta but Mattias, an admirer whom Lucetta's servant had surreptitiously allowed into her lady's chamber. Edwardo and Mattias first kiss

---

[45] I draw this conclusion from Harbage's observation that Killigrew and Davenant alone received patents, yet Killigrew's theater received special privileges even beyond that: "His was the royal theatre," Harbage sums up, "and when the audience came, it was a brilliant one." Ibid., 121.

[46] See DeRitter, "The Gypsy."

[47] Harbage asserts that for Killigrew, "there were two kinds of women: angelic women, and courtesans, with the latter class subdivided into good courtesans and bad courtesans." *Thomas Killigrew,* 230. In *Thomaso,* I argue, the distinction between the latter two collapses.

in the dark, then fight when they feel each other's beards. Lucetta's men throw them out in their drawers. An embarrassed Edwardo curses Lucetta as a "picaroon," believing she had planned to cheat him. Even though Lucetta *had* intended to have sex with him (as well as providing Phillipo and Sancho with the chance to take his money), Edwardo destroys Lucetta as sexual property by hiring men to slash her face. Thomaso himself eerily stands behind this brutal attack on Lucetta by financing it: even though he recognizes Edwardo's foolishness, he takes it upon himself to help avenge this illegitimate seizure of white English masculine property. Edwardo subsequently attempts a series of failed plots to dominate nonwhite or non-Christian women, first by attempting to marry a deformed Jew for her money, and then by planning to travel to the Indies and marry six black wives.[48]

Edwardo further reveals his inability to distinguish ladies from whores and inappropriate from appropriate partners by twice mistaking for a whore the virtuous Serulina, who eventually marries Thomaso. Readers of Behn will recognize this scene with a different character: Edwardo stumbles drunkenly into Serulina's garden, attempts to rape her and threatens to stab her when she resists. Although she calls out, Edwardo persists: "Rape! you lye, Baggage; how now, as if you were not as willing as I; what do you do here alone else? in a Garden at this hour, and your door set open, good Spider, but to catch a Passenger? do you frown? By cock, I shall frown angry too; come and kiss me, and leave your fooling—Hold you, there's a piece of eight for you."[49] Don Johanne, a friend of Serulina's brother, rescues her. The joke lies in Edwardo's insufficient ability to evaluate: he takes a whore for a lady, then a lady for a whore.

His next mistake most clearly reveals the ideological significance of this particular form of blindness. Unlike Behn's Hellena, Killigrew's Serulina has no desire to leave her house and only surreptitiously ventures out when her brother resolves to marry her off to Don Alphonso. Disguised, she sneaks into public only to deliver a letter to Thomaso, warning him of this turn of events. Her brother, however, mistakes her

---

[48] Behn repeats some of this story in *Rover II*. See Heidi Hutner, "Revisioning the Female Body: Aphra Behn's *The Rover*, Parts I and II," in *Rereading Aphra Behn: History, Theory, and Criticism,* ed. Heidi Hutner (Charlottesville: University Press of Virginia, 1993), 102–120.

[49] Thomas Killigrew, *Comedies and Tragedies* (London, 1664), 358; 1.4.2. References are to page; part, act, and scene. Future quotations are cited in the text.

for Angellica Bianca, which forces her to take refuge (as in *The Rover*) with Edwardo and Ferdinando. Edwardo has been planning revenge on all women, insisting that "if I had got my Night for my money, it would never have grieved me" (408; 2.2.4). His earlier belief that Lucetta *loved* him as well as his conversation with Ferdinando, however, belie this claim. Edwardo does not blame Lucetta to the extreme of having her face slashed for simply neglecting to provide sex; rather, he condemns her as a picaroon. He can extend this hostility to *all* such women out of the conviction that whores are *necessarily* thieves: they have an inappropriate relationship to property. When attacking Serulina, Edwardo and Ferdinando assume her lack of virginity and thus her inability to make a trustworthy exchange: "there are of her Tribe about the Town such excellent Thieves they'll geld a man ere he feel them: I have heard of one that robb'd a mans mouth, while he slept, of a row of teeth; another stole *Jack Smith's* Eye out of his Head at noon-day, and he never miss'd it till he felt the cold; Nay, she made him buy it again" (411; 2.2.4). Whores are such violators of property that they won't even stop at body parts. A whore in *Thomaso* is also *necessarily* a cheat because she does not deliver the subordination she promises. (Edwardo ultimately tries to solve this problem by attempting to acquire women who will be both wives and slaves.) The degree to which the male characters understand this structure distinguishes them from each other: in order to merit their own property rights, they must demonstrate a capacity to recognize the various types of sexual transactions. Edwardo cannot tell the difference between Lucetta and Serulina, who saves herself by offering one jewel as proof of her possession of another. But what kind of evidence does a jewel offer when a whore could also, in theory, defend herself in the same way? Only a patriarchal logic of property makes Serulina's jewel an acceptable defense, for a true whore would take and never give—not even what she seems to promise. For someone like Edwardo, who cannot distinguish among different kinds of women, the jewel offers all the proof he needs.

But this play articulates another anxiety, greater than but related to anxiety about the untrustworthiness of prostitutes. In both the contexts of exile and the author's impending lucrative marriage, *Thomaso* passionately insists upon the inalienability of male sexuality. Edwardo reveals his inability to inhabit the position of proper and proprietary masculinity in his incapacity to distinguish among women and also in his scheme to marry one of the Jews for her money. Still, he literally cannot trade sex for money in the latter case, for one of the Jews is too big and the other too small for intercourse. But while Edwardo can no more marry a beautiful and appropriate heiress than he can enjoy sex with a prostitute, Thomas(o) can do both. In *Thomaso*, the Angellica Bianca plot serves to demonstrate the inalienability of male sexuality, thus paving the way for the impoverished cavalier's marriage to the virtuous heiress. Angellica Bianca's affection for Thomaso at one level constitutes an amazing act of egotism on the author's part: this beautiful prostitute not only makes love to him for free, but also gives him a bag of gold to relieve his poverty. Like Serulina, she also attempts to define her position as not-whore by offering wealth. Yet Thomaso condemns Angellica Bianca not for her sexuality—Angellica, in fact, argues against the double standard—but for her mercenary practice or the *alienability* of her sexuality. He protests that *he*, in contrast, is not a prostitute: "When I hang out my picture, and at a rate expose my self to all comers, then I will not wonder if you despise me" (339; 1.2.4).[50] Thomaso compares his sexuality with his political position, claiming the higher virtue to engage in neither military or sexual alienation. His cavalier loyalty remains inalienable, as opposed to that of the professional or mercenary soldier;[51] his sexuality remains equally inalienable, even if he accepts money after providing sexual pleasure. The inalienability of male sexuality must be established so vehemently to set up the legitimacy of Thomaso's marriage to the wealthy heiress, upon which he graciously returns Angellica Bianca's gold. Killigrew represents the male cavalier as one who fully and constantly inhabits the position of owner, even if he may temporarily have no access to property. He deserves Angellica's love and property as much as he deserves those of Serulina.

The Angellica Bianca plot not only serves to demonstrate the inalienability of male sexuality, but also echoes the profound untrustworthiness of whores signified in the Lucetta plot. While Lucetta disguises prostitu-

[50] Anxiety over the possibility that men could be prostitutes comes up again in part 2, when Angellica tells Pedro that men could "set a price upon your selves" as well as women. Ibid., 393.

[51] See J. G. A. Pocock, *Virtue, Commerce, and History: Essays on Political Thought and History, Chiefly in the Eighteenth Century* (Cambridge: Cambridge University Press, 1985), especially "The Varieties of Whiggism from Exclusion to Reform: A History of Ideology and Discourse," 215–311. Pocock points out that by the end of the seventeenth century, the question of a professional army had become a significant line dividing political perspectives.

tion as love, Angellica Bianca attempts to transform her affair with Thomaso from property exchange into a gift economy: "Can you forgive a fault, and love for love? can you forget I was to be sold, and value this gift?" (340; 1.2.4). Thomaso humors her, but knows better than to trust a whore. As Thomaso would have predicted, Angellica reveals her untrustworthiness when she betrays Thomaso by sending Serulina's love letter to Pedro (Serulina's brother and guardian) and joins in an ultimately unsuccessful plot, initiated by Lucetta and Saretta (another prostitute), against Thomaso's life. None of these women, finally, accepts the subordination that their position demands. Unlike his friends, though, Thomaso never wavers in his capacity to distinguish among women, and unlike women, he accepts sex and money without the threat of self-alienation. In a historical situation in which rank and actual access to property had been severed for many royalists, Killigrew insists on (self-) ownership as a personal, inherent quality of certain men. Thomaso's marriage to an heiress cannot (the play protests too much) place him in the position of a prostitute, for he simply assumes in the marriage a position he already deserves.

The Restoration constructed female authorship as plagiaristic in the same sense that it constructed prostitution as piracy: representations of both commonly implied the violation of property. But if we take Behn's word for it—and on this point, there is no reason to do otherwise—her play points to, rather than attempts to hide, its intertextuality. Thomas M. Greene has characterized Renaissance imitation as the incorporation of a "subtext" in the text, and Leonard Barkan has demonstrated the ways in which these relationships often involve complicated and competitive struggles.[52] While perhaps not an "imitation" in the same sense as the texts that Greene and Barkan address, *The Rover* nevertheless embeds *Thomaso* as a subtext. Behn revises the sexual politics of *Thomaso*,[53] but in doing so she (consciously or not) attacks Killigrew himself in a way

---

[52] Thomas M. Greene, *The Light in Troy: Imitation and Discovery in Renaissance Poetry* (New Haven: Yale University Press, 1982); Leonard Barkan, *The Gods Made Flesh: Metamorphosis and the Pursuit of Paganism* (New Haven: Yale University Press, 1986). It might seem odd to write of Behn's *Rover* as similar to the kinds of texts that Greene addresses. Behn herself, however, questions the difference between commercial adaptation and elite imitation. The duchess of Newcastle similarly questions the difference between imitation and lack of originality.

[53] See DeRitter, "The Gypsy."

that becomes visible only by comparison. Killigrew's Thomas(o) demonstrates his inherent superiority—a superiority that merits both Serulina and her wealth—by his unique and characteristic skill of distinguishing ladies from whores. Behn's *Rover* destabilizes this privilege, however, for her Willmore constantly demonstrates his blindness.

Thomaso swaggers through *The Wanderer* on his way to Serulina's arms and fortune; Willmore, on the other hand, both blunders and connives his way to Hellena, unable to read the signs along the way. For most of the play, Willmore accepts Hellena's gypsy disguise at face value. Willmore and Blunt (Killigrew's Edwardo) articulate equal confusion at the women at Carnival, unable to decipher their code. Only Belvile can offer a reading:

> WILLMORE: Fine pretty creatures! May a stranger have leave to look
> and love? What's here? "Roses for every month." [Reads the papers.]
> BLUNT: Roses for every month? What means that?
> BELVILE: They are, or would have your think they're courtesans, who
> here in Naples are to be hired by the month.[54]

Belvile understands not only their semiotics but also the instability of the meaning they claim. Belvile and Willmore split the characteristics and plot functions of Thomaso between them; yet Willmore, in his philandering and adventuring, echoes Killigrew's autobiographical hero more closely. Behn's blundering rake, as opposed to Killigrew's slick one, cannot comprehend the possibility that a lady and a whore might circulate similar signs.[55] Later in the same scene, Willmore assumes that Belvile's lover Florinda will "oblige" him as well if he helps Belvile rescue her from her brother (1.2.258–264). When Belvile admires a picture of Florinda, Willmore cannot distinguish it from his own pilfered portrait of Angellica. Killigrew parallels the virtuous Serulina with the prostitute Angellica to demonstrate his Wanderer's acute capacity to distinguish; Behn, though, exploits this parallel to show Willmore's blindness *as well as* the genuine ambiguity of the difference between the positions of these

---

[54] Aphra Behn, *The Rover*, ed. Frederick M. Link (Lincoln: University of Nebraska Press, 1967), 1.2.82–86. References are to act, scene, and line. Future references to this play are from this edition and are cited in the text.

[55] See Diamond, "*Gestus* and Signature"; Diamond demonstrates the ways in which women circulate as signs in *The Rover*.

women. Like the foolish Edwardo in *The Wanderer*, Willmore drunkenly stumbles into a virtuous lady's garden, takes her for a whore, and attempts to rape her. His attempted rape raises questions about his humanity: Florinda calls him a "filthy beast" (3.5.33); Belvile calls him a "senseless swine" (3.6.3); Willmore calls himself an "unlucky dog" (3.3.9). Willmore can only apologize to Belvile by insisting that he did not know she was Florinda. But for Belvile, Willmore's imperfection as a reader misses the point: "Ah, plague on your ignorance! If it had not been Florinda, must you be a beast? A brute?" (3.6.2–3). Willmore constantly reveals himself as a notoriously inept reader of signs, and Thomas(o)'s position of *definitive* reader of women becomes unavailable in *The Rover*, for even Belvile mistakes Florinda in disguise.

Killigrew's autobiographical Thomaso stands at the center of the play, drawing desire from all the women and admiration from all the men. Behn's *The Rover*, however, challenges the basis on which Thomas(o) claims his privileges. The oblivious Willmore inadvertently blocks Belvile's marriage and thus functions as an obstacle to this play's sentimental plot. He stabs Antonio the Viceroy's son in a sword fight, for which Belvile is blamed: Willmore can no more recognize an unknown man's status than an unknown woman's. The one time he actually *does* recognize a disguise, he ruins Belvile's plan to marry Florinda. Willmore's inability to read signs complicates his own romances as well: when Hellena, disguised as a boy in Angellica's house, tells him that a rich young lady loves him, he makes a fool of himself trying to discover the lady's identity. Killigrew compares the foolish Edwardo to the savvy Thomaso in terms of their relative abilities to read the social world; Behn, however, rewrites them as parallel characters, for in spite of Willmore's charm and endearing foibles, he shares Blunt's blindness. To recharacterize the Wanderer in this way not only challenges the assumptions about gender in Killigrew's play, but also encodes an attack on the author himself.[56]

In *The Rover*, Behn both articulates a nostalgic loyalty to royalist politics

---

[56] I realize that this reading conflicts with the nearly standard assumption that Willmore represents the earl of Rochester. See, for example, Maureen Duffy's identification in *The Passionate Shepherdess: Aphra Behn, 1640–89* (London: Methuen, 1977), 153–154. Behn may indeed have intended to include a reference to John Wilmot with her Willmore, but such a reference would not have been entirely flattering. The more obvious reference—since *The Rover* rewrites *Thomaso*, which tells its author's adventures in idealized terms—has for some reason received less attention.

and attacks the elite masculine privilege within this system, which allowed men like Killigrew to claim exteriority to the emergent market economy.[57] Killigrew flaunted his (desired) position through Thomaso's sexuality: whether expressed to street whores, courtesans, "lady-whores," or ladies, his body remains inalienable. Thomaso cannot be commodified. Behn's Willmore, by contrast, can no more escape the commercial world than can Angellica Bianca. Belvile, who takes on *some* of Thomaso's qualities, mitigates this attack and his dignity may even have compensatorily flattered Thomaso's author. Belvile and Florinda provide an alternative that combines emergent ideals of the affective marriage[58] and a woman's privilege to select her husband[59] with highly traditional ideals about respect for virtuous women. But they seek nothing so progressive as passion outside of property, for both ultimately want (and receive) Don Pedro's approval. Willmore and Angellica Bianca, however, challenge cultural inscriptions of gendered differences in sexual alienability.

As in Killigrew's play, Behn's Angellica Bianca attempts to transform her relationship with Willmore from commerce to gift. Behn contrasts Angellica's sincere desire to trade love for love with Lucetta's trick of giving Blunt a bracelet, which fools him into thinking her advances have nothing to do with profit. Like Thomaso, Willmore also insults Angellica for self-commodification, claiming for himself the moral high ground: "Poor as I am I would not sell myself" (2.2.56). As asserted earlier, this statement could stand as a theme for Killigrew's play: however desperate certain men become, their sexuality and their very selves remain inalienable. Thomaso deserves Serulina for his position alone. But Behn's Angellica argues back to Willmore: "Pray tell me, sir, are not you guilty of the same mercenary crime? When a lady is proposed to you for a wife, you never ask how fair, discreet, or virtuous she is, but what's her fortune; which, if but small, you cry 'She will not do my business,' and basely leave her, though she languish for you. Say is not this as poor?"

[57] For another reading of the problem of gender and property in *The Rover*, see Hutner, "Revisioning the Female Body."

[58] See Lawrence Stone, *The Family, Sex, and Marriage in England, 1500–1800* (New York: Harper & Row, 1977).

[59] See Susan Staves, *Players' Scepters: Fictions of Authority in the Restoration* (Lincoln: University of Nebraska Press, 1979). Staves demonstrates the important relationship between political changes and women's domestic position in the late seventeenth century.

(2.2.90–95).[60] Willmore instantly denies any complicity with such a practice ("It is a barbarous custom, which I will scorn to defend in our sex, and do despise in yours"), yet the events of the play belie his claim to superiority on this account. His decision to marry Hellena seems, and has been read as, a spontaneous and affectionate second choice to free love.[61] Hellena insists on the rites of Hymen, for otherwise she would find herself with "A cradle full of noise and mischief, with a pack of repentance at my back" (5. 453–4). Readers have paid less attention, however, to the fact that Willmore's attitude toward marriage changes immediately upon the discovery of his gypsy's wealth. Angellica inadvertently gives Willmore away to her rival when she wishes aloud that he only courted Hellena for her two hundred thousand crowns:

WILLMORE. Two hundred thousand crowns! What story's this? What trick? What woman, ha?

ANGELLICA. How strange you make it. Have you forgot the creature you entertained on the Piazzo last night?

WILLMORE (aside). Ha! My gipsy worth two hundred thousand crowns! Oh, how I long to be with her! Pox, I knew she was of quality. (4.2.186–192)

That Willmore had not yet figured out Hellena's financial worth does not occur to Angellica, but it remains consistent with the Rover's inability to read signs. Hellena, in fact, immediately enters this scene dressed as a boy, a disguise Willmore cannot see through until she looks him full in the face. By the end of the scene, however, he swears to marry Hellena and takes the first opportunity to escape Angellica in pursuit of his rich gypsy.[62] Interestingly, in his next scene with Hellena he no longer demands sex, but rather "the pleasure of working that great miracle of making a maid a mother" (5.1. 450–451). Thus it is Willmore, rather than Hellena, who first raises the issue of reproduction: *he* reminds *her*

---

[60] Killigrew's Angellica, in contrast, points out that men are equally guilty of lust. *Thomaso*, 1.2.4.

[61] See, for example, DeRitter, "The Gypsy"; and Duffy, *The Passionate Shepardess.*

[62] "If it were possible I should ever be inclined to marry," Willmore swears, "it should be some kind young sinner: one that has generosity enough to give a favor handsomely to one that can ask it discreetly, one that has wit enough to manage an intrigue of love. Oh, how civil such a wench is to a man that does her the honor to marry her." Behn, *The Rover*, 4.2.374–379.

of the consequences of sex. He withholds his knowledge of her financial worth, with which Hellena gleefully "surprises" him at the end.

Willmore not only manipulates his willing heiress, but also earns a small profit from his affair with Angellica. After their night of love, Willmore boasts to his friends of financial, rather than sexual, conquest: " 'Tis he and she gold whilst here, and shall beget new pleasures every moment" (3.1.116–117). Alarmed at his sudden wealth, Blunt wonders: "But hark'ee, sir, you are not married, are you?" Willmore replies, "All the honey of matrimony but none of the sting, friend" (3.1.119–120).[63] Ordinarily, we might read the "honey of matrimony" as sexual pleasure. In this particular scene, however, the honey refers most immediately to the gold he jingles in his hand. Blunt's own subplot echoes this: he refers to Lucetta as his "lucky bargain," celebrating with Willmore that "here's two provided for!" (3.1.125, 127). Once at Lucetta's house, though, she confesses that she has "nothing to pay for so great a favor, but such a love as cannot but be great, since at first sight of that sweet face and shape it made me your absolute captive" (3.2.11–13). Blunt agrees to make love to her for free, but clearly her appearance of wealth draws him. He compares her to the "mercenary prodigal whores" in England who expect payment to "this, that free and generous . . . Why, what a house she has, how rich and fine!" (3.2.27–29). In Behn's play, then, Willmore and Blunt differ in degree rather than in kind: both expect payment for sex, but only Willmore's charm merits the reward of an heiress.

Willmore, in conclusion, is a whore.[64] The line he uses to seduce Angellica, in fact, is similar to the one Lucetta uses to seduce Blunt: "Throw off this pride, this enemy to bliss,/ And show the power of love: 'tis with those arms/I can be only vanquished, made a slave" (2.2.130–132), similarly encouraging his partner to subordinate financial to sexual interests, as he has. Like Lucetta, he offers subordination; like Lucetta, he doesn't mean it. Angellica's woman Moretta, in fact, calls Willmore a "picaroon" (2.2.164), Killigrew's word for Lucetta and Behn's own word for prostitute in her first prologue. Moretta sums up "the fate of most whores" as follows: *Trophies, which from believing fops we win,/ Are*

---

[63] As in Killigrew's play, Willmore eventually gives the money back.

[64] This reading of Willmore has benefited from the comments of my spring 1994 class on gender theory and from Donna Long in particular, who put the Rover's identity this succinctly.

spoils of those who cozen us again" (2.2.168–169). Indeed, Angellica, like Blunt, attempts violent revenge on the one who tricked her. Hellena's fortune offers more gold than Angellica's profits from other men; Willmore goes to the highest bidder.[65] In associating Willmore with prostitution, Behn does not charge *all* men with the same practice (think of Belvile) nor does she necessarily even condemn the Rover for self-commodification. She gives him enough charm and seductiveness to avoid a bald insult to any man who might recognize his own position in the Rover's. Nevertheless, *The Rover* refutes the central anxious claim of *Thomaso*: the hero's masculine ability to avoid alienating himself or his sexuality. In this way, *The Rover* challenges the naturalness of gendered divisions between owners and the owned. When Angellica confronts Willmore at gunpoint upon the discovery that he has cheated her—that he really *is* a picaroon—he offers her money back as amends. These are the terms he understands. Unlike Killigrew's Thomaso, Behn's Willmore unabashedly belongs to the same marketplace of alienable sexuality as Angellica.

Gendered positions of alienability have consequences for authorship as well as sexuality. Elin Diamond reads Angellica Bianca as in some ways a "signature" for Behn herself, and I have suggested that Willmore rewrites Killigrew's idealized self-representation in *Thomaso; or, The Wanderer*. In her fictional world, then, Behn closes the gap between the elite male amateur literary world and her own professional, public, and ill-reputed career; Killigrew participates in the same marketplace as does she. In her postscript, in fact, Behn suggests that Killigrew practices the same kind of literary appropriation: "if the *Play of the Novella* were as well worth remembering as *Thomaso*, they might (bating the name) have as well said I took it from thence." By mentioning this play as another possible source for her own, she also reminds the readers that *Thomaso* itself borrows incidents from an earlier text. Behn nevertheless declares the "plot and business . . . my own," perhaps appropriating Killigrew's text as fair payment for the suffering he brought upon her with the spying mission. Whether this incident motivated her or not, she rewrites Killigrew's charming hero as both a fool and a whore, as an inept reader and a peddler of alienated selves and texts. By deconstructing the gen-

---

[65] In "*Gestus* and Signature," Elin Diamond significantly points out that in fact all the money ultimately comes from Don Pedro, which destabilizes the difference between the positions of Hellena and Angellica and even Florinda.

dered opposition between those who can alienate sexual property and those who cannot, Behn by implication deconstructs the opposition (informed by both class and gender) between elite, amateur economies of privilege and the professional circulation of texts for money. Behn fully participated in the commodification of letters.[66] Yet for all the independence that the literary marketplace offered, Behn nevertheless continued to regard her own participation in it with an ambivalence only partially explained by her aristocratic ideology. Her *Oroonoko* documents this ambivalence, and its subsequent dramatic appropriation by Thomas Southerne reinvents, though in a different ideological framework, cultural divisions between owners and the owned.

Owning Oroonoko

The adventures of Oroonoko tell a story about property. In the first half of Aphra Behn's novel, which takes place for the most part in Africa, Oroonoko struggles against his royal grandfather for possession of Imoinda, the woman he loves; in the second half, the now enslaved prince fights English colonists in Surinam for possession of himself as well as his wife. This drama unfolds in the context of two pressing issues of ownership in the late seventeenth century: slavery and colonialism. While Oroonoko's place in a kinship system denies him access to Imoinda in Africa, the intrusion of English colonial slave traders at once offers and dispels the possibility of uniting the two lovers abroad. Aphra Behn's novel confronts the ownership of Africans by the English, the ownership of American land by European colonists, and the ownership of women by men.

Property becomes not just an issue of gender and national origin in *Oroonoko*, but also an issue of writing: Behn's English woman narrator opens by claiming no originality and closes by lamenting the inadequacy of her "wit" to tell a story that belongs to a great African man and woman. Behn's own capacity to claim literary property continues as a problem in the eighteenth century. Although most modern readers associate this story with Aphra Behn, for eighteenth-century readers, Behn's property in *Oroonoko* would have been overshadowed by Thomas Southerne's

[66] See Gallagher, "Masked Woman," and also Ferguson, "Juggling the Categories of Race, Class, and Gender."

successful play (first performed in 1695, published in 1696) of the same name. Behn's reputation suffered in the eighteenth century: *Oxford Magazine* and later *Ladies Magazine* serialized her *Oroonoko*, but critics nevertheless denounced her plays as indelicate and her novels as ephemeral.[67] Southerne, however, became one of the century's most respected dramatists, largely as a result of his appropriation of *Oroonoko*.[68] Southerne's *Oroonoko* played at least once a year from its initial appearance in 1695 until as late as 1829, becoming one of the two or three most popular plays of the eighteenth century.[69]

The difference between Southerne and Behn, I argue, lies in the particular way that each represents human, literary, and real property. Both versions of *Oroonoko* appear in a cultural moment of property consciousness that also gave rise to John Locke's *Two Treatises of Government*. Locke proclaims an equality of access to property, particularly to one's own body, and locates the ownership of land in its use. Thus, Locke's treatise offers its readers a mandate for the cultivation of any apparently unclaimed land, providing an ethical as well as economic justification for colonialism. Behn's novel resists this ideology, which Michael McKeon has called "progressive" (for its self-conscious belief in its superiority to the past); the novel's resistance partly comes, however,

[67] See Mary Ann O'Donnell, *Aphra Behn: An Annotated Bibliography of Primary and Secondary Sources* (New York: Garland, 1986), 327–353. O'Donnell lists these editions and notes the negative critical responses to Behn in the eighteenth century, which characterize Behn's writing as loose and frivolous. For defenses of Behn, however, see John Pearson, *Two Centuries of Testimony in Favour of Mrs. Aphra Behn* (London, 1872).

[68] Colley Cibber, for example, says it was a turning point in his literary career when Southerne decided to support the production of *Love's Last Shift*. Cibber introduces his mentor to the reader as "Mr. *Southern*, the Author of *Oroonoko*." *An Apology for the Life of Colley Cibber, Written by Himself*, ed. Robert W. Lowe, 2 vols. (London, 1889; reprint, New York: AMS Press, 1966), 1:212.

[69] Southerne's *Oroonoko* generated several spin-offs as well: Southerne's added comic plot became *The Sexes Mismatch'd*, printed in *The Stroller's Pacquet Open'd* (London, 1742). Francis Gentleman (1760) and John Hawkesworth (1759) each adapted the tragic scenes into somewhat altered versions; and John Ferriar transformed the play into an antislavery protest in his *Prince of Angola* (1788). Southerne wrote, Ferriar argues, "a groveling apology of slave-holders" that Hawkesworth merely repeated. Ferriar made it his own task to supply "the reflexions . . . which . . . had escaped the dramatic attempt of Southerne and Hawkesworth" (i). Ferriar treats the novel as a source study for the play: "Southerne copied," he complains, "with injudicious fidelity from Mrs. Behn's Novel" (iii). As Ferriar's attack indicates, Southerne successfully appropriated Behn's story as his own for eighteenth-century audiences.

from a conservative perspective.[70] Still, neither conservative ideology nor the related nostalgia for an aristocratic ethos can entirely contain the complexities of Behn's narrative. Southerne's play, by contrast, not only embraces "progressive" ideology, with its emphasis on private property, but also parallels Lockean rhetoric, which, as C. B. Macpherson has demonstrated, proclaims equality but constitutively depends upon limiting the category of the individual and by extension the category of potential owner.

Both texts of *Oroonoko* offer vivid negotiations of human property, both in slavery and in marriage. Here, "race," class, and gender intersect in each text to produce complex positions in relation to ownership.[71] Neither narrative protests slavery, but Behn's *Oroonoko* problematizes human commodification, while Southerne's seeks complex ways to justify it. Behn begins her main narrative in Africa, giving the two African lovers a cultural context—however ethnocentrically drawn—prior to their struggles against English mercantilism. Her African setting and African lovers create a fictional alternative to the pervasive commodification brought by English colonialism, which dominates the second half of her novel. The dramatic version, by contrast, takes place entirely in a colonial setting. Southerne transforms Imoinda from Oroonoko's black African lover and later wife (in Behn's version) into a white European, presumably an Englishwoman, whom Oroonoko meets when she accompanies her father to Africa.[72] By eliminating the history of the African characters and by changing Imoinda into an Englishwoman, Southerne inscribes

---

[70] Michael McKeon distinguishes three major ideologies for the Restoration. Aristocratic ideology naturalized elites as the embodiment of a static unity of status and virtue; progressive ideology advocated mobility through individual accumulation and other forms of virtue; and conservative ideology arose as a nostalgic attack on class mobility and capitalist circulation. See his *Origins of the English Novel, 1600–1740* (Baltimore: Johns Hopkins University Press, 1987).

[71] I put the word *race* in quotation marks because, as much recent scholarship has argued, the sense of difference that Behn and Southerne articulate is not the same as the modern construction of "race," which is itself being held up for scrutiny. See *"Race," Writing, and Difference,* ed. Henry Louis Gates, Jr. (Chicago: University of Chicago Press, 1986), intro.; and Kwame Anthony Appiah, "Race," in *Critical Terms for Literary Study,* ed. Frank Lentricchia and Thomas McLaughlin (Chicago: University of Chicago Press, 1990), 274–287.

[72] Southerne does not actually specify that Imoinda is English, only that she is white. From the context of play, it seems reasonable to assume that both author and audience would have understood Imoinda as English. Still, her lack of national

precisely the progressive ideology that helped enable colonialism and that Behn's novel holds up for scrutiny. Further, authorship itself becomes a site of contestation over property as these writers take up various strategies to negotiate their differently gendered positions and thus their differing capacities to own literary property. Behn's own vulnerability to accusations of plagiarism and the complex strategies of authority she found necessary to adopt,[73] compared to Southerne's strategies for appropriating her novel, demonstrate the way a progressive ideology of property undermined Behn's ability to claim property in the narrative itself.

Aphra Behn's representation of slavery has been debated extensively, with insight but without resolution.[74] Nearly all critics acknowledge this novel's outright ethnocentrism as well as its failure to condemn human ownership, but Laura Brown and Charlotte Sussman have shown the text's glimpses of resistance to dominant paradigms as well. I hope to

---

identity suggests that she comes to signify, through the color of her skin, a more general European identity formed in opposition to non-Europeans.

[73] For Behn's authorial strategies, see, for example, Payne, "Aphra Behn and Patronage"; Kavenik, "Aphra Behn"; and Munns, "Aphra Behn and Sexual Space" in *Curtain Calls;* see also Gallagher, "Masked Woman."

[74] Wylie Sypher, for example, objects that the choice to make Oroonoko a prince obviates any potential antislavery stance, for the hero becomes a noble exception in contrast to the ordinary African. *Guinea's Captive Kings: British Anti-Slavery Literature of the XVIIIth Century* (Chapel Hill: University of North Carolina Press, 1942), 116, 108. See also Ferguson, "Juggling the Categories of Race, Class, and Gender"; William C. Spengemann, "The Earliest American Novel: Aphra Behn's *Oroonoko*," *Nineteenth Century Fiction* 38 (1984): 384–414; Laura Brown, "The Romance of Empire: *Oroonoko* and the Trade in Slaves," in *The New Eighteenth Century: Theory, Politics, English Literature,* ed. Felicity Nussbaum and Laura Brown (New York: Methuen, 1987), 41–61; George Guffey, "Aphra Behn's *Oroonoko*: Occasion and Accomplishment," *Two English Novelists, Aphra Behn and Anthony Trollop: Papers Read at a Clark Library Seminar, May 11, 1974* (Los Angeles: William Andrews Clark Memorial Library, 1975), 3–41; Heidi Hutner, "Aphra Behn's *Oroonoko*: The Politics of Gender, Race, and Class," in *Living by the Pen: Early British Women Writers,* ed. Dale Spender (New York: Teachers College Press, 1992), 39–51. More recent contributions include Charlotte Sussman, "The Other Problem with Women: Reproduction and Slave Culture in Aphra Behn's *Oroonoko*" (212–233); Ros Ballaster, " 'Presences of State': Aphra Behn and the Female Plot" (187–211), both in Hutner, *Rereading Aphra Behn*; and Catherine Gallagher's reading of *Oroonoko* and commodification in *Nobody's Story*, chap. 2.

offer another such reading by looking closely at Behn's representations of slavery and colonialism in the context of other contemporary possibilities. The general term "slavery" elides two distinct practices in the novel—one English and one "African"—that Behn represents as having different social meanings within their different cultures and economies. Behn structures her "Africa" as an oppressive and elitist society, but one that primarily circulates goods—including slaves—as gifts. So although Behn narrates little about the institution of slavery within Africa, especially in comparison to the strikingly graphic picture of English colonial slavery she offers, the novel does provide several points (which I will discuss later) where the differences between these two institutions become visible. Behn's fictional, pseudo-anthropological, and ethnocentrically imagined "African" culture maintains a rigid hierarchy based on rank and kinship—a hierarchy respected across enemy lines, enabling different communities to circulate low-ranking prisoners of war as slaves.[75] This hierarchy creates the problem of the romance plot: Oroonoko cannot live with his wife because his grandfather the king has claimed her for himself. Most of the English colonists, by contrast, indiscriminately understand all Africans as commodities or potential commodities. In the first half of the novel, the enslaved prisoners only become *commodities*—that is, measured by an exchange value that does not recognize their African cultural position—upon contact with the English. Oroonoko's life and body become such an explosive site of contradiction because he attempts to participate fully in both economies. He ends up, however, with neither the romantic and kinship ties that "Africa" offers, nor the economic and political rights that English colonialism offers to other slave traders. Behn grotesquely literalizes this fragmented subject position in the final scene, in which the colonists slowly dismember the African prince.

Laura Brown has argued that in spite of *Oroonoko's* "racism"—Behn,

---

[75] The debate over Behn's accuracy in representing Africa has a long history; Moira Ferguson makes the latest contribution to this debate in *Subject to Others: British Women Writers and Colonial Slavery, 1670–1834* (New York: Routledge, 1992), chap. 2. I am interested, however, in Behn's narrative as a *representation* that repeats and revises other representations of Africa. See also Katherine M. Rogers, "Fact and Fiction in Aphra Behn's *Oroonoko,*" *Studies in the Novel* 20 (1988): 1–15. Rogers accepts European travel narratives as transparently factual; she does, however, demonstrate how closely Behn engaged them.

for example, praises her hero for the Roman nose and thin lips that distinguish him from other Africans[76]—the text resists English colonialism at the level of ideology by yoking the African prince to England's own martyred king, Charles I. As Brown has convincingly argued, "Charles I and Oroonoko are victims of the same historical phenomenon—those new forces in English society loosely associated with an antiabsolutist mercantile imperialism."[77] Behn's gesture of linking these figures mourns the way mercantile capitalism has destroyed an earlier royalist culture and an aristocratic ideology. Although I agree that much of *Oroonoko*'s accomplishment consists of an ambivalent critique of an emergent mercantilism, the economy to which Behn opposes colonialism does not entirely characterize an aristocratic ideology that existed in the time of Charles I. To settle on aristocratic ideology and nostalgia for an earlier English regime as Behn's conceptual framework leaves out the significance of the first half of the story's "African" location.

In *Oroonoko*, Behn uses myths and narratives of "Africa" to imagine a "precapitalist" economy that did not entirely exist in England at the time of the royal martyr; her novel, unlike Southerne's play, imagines African characters belonging to a culture prior to and independent of English colonialism. Behn's representation, however, repeats and contributes to English ethnocentrism. The sexual greed of Oroonoko's grandfather, for example, resembles contemporary travel narratives that describe the excessive sexual indulgence of tyrannical African kings.[78] These narratives commonly describe the huge seraglios kept by the king and the limited access to women suffered by other men; several represent murderous and sadistic kings as part of an argument that the English slave trade actually rescues Africans.[79] Although Behn participates in

[76] Aphra Behn, *Oroonoko, or, The Royal Slave*, ed. Lore Metzger (New York: W. W. Norton, 1973), 8. Future references are from this edition and are cited in the text.

[77] Brown, "The Romance of Empire." The colonists rename Oroonoko as Caesar, a name also given to Charles I; the death scene itself, Brown points out, would have evoked images of the suffering of Charles I for contemporary readers.

[78] See also Ferguson, "Juggling the Categories of Race, Class, and Gender," on the ways in which *Oroonoko*'s ethnocentricity takes a sexualized form.

[79] William's Smith, *A New Voyage to Guinea*, ed. John Ralph Willis (1744; reprint, London: Cass Library of African Studies no. 22, 1967), for example, describes a bloodthirsty African king's house that is filled with human skulls. Upon the king's death, his thousands of wives attempt to kill each other. Smith's *Voyage* is an explicit plea for slavery as a more humane way of life than subjugation to the violent, despotic, and sexually voracious kings Smith represents. Similar descriptions appear in William

this ethnocentric discourse, she also at times departs from dominant representations. In spite of his acquisition of women, Behn's African king, Oroonoko's grandfather, is literally impotent, and her hero is passionately monogamous. The novel indeed exploits, as Margaret W. Ferguson shows, the stereotype of sexually threatening black African men, yet the novel's constant return to Oroonoko's love for Imoinda to the exclusion of all others at the same time disrupts it. Charlotte Sussman, Ros Ballaster, and Margaret Ferguson have all suggested different ways in which the novel silences and sacrifices Imoinda: Behn empowers her white narrator at a black woman's expense. Without disagreeing with this point, I believe it is nevertheless important to notice the ways in which Oroonoko's love for an African woman and Imoinda's presence itself have significance within the novel's historical context.[80] Behn did not hesitate to tell stories of "miscegenation" elsewhere and could easily have done so in *Oroonoko*.[81] I take her choice to create faithful African lovers—literally to *romanticize* what most other contemporary narratives represent with disgust—as one both embedded in and distinct from stereotypes of African sexuality. Behn uses myths of Africa—the only Africa to which she has access—to represent an alternative to the brutality of English commodification and a place from which to offer a critical view of colonialism.

If Behn does not escape ethnocentrism when she inverts a negative stereotype of African sexual voraciousness into a utopian monogamous romance, neither does she do so when she rewrites a stereotype of the African inability to comprehend European trading practices as an admirable freedom from commodity culture: the ideals themselves remain those of her own culture. Behn's myths idealize, whereas prevailing myths denigrate. In *The Golden Coast, or a Description of Guinney* (1665)— a text sometimes cited as a source for *Oroonoko*—European conceptions

---

Bosman, *A New and Accurate Description of the Coast of Guinea,* ed. John Ralph Willis (1704; reprint, London: Cass, 1967). See also Dorothy Hammond and Alta Jablow, *The Myth of Africa* (New York: Library of Social Science, 1977); Robert Norris, *Memoirs of the Reign of Bossa Ahádee, King of Dahomy* (1789; reprint, London: Cass, 1968); William Snelgrave, *New Account of Some Parts of Guinea and the Slave-Trade* (1734; reprint, London: Cass, 1971).

[80] Sussman emphasizes the violence and proprietorship of that love. "The Other Problem with Women."

[81] For example, Behn's plays *Abdelazar* and *The Widow Ranter* have mixed-"race" romances, as does her novel *The Blind Lady.*

of property meet with confusion in Africa. The author reports how easily his party fooled the people they traded with: "At first wee used many times to deceive them, not only in the measuring of Linnen, but in delivering them broken and patch'd Basons, and peeced Kettles for their mony; rotten Cloath, through which they might have sifted Beans; Knives that were so Rusty, that they could hardly, without breaking, pull them out of their Sheaths."[82] Eventually, however, the Africans become overly scrupulous and thus excessively difficult. Both extremes, however, inhibit trade. The author further describes the African expectation of a gift that accompanies trade: "when they have bestowed their mony, then wee must give them something to boot, which they call *Dache*" (57). The Europeans figure out ways to exploit the "*Dache*" expectation. Trade among Africans themselves devolves into a cheating contest: "Whiles [a merchant] looks about, or turns to spue, [another] steals a peece of the Merchants Gold, and puts it into their Mouths, Ears and Nostrils, making the Merchant beleeve that his mony is two [sic] light; the Merchant for his part, seeing that by means of their theevery his mony will not hold out, because it is too light . . . blows into the Ballance" (60). Finally, the author concludes that these Africans have no respect for property at all: "On my conscience I think there are not such Theives in the world, they are not more ashamed to steal from one another, which they reckon dishonesty . . . than they are proud to steal from strangers, which they esteem as policy, and look for honours as the reward of so brave an action. . . . yea, though they bee never so great Merchants, and bestow three or four pound of Gold with you for Merchandize, their opinion being that they may steal, and wee not; I asked them the reason, and they said, *wee were rich, and brought great store of Ware, which would stand upon our hands, if they took not some away, and they naked*" (71–72).

As in this narrative, *Oroonoko* brings the English and African cultures into sharpest contrast in their economic practices. But whereas *The Golden Coast* ridicules Africans for their initial ignorance of property and their later refusal to abide by English practices, Behn—with equal ethnocentrism—idealizes this difference, depicting Africa as an economically innocent world. While colonial culture in the novel's second half treats bodies and land as commodities, Behn's "Africa" operates on a gift economy. "Africa" becomes a place in which objects and human bodies circulate without commodification. *Oroonoko*'s pseudo-anthropology re-

---

[82] *The Golden Coast* (London, 1665), 18–19. Future references are cited in the text.

fers to this "African" gift economy in a spirit similar to Jean Baudrillard's vague historical reference to a lost symbolic economy: both writers visualize a precapitalist world in which objects retain a value other than their commodity value, an economy that operates on "the presentation, the gift, the festival [,] . . . the ambivalence (positive and negative) of personal exchange."[83] Behn's "African," like any symbolic or gift economy, does not eliminate conflict, for exchanges, as Baudrillard argues, create great personal disturbances. Behn's "African" culture, in fact, oppresses people through stifling kinship networks and inviolate hierarchies. Still, those conflicts recede before the violence of human commodification. Like Baudrillard, Behn represents an alternative "primitive" economy as a critique of a colonialist economy in which even a prince becomes vulnerable to commodification.[84]

The first half of the novel figures human bodies as gifts. Oroonoko first meets Imoinda because her father sacrificed his own life in battle to prevent the prince's death. Other bodies must now circulate back to Imoinda's family as compensation for this loss: Oroonoko brings to Imoinda, as a gift, 150 slaves (9). When Oroonoko's grandfather and king desires Imoinda, he does not attempt to buy or bribe her but rather indicates that she must give herself to him. The grandfather discovers Oroonoko's transgressive love for her, in fact, by exploiting the gift economy: the king sends a man to "make a Present to *Imoinda*, as from the Prince; he should then, unknown, see this fair Maid, and have an opportunity to hear what Message she wou'd return the Prince for his Present, and from thence gather that state of her Heart" (12). Oroonoko,

---

[83] "For a Critique of the Political Economy of the Sign," *Jean Baudrillard: Selected Writings*, ed. Mark Poster (Stanford: Stanford University Press, 1988), 58, 61.

[84] See Marcel Mauss, *The Gift: The Form and Reason for Exchange in Archaic Societies*, trans. W. D. Halls (1950; reprint, New York: Norton, 1990). Mauss describes such gift economies in societies based on complex exchanges that cement social relations. Although a gift economy can exist simultaneously with a merchant economy, the obligation to keep the gift in circulation—although not necessarily by returning a gift to the same person or group—binds the community together. The objects themselves become endowed with ritual and even sacred significance. See also G. A. Starr, "Aphra Behn and the Genealogy of the Man of Feeling," *Modern Philology* 87 (1990): 362–372. Starr argues that Behn's rhetoric "is distinctly Tory; the object of its disdain is not slavery per se but the Whiggish spirit that reduces everything including human beings to objects of commerce" (365). Starr contends that Behn's *Oroonoko* supports slavery by representing it as "so solid and impervious an institution that any attempt to alter or eliminate it would seem doomed" (366).

in turn, surreptitiously gains the opportunity to consummate his secret marriage to Imoinda by another exchange of bodies: his loyal friend Aboan agrees to give himself in love to Onahal (the king's older, discarded wife, who guards the young wives), and Onahal in return admits Oroonoko into Imoinda's chambers. Once Oroonoko violates the gift economy that his grandfather controls, the grandfather converts Imoinda from gift to commodity by selling her into English colonial slavery (26). The king, however, comes to see this conversion of Imoinda as a crime of an entirely different order than Oroonoko's love for her. He realizes that he "ought to have had so much Value and Consideration for a Maid of her Quality, as to have nobly put her to death, and not to have sold her like a common Slave; the greatest Revenge, and the most disgraceful of any, and to which they a thousand times prefer Death, and implore it; as *Imoinda* did, but cou'd not obtain that Honour" (27). So even though Imoinda becomes enslaved on both continents, Behn distinguishes between Imoinda's captivity in Africa, where she circulates as a gift, and her captivity in America, where she circulates as a commodity.

Oroonoko as well as Imoinda falls victim to English exploitation of the "African" gift economy. And, although Oroonoko sells slaves to Europeans, his aristocratic conception of honor prevents him from understanding Africans indiscriminately as commodities and prevents the practice of slavery from destroying the "African" symbolic culture. Thus, Oroonoko withholds the captured enemy leader from commodity circulation. This Jamoan "afterwards became very dear to [Oroonoko], being a Man very gallant, and of excellent Graces, and fine Parts; so that he never put him amongst the Rank of Captives, as they used to do, without distinction, for the common Sale, or Market, but kept him in his own Court, where he retain'd nothing of the Prisoner but the Name, and returned no more into his own Country, so great an Affection he took for *Oroonoko*" (30–31). Oroonoko resists pervasive commodification but embraces a hierarchy based on rank—the same hierarchy, ironically, that takes Imoinda away from him. Further, in "African" slavery, affective ties can transcend the distance between owner and owned. This, for Behn, remains impossible in the English mercantile institution: Oroonoko's refusal to commodify Jamoan thus provides a sharp contrast to Oroonoko's own capture. The prince at first understands his relationship to the English sea captain, to whom he sells slaves, as part of a gift economy: Oroonoko grows fond of the captain and "for the Favour and

Esteem he had for him, made him many Presents, and oblig'd him to stay at Court as long as possibly he cou'd" (32). The captain appears to reciprocate with the gift of a feast, but then abruptly violates the symbolic economy by capturing Oroonoko into slavery. Appropriately, Oroonoko and his entourage will not accept the sea captain's further offerings of food until the captain tricks them with the illusion that they have returned to a gift economy: he frees the prince and insists that the other Africans are his guests to be freed once they reach land. So while this gift economy has profound internal conflicts, nothing becomes more pernicious in Behn's novel than when English commodification violates it.[85]

In *Oroonoko*, stories as well a human bodies ideally belong to a symbolic or gift economy. The entire "African" half of the novel, after all, only comes to the narrator through Oroonoko's storytelling. Yet the narrator learns this from an *exchange*, for she tells as many stories as she receives: "I entertained [Oroonoko and Imoinda] with the Lives of the *Romans*, and great Men, which charmed him to my Company; and [Imoinda], with teaching her all the pretty Works that I was Mistress of, and telling her stories of Nuns . . ." (46).[86] Trefry, one of the few colonists sympathetic to the prince's plight, befriends Oroonoko by exchanging narratives with him: Trefry "entertain'd *Oroonoko* so agreeably with his Art and Discourse" that Oroonoko "made no scruple of declaring to *Trefry*

[85] Although Behn provides only glimpses of the Surinam natives, they too seem to participate in a gift economy, although the narrator's reports of them are contradictory. Early in the novel, she says that the English keep peace with them by giving "small and unvaluable Trifles" (4) and the natives bring them delicate food in return. In the beginning the narrator reports that the English do not enslave them, but later she mentions Indian slaves (59). For an interesting discussion of these narrative contradictions, see Jacqueline Pearson, "Gender and Narrative in the Fiction of Aphra Behn," *Review of English Studies*, n.s. 42 (1991): 40–56, 179–190. When the narrator visits them, she and her party give pieces of their clothing and the natives give food. Their warriors have a custom that borders on a parody of the human-body-as-gift motif in the African tale: these men slice off *parts* of their bodies and offer them up as ways of demonstrating their courage.

[86] The narrator is, as Jacqueline Pearson points out in "Gender and Narrative," nevertheless ambivalent about this exchange, which renders her complicitous with the enslaving institution. In "Juggling the Categories of Race, Class, and Gender," Margaret W. Ferguson makes the important observation that Imoinda remains silent during these exchanges. In the quoted passages, I have changed "Loves" back to "Lives" in accordance with the 1688 edition. I wish to thank Joanna Lipking for pointing out this discrepancy to me.

141

all his Fortunes" (38). Jamoan similarly had offered stories to his friend when the loss of Imoinda immobilized him with grief: "by a thousand Tales and Adventures of Love and Gallantry, [Jamoan] flatter'd [Oroonoko's] Disease of Melancholy and Languishment: which I have often heard him say, had certainly kill'd him, but for the Conversation of this Prince and *Aboan*" (31). Each of these three friendships, then, becomes cemented through an exchange of stories.

Much in the same way that this novel uses "Africa" to offer a nostalgic, even primitivist alternative to English capitalism, *Oroonoko* also offers an alternative literary economy, part nostalgia for an aristocratic circulation of writing without payment, part primitivist mythology of an idealized, preprint exchange that binds communities and creates noble friendships. Just as commodification both offers and dispels the possibility of happiness for Imoinda, the circulation of writing as commodity (economic capital) rather than gift (social capital) both advances and undermines Behn's position as an author. A professional writer had to be an owner, both of the manuscript itself and the cultural texts that the manuscript repeats. Although Behn's position as widow may have provided a greater opportunity (and necessity) to inhabit the legal position of owner, her need to inhabit the cultural position of owner (and thus individual) provided another, perhaps greater, challenge.

Oroonoko betrays Behn's uneasiness with ownership through her narrator. In the opening of the novel, the female narrator disclaims literary property in two ways. First, she insists that she did not invent anything in the novel: "I do not pretend, in giving you the History of this *Royal Slave*, to entertain my Reader with Adventures of a feign'd *Hero*, whose Life and Fortunes Fancy may manage at the Poet's pleasure . . . it shall come simply into the World . . . without the addition of Invention" (1). Whereas Behn fully claimed the position of appropriator in her *Rover*, here she configures herself as no more than a conduit for the simple truth. In fact, the narrator attributes the first half of the novel, which she did not witness, to Oroonoko himself. Finally, the narrator ends by insisting, "thus died this great Man, worthy of a better Fate, and a more sublime Wit than mine to write his Praise" (78). The parallel structure implies that Oroonoko's miserable death by torture is just as undeserved as his misfortune to have a (European) woman tell his story.

The narrator's disclaimers not only express the uneasiness with which an English woman inhabits the position of ownership, but they also recognize and problematize Behn's own position in a literary economy.[87] If the author owns *Oroonoko*, then she participates in the same economy as the men who own Oroonoko. Just as the English body-as-commodity trade violates the African body-as-gift economy within the novel, so the narrative-as-commodity trade exploits the literary gift economy that the novel itself idealizes. Consciously or not, Behn expresses some distress in her own inevitable participation in the commodification of Oroonoko. If we can for a moment enter the fiction of the novel and identify the narrator with Behn herself (as the book encourages us to do), then the publication of *Oroonoko* appears as both an attempt to honor Oroonoko and as an exploitation of his story and his friendship. With this novel, the historical Aphra Behn participated, as Margaret W. Ferguson writes, "in the process of extracting surplus in Britain's early colonial economy."[88] As if to deny her own potential commodification of discourse, the narrator locates herself squarely in a gift economy when she refers to her own connection to the English literary marketplace. In Surinam, "I had a Set of [feathered apparel] presented to me [by the Surinam natives], and I gave 'em to the King's Theatre, and it was the Dress of the *Indian Queen*, infinitely admired by Persons of Quality" (2). Here the narrator represents herself as a diplomatic mediator rather than an enterprising playwright, circulating a gift between native Americans and the London stage to earn only the social capital of approval from "Persons of Quality," and implicitly from Killigrew himself, for her efforts.

Laura Brown has observed that Behn's novel explores parallels between the kinds of oppression suffered under mercantile capitalism by an African man and an English woman: "Though Behn never clearly sees herself in the place of the African slave," the text "uncovers a mutuality beyond her conscious control."[89] Yet any spark of mutuality remains in tension with the cultural differences, however fictive, on which the author insists. In my reading, mutuality emerges in a similar

[87] For an alternative view of Behn's representation of her authorship, see Ferguson's essay, which suggests that Behn competes for authorship—that is, the ability to carry on Oroonoko's name after his death—with Imoinda. Ferguson further argues that Behn offers "a representation of an economy in which the white woman's book is born, quite starkly, from the death and silencing of black persons." "Juggling the Categories of Race, Class, and Gender," 172.

[88] Ibid., 164.

[89] Brown, "The Romance of Empire," 61.

problem of property: as the accusations of plagiarism leveled against Behn evidence, contemporaries represented her as failing to comprehend or obey a system of literary property much in the same way that *The Golden Coast* represents Africans as unable to fully comprehend or obey the rules of mercantile property. The tensions between the narrator and Oroonoko, however, insist on the difference between the positions of an English woman and an African man. The narrator befriends Oroonoko through stories, but her role as entertainer makes her complicitous with the men who enslave him.[90] She even threatens the prince: when he expresses his distrust of his captors, she tells him that such doubts would "possibly compel us to treat him so as I should be very loth to behold" (46). The narrator regards Oroonoko as a fascinating but dangerous presence. His beauty strikes her with "Awe and Reverence" (6), but when she hears he has escaped, she fears "he would come down and cut all our Throats. This Apprehension made all the Females of us fly down the River, to be secured" (68). While the English women hide, the English men capture and torture Oroonoko. "I suppose," the narrator confesses, "I had Authority and Interest enough there, had I suspected any such thing, to have prevented it" (68). So although the novel inscribes flashes of political mutuality, the narrator fears and abandons Oroonoko at the same time that she adores and celebrates him for his otherness.

The narrative reveals an equivalent ambivalence of competition and identification in its representation of the white English female colonist and the black African female slave. Margaret W. Ferguson argues that, as the author, Behn competes with the pregnant Imoinda for the capacity to honor Oroonoko and memorialize his reputation. Yet at the same time, Imoinda's two forms of subjugation articulate the very situation of Behn's authorship and English women's relationship to property in general: disempowered by both traditional and commercial economies, Behn and Imoinda nevertheless find the new world more violent than the gift economy. By locating Imoinda *differently* in her two forms of captivity and by crafting such a complicated relationship between the narrator and Oroonoko, *Oroonoko* ultimately thwarts facile comparisons made by other seventeenth-century English women writers between the positions of white English women and black African slaves. If we cannot praise *Oroonoko* as an abolitionist, antiracist, or even feminist text, we can

[90] See Pearson, "Gender and Narrative."

144

recognize its ambivalence toward colonialism and its representation—
however ethnocentric—of an Africa with a culture prior to and independent of the English colonial slave trade. This becomes possible through
the narrative centrality of an African woman. The passionate love between Oroonoko and Imoinda, who prefer each other before anyone
else, emerges as an emblem for this cultural independence. Oroonoko
becomes immobile with grief when his grandfather sells Imoinda into
slavery and again when Imoinda submits to death by his hands before
allowing their child to be born into slavery.[91] Oroonoko loves only "this
fair Queen of Night" who was in turn "too great for any but a Prince of
her own Nation to adore" (9). But just as "Africa" itself disappears from
the narrative when Thomas Southerne brings this story to the stage, so
does Oroonoko's desire for an African woman.

"The concept of man as a material possession," David Brion Davis has
argued, "has always led to contradictions in law and custom."[92] According
to Davis, these contradictions became pressing with the early eighteenth-
century philosophies of moral sensibility, on the one hand, and the
Lockean definition of humans as self-governing individuals, on the other.
These are the contradictions that Thomas Southerne attempts to repress
in his adaptation of *Oroonoko*.[93] In this play, Southerne tries to reconcile

[91] To note their love and mutual attraction is not, however, to deny the violence
of their relationship. See Sussman, "The Other Problem with Women."
[92] David Brion Davis, *The Problem of Slavery in Western Culture* (Ithaca: Cornell
University Press, 1966), 223.
[93] Eighteenth-century disagreements over the position that Southerne's *Oroonoko*
takes on slavery, however, indicate the complexity with which the play represents the
institution. In spite of Ferriar's scathing critique, Mrs. Inchbald praised Southerne's
antislavery sentiments, suggesting that *Oroonoko* be produced for the traders of Liver-
pool. Similarly, Hannah More appreciated Southerne's sympathetic portrayal of the
royal slave:

O, plaintive Southerne! whose impassion'd strain
So oft has wak'd my languid Muse in vain! . . .
For no fictitious ills these numbers flow,
But living anguish, and substantial woe; . . .
For millions feel what Oroonoko felt:
Fir'd by no single wrongs, the countless host
I mourn, by rapine dragg'd from Afric's coast.

Quoted by Sypher, *British Anti-Slavery Literature*, 117–118.

Enlightenment individualism with human commodification.[94] Southerne's *Oroonoko*, like John Locke's *Two Treatises*, holds that all people may
occupy the position of owner; at the same time, both use Enlightenment
conceptions of reason to exclude certain groups from this possibility.
Like Locke, Southerne deploys a double discourse of ownership: *Oroonoko* represents an economy in which the privilege of ownership appears
to be available to all, but nevertheless consistently turns out to be socially
contingent. In both Locke and Southerne, self-possession extends only
to the self-possessed.

Southerne's *Oroonoko* wildly succeeded in pleasing audiences in general, but the author was probably hoping to please one man in particular.
It seems likely that Southerne at the time aspired to the patronage of
Christopher Codrington—a reward he eventually received.[95] Codrington,
a slave owner fashioning himself as a man of feeling and a man of letters,
was heir to the greatest individual fortune in the West Indies. At the
height of his military success, he was appointed governor-general of
Leeward Island in 1699 upon the death of his father, who had previously
held the post. Codrington did not question the practice of slavery, but
he publicly opposed cruelty to slaves and advocated their education and
Christianization. Codrington, in fact, left a substantial amount of money
in his will to bring scholars and clergymen to his plantations, where they
would set up a school for slaves to teach reading and religion. (The
project failed dismally; not a single slave was converted.) Codrington's
combination of sentimental charity and slave ownership was not un-

[94] Twentieth-century commentators have been divided on Southerne's politics.
Whereas Jacqueline Pearson, *The Prostituted Muse*, 114–115, finds antislavery and even
feminist sentiments in Southerne's *Oroonoko*, Wylie Sypher argues in *British Anti-
Slavery Literature* that in Southerne, as in Behn, Oroonoko's royal status prevents the
play from launching a genuine critique of slavery. For Sypher's view, see above, n.74.
In their preface to Southerne's *Oroonoko* (Lincoln: University of Nebraska Press,
1976), editors Maximillian E. Novak and David Stuart Rodes contend that Southerne's play is neither antislavery nor proslavery. For a formalist reading of the play,
see Julia A. Rich, "Heroic Tragedy in Southerne's *Oroonoko* (1695): An Approach to
Split-Plot Tragedy," *Philological Quarterly* 62 (1982): 187–200. Rich finds Southerne's
play innocent of "social commentary." See also John Wendell Dodds, *Thomas Southerne,
Dramatist* (New Haven: Yale University Press, 1933); and Robert L. Root, Jr., *Thomas
Southerne* (Boston: Twayne, 1981).
[95] *The Works of Thomas Southerne*, ed. Robert Jordan and Harold Love, 2 vols.
(Oxford: Clarendon Press, 1988), 2:95.

usual.[96] As David Brion Davis has documented, theological changes that emphasized good works ushered in a cult of sympathetic feelings for, if not treatment of, slaves. The church had previously excused slavery as one more evil in the temporary, corrupt life on earth; new doctrines of individual responsibility, however, emphasized charity in the present life.[97] Southerne's *Oroonoko* addresses the contradiction exemplified by Codrington between sentimental self-fashioning and slave owning. The play indulges its audiences in tearful sympathy for Oroonoko's suffering, heightened by the prince's separation from his true love. By reconfiguring the character of his hero, Southerne invites sympathetic passions for Oroonoko's death while at the same time accomplishing poetic justice.

Southerne makes a few key changes in Behn's plot that help achieve this effect: the African half of the novel, except for a few lines when Oroonoko recalls his home, disappears, and Imoinda becomes the white European daughter of a white European man visiting Africa. Thus, Southerne erases the "African" culture and economy that for Behn provide a context outside of the indiscriminate commodification of Africans by the English. Southerne's new comic plot, which I will discuss later, explores the possibility of English women inhabiting the position of owner. The tragic plot appropriated from Behn, in a parallel exploration of property, glamorizes English colonial slavery through sentimental tragedy and both suggests and dispels the possibility of Oroonoko's self-possession. Southerne's tragic plot begins when Captain Driver brings the slaves to market in Surinam. Blanford, who replaces Trefry as the English man who befriends Oroonoko, takes charge of the royal slave for the absent governor, and the lieutenant-governor unsuccessfully attempts to buy Imoinda as his personal sex slave. Oroonoko and Imoinda discover each other and resume their marriage, but the lieutenant-governor continues to pursue Imoinda and finally attempts to rape her. In a fit of jealousy, Oroonoko leads a rebellion that fails through the cowardice of the other slaves. Recognizing the futility of his situation, Oroonoko kills Imoinda to prevent further attempts on her honor. But while in Behn's novel Oroonoko then falls victim to the English, who

[96] Vincent T. Harlow, *Christopher Codrington, 1668–1710* (Oxford: Clarendon Press, 1928), 11, 122–123.

[97] Davis, *Slavery in Western Culture*, 291–482.

torture him to death, in Southerne's play Oroonoko kills himself as proper punishment for the death of Imoinda.

Southerne's play insists that anyone, English or African, can inhabit the position of owner: as in Behn's novel, Oroonoko trades slaves, but Southerne emphasizes that Oroonoko *owns* slaves. When Blanford decides to become Oroonoko's advocate, he attempts to restore Aboan (a loyal friend in Behn, a slave in Southerne) to Oroonoko's ownership. Further, the position of slave, like the position of owner, at first glance has no "racial" identification: Southerne populates the colony with black *and* white slaves.[98] Imoinda herself, surprisingly, turns out to be one of the latter. Still, just as alienated labor in Locke assumes a hierarchy of class, so the position of slave turns out to be the only one available to a black African. Ultimately, Southerne's Oroonoko cannot possess himself because, as an African, he is incapable of self-possession.

Southerne's *Oroonoko* achieves much of its ideological shape through the way in which it self-consciously echoes Shakespeare's *Othello*.[99] Behn's hero demonstrates his greatness in various ways—his extraordinary beauty, his peacetime conquest of threatening animals, his entertainment of the women colonists, his gracious manners, his diplomacy with the natives—whereas Southerne's Oroonoko becomes the consummate warrior. This Oroonoko associates with no women except his wife, defeats the American natives in battle instead of befriending them, and partakes of no adventures in the forest. And in the end, Southerne's Oroonoko comes to respect the justice of his captors in the same way that Othello accepts the laws of Venice. While Behn represents Oroonoko's rebellion as heroic, if quixotic, Southerne characterizes this rebellion as Oroonoko's moral weakness, the final evidence that he does not possess the rationality for self-possession. For Southerne's Oroonoko, the contracts of mercantile capitalism are sacred—even those of slavery itself. To deny the contract of slavery, in fact, would reveal the genuine barbarity of the African. So when Aboan implores Oroonoko to rebel, Oroonoko

[98] When the Surinam natives attack, the Governor assures the others that "there's no danger of the White Slaves . . . Some of you stay here to look after the Black Slaves." *The Works of Thomas Southerne*, 2.4.43–45. References are to act, scene, and line. Future references are from this edition and are cited in the text.

[99] Jordan and Love (*Works of Thomas Southerne*) suggest *Oroonoko's* recollection of *Othello*, 2:93. See also Ferguson, "Juggling the Categories of Race, Class, and Gender." Ferguson argues that Behn's novel itself echoes *Othello*, especially in the way Oroonoko woos the English ladies with stories of his adventures.

says that he wishes for his liberty, but would not buy it at the price of "black Ingratitude":

> they shannot say,
> That we deserv'd our Fortune by our Crimes. . . .
> If we are Slaves, they did not make us Slaves;
> But bought us in an honest way of trade:
> And we have done before 'em, bought and sold
> Many a wretch, and never thought it wrong.
> They paid our Price for us, and we are now
> Their Property, a part of their Estate,
> To manage as they please. (3.2.104–114)

Aboan can only incite Oroonoko to rebellion through Iago-like insinuations of other men's desires for the now-white Imoinda.[100] In fact, the way this scene echoes *Othello* reconfigures Oroonoko as a man too noble for rebellion, yet goaded into an irrational crime of passion by the threat of a white man bedding his white wife. Aboan can tempt Oroonoko only through jealousy:

> I rather fear
> More mischiefs from [the Governor's] coming: he is young,
> Luxurious, passionate, and amorous:
> Such a Complexion, and made bold by power,
> To countenance all he is prone to do;
> Will know no bounds, no law against his Lusts:
> If, in a fit of his Intemperance,
> With a strong hand, he should resolve to seize,
> And force my Royal Mistress from your Arms,
> How can you help your self? (3.2.197–206)

Southerne had already introduced the threat of an English colonist raping Imoinda when the lieutenant-governor tried to buy her. But because Oroonoko advocates waiting for the true governor, who will surely bring justice, Aboan ignites jealousy in his leader by punning on

---

[100] In Behn's novel, Oroonoko's stated reason for rebelling is that his child will become a slave as well. Southerne's play *does* have Aboan repeat this point and it angers Oroonoko, but the royal slave resolves to rebel only when Aboan convinces him that the governor would eventually rape Imoinda.

the governor's "complexion" to remind the prince that as an African, he can never truly possess the white Imoinda.[101] Because of this anxiety and not, as in Behn, because of the realization that his children will become slaves, Oroonoko gives up his "rational" attachment to mercantile capitalism and becomes a jealous, raging animal: "Ha! thou hast rouz'd/The Lion in his den, he stalks abroad,/And the wide Forrest trembles at his roar" (3.3.207–208). In Behn the rebellion confirms Oroonoko's nobility; in Southerne it reveals his fatal weakness, the key vulnerability in an apparently "civilized" foreigner. And as in *Othello*, Oroonoko punishes himself for the murder of his wife with a dignity that Behn's novel represents as impossible within the English institution of slavery:

> The Deed was mine:
> Bloody I know it is, and I expect
> Your Laws shou'd tell me so. Thus self-condemn'd,
> I do resign my self into your Hands,
> The Hands of Justice—But I hold the Sword
> For you—and for my self. (5.5.297–302)

Like Othello, Oroonoko recovers his civilized rationality just long enough to destroy himself in accordance with the laws of the colonizing culture.[102] At the end of Southerne's *Oroonoko*, the tragedy becomes not the institution of slavery but an African man's inability to possess a white woman. With this change, Southerne privileges Shakespeare over Behn as his precursor. In the tragic plot, then, Southerne rewrites the politics of Behn's novel in two significant ways. First, instead of confronting the problem of human commodification, Southerne deflects this public controversy into the private terms of erotic possession. Second, Southerne confirms an ideology that allows only certain European men the capacity for reason and consequently the capacity for ownership.

The comic plot of Southerne's *Oroonoko*, which has puzzled critics for its apparent irrelevance to the tragic plot,[103] offers in fact a parallel inscription of Lockean contingencies of ownership. Briefly, two English women, Charlotte and Lucy Welldon, come to Surinam in a desperate

[101] *Complexion,* according to the *Oxford English Dictionary,* 1985, could also mean balance of humors, and thus temperament as well as skin color.

[102] Oroonoko *does,* however, destroy his enemy at the last moment, as well as himself.

[103] For a more detailed exploration of this debate, see Rich, "Heroic Tragedy."

husband-hunting expedition. Charlotte dresses as a man to court the Widow Lackitt in the hope of securing a lucrative marriage between the widow's son Daniel and Charlotte's sister Lucy. Charlotte marries the widow, but hires Jack Stanmore, who had long courted the widow himself, to substitute for her on their wedding night. Meanwhile, Charlotte arranges a marriage for herself with Jack's brother (known simply as Stanmore) by promising to him her beautiful "cousin," who is, of course, Charlotte herself back in women's clothes. Charlotte's return to femininity, however, exposes the widow as a foolish, lascivious dupe caught by a humiliating swindle. The common theme of human property—marriage in the comic plot, slavery in the tragic plot—has been observed, and in fact critics have praised Southerne for protesting, as does Charlotte herself, that women should not be treated like slaves.[104] Yet this argument simply accepts Southerne's own erasure of enslaved African women: Charlotte and Lucy (and for that matter, Imoinda) are not simply "women," but white women. The point, then, belongs less to feminism than to an argument for European privilege.[105] The comic plot's ideology, in fact, relies on the absence of African women as characters. This play parallels the situations of Charlotte and Oroonoko—and by implication, "women" and "Africans"—as being offered equal access to ownership but lacking the rationality to fill that position. The parallel between the characters in turn allows Southerne to analogize marriage and slavery as affectionate and erotic institutions of ownership.

The tragic plot's central character is both a slave and a trafficker in slaves; the comic plot's central character—Charlotte—is both a woman and a trafficker in women. Both Charlotte and Oroonoko have the opportunity to inhabit the position of owner, confirming the Lockean illusion of equal access to appropriation. But just as Oroonoko's moments of irrationality disqualify him from owning, so any sympathetic female character in the comic plot must abandon this privilege as well. The comic plot opens with Charlotte and Lucy's arrival in Surinam, and Charlotte's resolution to secure a mate for her sister—a role traditionally played by a father. Charlotte describes *men* as commodities: in America,

---

[104] See, e.g., Novak and Rodes's introduction to Southerne's *Oroonoko*; and Pearson, *The Prostituted Muse*, 144–145.

[105] I am using the term "feminism" here in the most optimistic and contemporary sense. It is entirely possible that for Southerne and for numerous subsequent writers, feminism could indeed be itself an argument for European privilege.

she insists, husbands grow on plantations "as thick as Oranges, ripening one under another. Week after week they drop into some Woman's mouth: 'Tis but a little patience, spreading your Apron in expectation, and one of 'em will fall into your Lap at last" (1.1.4–7). Charlotte commodifies and eroticizes men by comparing them to an edible colonial product. Women, however, remain commodities as well: "Women in *London* are like the Rich Silks, they are out of fashion a great while before they wear out" (1.1.19–20). In the traditional kinship relationships that tend to operate in late seventeenth-century comedy, men exchange women in order to establish particular social and economic relations with each other.[106] In male drag, Charlotte replaces an actual brother for Lucy and arranges a marriage that financially benefits their family. Southerne, then, represents Charlotte as well as Oroonoko as both trader and commodity. Charlotte is not the only woman who inhabits this role, for the widow uses her money to acquire a husband and uses her son as an item of exchange. Southerne thus initially represents the position of the patriarchal trafficker as a role inhabitable by women as well as men.

Charlotte's drag role teases the audience with the possibility that women could sympathetically occupy the position of owner, which may account for the play's reputation as a favorite of the ladies.[107] Still, that position itself remains gendered as masculine. Property consistently ends up in the hands of those signified as male; the Widow turns over her money to Charlotte (as Mr. Welldon), but Charlotte herself turns the money over to Stanmore when she changes back into women's clothes. So although Charlotte appears to be able to inhabit the position of either owner or owned, she ultimately gives up the money in the hope of becoming a married woman. Nevertheless, by placing Charlotte in the position of both trafficker and trafficked in, Southerne, like Locke, creates the illusion that the patriarchal position of ownership can easily be inhabited by men or women. This, in turn, feeds the tragic plot, in

[106] See, for example, Eve Kosofsky Sedgwick's reading of *The Country Wife* in *Between Men: English Literature and Male Homosocial Desire* (New York: Columbia University Press, 1985).

[107] In Charles Gildon's *Comparison between the Two Stages*, Ramble declares, "Oh! the Favourite of the Ladies," when Sullen mentions *Oroonoko*. See also Daniel Kendrick in *A New Session of the Poets* (London, 1700). Kendrick writes, "Next *Southern* to the Judge himself apply'd,/ With haughty *Oroonoko* by his side/ The Ladies Pity, and the Author's Pride." Both cited by Jordan and Love, *Works of Thomas Southerne*, 2:94.

which the position of slave and slaver is equally inhabitable (in theory) by an English or African person. So whereas Behn's novel explores the ways in which an English woman, an African man, and an African woman all suffer in very different ways from their exclusion from the rights of ownership, Southerne's play naturalizes ownership as tragically illegitimate for Oroonoko and comically illegitimate for Charlotte.

The comic plot further associates ownership with European masculinity by representing it as a form of sexual subjectivity. When Charlotte temporarily inhabits the position of owner, she also (temporarily) inhabits the place of sexual subject: she circulates men as sexual objects, and even chooses one for herself (Stanmore). The widow becomes the comic plot's butt, however, because she attempts to inhabit the masculine position of owner and sexual subject without the excuse of a temporary drag role. The widow attempts to use her money to acquire "Mr. Welldon" as a sexual object, but Mr. Welldon—appropriately enough for one who has been signified as an object—turns out to be a woman. The widow also sexually commodifies her son Daniel by forcing him to marry Lucy as part of her agreement with Mr. Welldon. Although Daniel does not turn into a woman, the bargain emasculates him: he cannot perform his conjugal duties. The Widow Lackitt (lacks "it") aggressively objectifies male bodies; unlike Charlotte, however, she will not give up her position of ownership, and for this intransigence the play ultimately humiliates her. Charlotte only temporarily impersonates the masculine position in order to improve her estate: "Theirs is a trading Estate, that lives upon credit, and increases by removing it out of one Bank and into another" (4.1.52–53). Male ownership and sexuality proliferate together; female sexuality, on the other hand, inhibits prosperity: "Poor Women have not these opportunities: we must keep our stocks dead by us, at home, to be ready for a purchase, when it comes . . . or venture our Fortunes abroad on such rotten security, that the principal and interest, nay very often our persons are in danger" (4.1.54–58).

While Oroonoko's passion and irrationality demonstrate his unfitness to own in the tragic plot, ownership itself becomes a form of sexual transgression for English women in the comic plot. As noted, Charlotte's disguise playfully mocks patriarchal control of women and allows her briefly to inhabit the position of owner and sexual subject. She enjoys the rewards of marriage and money because she relinquishes her position as owner by the end of the play. The widow, on the other hand, tries permanently to inhabit the positions of owner and sexual subject; she ends up sexually and financially exploited. Southerne represents the widow's commodification of men as self-implicating, revealing a lasciviousness that justifies Charlotte Welldon's public humiliation of her. In one of the rare scenes in which the tragic and comic plots meet, then, the widow's complaint that she has "six Slaves in my Lot, and not a Man among 'em" (1.2.9–10) takes on a lubricious meaning, especially since it follows the lieutenant-governor's explicitly lustful disappointment that Clemene/Imoinda has not fallen to his lot. When the widow then tries to buy Oroonoko, the Captain assumes that she wants him for sexual purposes: "Have you a mind to try what a Man he is? You'll find him no more than a common Man at your business" (1.2.44–45). Whereas the English object of the widow's erotic desire reveals herself as a woman, though, the African object of her desire need not change his sex to become an erotic commodity.

The widow's sexual desire for Oroonoko most explicitly bridges the racial and gendered contingencies of ownership in this play, suggesting the scandalousness of the widow's lascivious desire to own and Oroonoko's position as an eroticized object. Southerne's play represents, as Homi K. Bhabha says is characteristic of all colonial discourse, an " 'otherness' which is at once an object of desire and derision."[108] Through Charlotte's masquerade, the comic plot explores the process that genders owner as masculine and owned as feminine, while the tragic plot explores an eroticized masculine economy of owners and slaves. Oroonoko's position as both husband (owner/subject) and slave (owned/object) becomes untenable. Yet Blanford, who acts as Oroonoko's owner, sees the prince as an object of fascination and affection. Not only does Oroonoko become a desirable object to Blanford, but also Blanford performs the masculine functions that Oroonoko, as a slave, cannot. Blanford protects Imoinda from being sold to the lieutenant-governor; he rescues Imoinda from rape while Oroonoko struggles helplessly in chains after his failed rebellion.[109] Oroonoko's marriage is doomed

---

[108] Homi K. Bhabha, "The Other Question—the Stereotype and Colonial Discourse," *Screen* 24 (1983): 19. Bhabha goes on to argue that "caught in the Imaginary as they are, these shifting positionalities will never seriously threaten the dominant power relations, for they exist to exercise them pleasurably and productively."

[109] Southerne, *Oroonoko,* act 5, sc. 4. Oroonoko literally belongs to the absent Lord Governor, but Blanford looks after the governor's property.

because he cannot occupy the husband/owner position in relation to Imoinda not just because he is a black African, but because she is a white European. Literal slave to Blanford (in his capacity as a functionary for the governor), Oroonoko is a metaphorical slave to Imoinda herself: "To Honour bound! and yet a Slave to Love!" (5.5.1), he cries out. "Honor" in this scene holds him back from rebelling: Southerne displaces Oroonoko's literal enslavement onto erotic enslavement. Oroonoko tells Blanford, in fact, that when he first met Imoinda he offered her slaves and then "I offer'd up my self/To be the Sacrifice" (2.2.90–91). Behn has a similar scene in which the institution of slavery and the romance slave-for-love cliché meet, but the relationship between a bond of ownership and a bond of eros becomes complicated in Southerne's version in that an African offers himself (and other Africans) as a slave to a European woman. Southerne's displacement, however, works in both directions: not only does love become a form of slavery, but slavery a form of love. Blanford's "heart drops blood" for Oroonoko (1.2.174) and he vows to "study to deserve" (2.2.20) Oroonoko's friendship; he rescues Imoinda because Oroonoko declares to him that this is the only way "To tye me ever to your honest Love" (5.3.34). Blanford's rescue of Imoinda enlists an unequal homosocial scenario in which the European man performs daring deeds to win the heart of an African man. In this play, then, marriage and slavery become analogies for each other not as a critique of either institution, but as similarly erotic, affectionate, and hierarchical bonds of ownership. As contracts, they similarly institutionalize relationships of subordination.

Thus, the widow's desire for Oroonoko not only characterizes her own sexual and proprietary subjectivity as the same transgression—a desire that parallels her lust for Mr. Welldon, a venture that ends in her humiliation—but it also establishes Oroonoko as an eroticized object. Still, the widow is not the only white woman from the comic plot who likes Oroonoko. In one of the few other scenes in which the comic and tragic plot meet, Charlotte and Lucy join the widow in begging for Oroonoko's freedom. The widow's lust finds a third parallel in another white woman: Imoinda herself. *Oroonoko* depends on the royal slave's larger-than-life romantic appeal and his powerful masculine desirability, which, coupled with the play's temporary fantasy of English women as owners, becomes an erotic objectification when the two plots meet. Oroonoko's eroticism is of course overdetermined and part of Southerne's exploitation of extant cultural stereotypes: the lasciviousness of African people had long been hypothesized in European colonial discourse.[110] The eroticization further originates in part from Behn's novel, in which Oroonoko's body, as either a beautiful object or a tortured object, remains central throughout the narrative. But while Behn's novel creates an independent African love relationship, Southerne's play indulges the audience's fascination with "miscegenation." This dynamic, I believe, accounts to a great extent for the play's extraordinary popularity. For English women, *Oroonoko* offers a temporary fantasy of sexual and proprietary subjectivity at the expense of a non-European "other." At the same time, the play articulates tremendous anxiety over this possibility.

When eighteenth-century artists such as Hogarth wished to show sexual deviance, Sander L. Gilman has demonstrated, they paired a white figure with a black figure of the opposite sex. The presence of the black figure came to signify the lasciviousness of the white figure. In the nineteenth century, the African woman (especially the "Hottentot") comes to represent African sexuality in general, but in "the eighteenth century," according to Gilman, "the sexuality of the black, both male and female, becomes an icon for deviant sexuality in general; ... the black figure appears almost always paired with a white figure of the

---

[110] As early as 1621, Richard Jobson took "the enormous Size of the virile Member among the Negroes" as "an infallible Proof, that they are sprung from *Canaan*, who, for uncovering his Father's Nakedness, had (according to the Schoolmen) a Curse laid on that Part." Women abstain from coition during pregnancy because of the "Danger of Abortion" from this member. Quoted by Davis, *Slavery in Western Culture*, 452. Later, in *The History of Jamaica: or, General Survey of the Antient and Modern State of that Island*, 3 vols. (1774; reprint, New York: Arno Press, 1972), Edward Long also reports that Africans have "no taste but for women; gormandizing, and drinking to excess" (2:353); they are "addicted to all kinds of lust, and ready to promote them in others" (2:354). William Smith's *New Voyage to Guinea* (1744) provides a glimpse of what kind of images Oroonoko's origins might conjure up for English audiences. Rape does not exist in Guinea because the "young Ladies are not taught by the Priests, that the Gratification of their darling Passion is a damnable Crime, as they are by the Christian Apostles in *Europe*" (246). The king has the right to all the virgins in the land, and keeps thousands of wives; other important men maintain hundreds of wives, and can sell any of their sons into slavery except the eldest (201–202). Even though African countries punish adultery, "If [the women] meet with a Man they immediately strip his lower Parts, and throw themselves upon him, protesting that if he will not gratify their Desires, they will accuse him to their Husbands" (221).

opposite sex."[111] While Imoinda remains perfectly chaste, *Oroonoko's* evo-
cation of *Othello* also invokes the sense of the heroine's sexuality that
Shakespeare's play suggests about Desdemona.[112] Desdemona, after all,
chooses her own husband against her father's wishes and refuses to leave
Othello's side or his bed. Southerne's Imoinda further becomes suspect
in her comic parallel to the Widow Lackitt, who wishes to buy Oroonoko.
If the audience misses these suspicions in the play, the epilogue, spoken
by Mrs. Verbruggen in the character of Charlotte Welldon, drives
them home:

> Wee, to those Islands, where Rich Husbands grow:
> Tho' they're no Monsters, we may make 'em so.
> If they're of English growth, they'll bear't with patience:
> But save us from a Spouse of *Oroonoko's* Nations!
> Then bless your Stars, you happy *London* Wives,
> Who love at large, each day, yet keep your lives:
> Nor envy poor *Imoinda's* doating blindness,
> Who thought her husband kill'd her out of kindness.
> Death with a Husband ne'er had shewn such Charms,
> Had she once dy'd within a Lover's Arms.

English husbands become one kind of monster: the cuckold. Yet a spouse
of "*Oroonoko's* Nation" can become another kind of monster, one who
will murder his wife when he finds her unfaithful. According to this
epilogue, then, Oroonoko kills Imoinda out of the jealous assurance
that sooner or later she would have "died" in another lover's arms. This
epilogue's accentuation of *Oroonoko's* repetition of *Othello* highlights
suspicions about the white Imoinda's motives in choosing a black love
object. Finally, as Mrs. Verbruggen speaks this epilogue, the audience
would have been aware that she herself was *married* to the actor who
played Oroonoko. Southerne, then, gives each of these three characters—Charlotte Welldon, Widow Lackitt, and Imoinda—some kind of
erotic connection to Oroonoko.

---

[111] Sander L. Gilman, "Black Bodies, White Bodies: Toward an Iconography of
Female Sexuality in Late Nineteenth-Century Art, Medicine, and Literature," in
"Race," Writing, and Difference, 223–261.
[112] For this reading of *Othello,* I am following Mary Beth Rose, *The Expense of Spirit:
Love and Sexuality in English Renaissance Drama* (Ithaca: Cornell University Press,
1988), 131–156.

Clearly Southerne transformed Imoinda to a white woman in part to evoke Shakespeare's *Othello* and the sexual suspicions that play evokes. But Thomas Brown, a contemporary of Southerne's, suggests a different reason why the playwright made his heroine white instead of black. Southerne made Behn's "*Imoinda*, not of the Complexion belonging to the Country she came from, but so very beautiful, as to give us a valuable Idea of the Fair Person that gave Being to her Character."[113] To Brown, Imoinda resembles not Desdemona but Aphra Behn herself! In his fictional letter from beyond the grave, Thomas Brown reports Southerne's adaptation of *Oroonoko* to Aphra Behn, whom he meets in the land of the dead: "After having ask'd me a thousand Questions about the Price of Wit, as where the Market was risen or fallen since her Time, and what Female Authors were in Being when I left my Territories, [Aphra Behn] sate down by me, and laid her Head in my Lap, as much to say she was at my Disposal, and had no manner of Aversion to a Stranger, who she had been told had none for her Sex. I perceived she retain'd the same Passions she had formerly been famous for, though she was not Mistress of the same Beauty." Upon hearing about Southerne's appropriation of her novel, the fictional Behn first expresses her concern for women's literary property and then makes herself sexually available. Brown links Behn's identities as writer, owner, and disgusting sexual object (she is, after all, dead). Imoinda, Charlotte, and Widow Lackitt may each establish a suspicious relationship with Oroonoko in the play, but in Brown's reading of Southerne, the strongest erotic bond arises between the royal slave and the earlier author, a woman famous for her passions and available, in his fantasy, without his even asking.[114]

Thomas Brown has, I believe, identified one of the central projects of Southerne's adaptation. In Southerne's play, Charlotte Welldon, Widow Lackitt, and Imoinda each in some way come to signify Aphra Behn. Behn was a widow, and the Widow Lackitt/Charlotte Welldon subplot derives in part—and without acknowledgement—from Behn's play *The Widow Ranter*. The white Imoinda, hopelessly (and foolishly, according

[113] *A Letter from the Dead Thomas Brown to the Living Heraclitus* (London, 1704).

[114] Similarly, Mary Vermillion has suggested that Southerne's play mourns the "cultural loss . . . of the strictly fraternal literary community." Vermillion concentrates on the character of Charlotte as a "mock Behn" demeaned by Southerne. See her essay, "Buried Heroism: Critiques of Female Authorship in Southerne's Adaptation of Behn's *Oroonoko*," *Restoration* 16 (1992): 28–37.

to the epilogue) in love with a black man, hints at contemporary gossip about a love affair between Aphra Behn and the "real" Oroonoko.[115] For Brown at least, Southerne's Imoinda *was* Aphra Behn. The Widow Lackitt's desire to buy Oroonoko, however, highlights the political complexities of such a relationship. Charlotte, as a single woman who has arrived in Surinam without her family and who pleads for Oroonoko, also invokes Behn by occupying a similar position to Behn's narrator in the novel.[116] Southerne establishes some kind of erotic connection between each of these three characters and the royal slave; each in some way evokes Aphra Behn.

What stake, though, would Southerne have in representing Behn as erotically entangled with her fictional hero? Just as he renders any female act of ownership as obscene within the fiction of the play, so Southerne, faced with the challenge of making this story his own, represents Behn as similarly disqualified from the ownership of *literary* property. The African man cannot possess himself because he lacks self-possession; the English woman remains similarly excluded from ownership, for her sexual desires keep her from acting in reasonable ways. Southerne acknowledges his play's debt to Behn, although he confesses to having failed to admit his use of her work on another occasion: "I stand engag'd to Mrs. *Behn* for the Occasion of a most Passionate Distress in my Last Play; and in a Conscience that I had not made her a sufficient Acknowledgment, I have run further into her Debt for *Oroonoko*, with a Design to oblige me to be honest; and that every one may find me out for Ingratitude, when I don't say all that's fit for me upon that Subject."[117] It seems that others had noticed that his debt to Behn in *The Fatal Marriage* was greater than the "Hint" he claims to have taken. In wondering why Behn herself failed to make this novel into a play, Southerne speculates

[115] The author of "The Life and Memoirs of Mrs. Behn. Written by One of the Fair Sex," prefacing *The Histories and Novels of the Late Ingenious Mrs. Behn* (London, 1696), vehemently denies this rumor but notes how widespread it has become. In "Juggling the Categories of Race, Class, and Gender," Ferguson similarly characterizes Southerne's motive in making Imoinda white as "a desire to capitalize" on the rumors of Behn's affair with Oroonoko. Whoever published Behn's *Histories and Novels* (perhaps Charles Gildon) may have in turn capitalized on the implications about Behn in Southerne's play, for it appeared a year after *Oroonoko*'s stage debut.

[116] See also Vermillion, "Buried Heroism."

[117] *Works of Thomas Southerne*, 2:102.

that she could not "bear [Oroonoko] represented" and insists that she always told his story "more feelingly, than she writ it."[118] Here again, Southerne (like Thomas Brown) hints at the familiar rumor that Behn told this story so passionately because she actually had a love affair with Oroonoko. This representation of property recalls the rhetoric of ownership in Locke. Any reasonable person can own property and himself; reason, however, turns out to be contingent on "race," class, and gender. Just as Oroonoko honors the contracts of mercantile capitalism but cannot even own himself, so Behn can have no property in *Oroonoko* for the same reasons that the widow can have no property in Oroonoko. Oroonoko's irrationality surfaces as jealousy; Behn's surfaces as lust. Southerne illegitimizes Behn's literary property in *Oroonoko* by reconfiguring this relationship as an English woman's desire for an African man. That Southerne underrepresents his use of Behn for *The Fatal Marriage* and fails to acknowledge his use of *The Widow Ranter* for *Oroonoko's* comic subplot indicate similar resistance to acknowledging Behn as a precursor.

Southerne's rewriting of Oroonoko as finally lacking the self-possession to possess himself (or anything else), as well as his representation of Behn as documenting her desires rather than creating literary property (re)produces the rhetoric of Locke's treatise on property. In a colonialist culture in which a small group of people profits from the labor of others, Locke and Southerne both found ways to claim a universal human potential to own while at the same time inscribing its constitutive inequality. Behn may take advantage of the same economy, but her text exposes, rather than attempts to resolve, its contradictions. That Aphra Behn's novel has enjoyed a revival in recent years while Southerne's play has remained obscure, however, does not mean that Southerne's ideological reconfiguration and appropriation of literary property have ultimately failed. In one instance, in fact, Southerne's version literally overlays Behn's telling of the story. On the cover of the recent Norton paperback of Behn's *Oroonoko*, the eponymous royal slave holds a dagger poised before his wife, Imoinda. Oroonoko wears the European doublet and hose; Imoinda looks upon him lovingly. Aboan lies dead in the background. The careful observer will note, however, that not only does this engraving capture the characters in highly theatrical poses, but it also depicts Imoinda as unmistakably European. This cover actually represents Thomas Southerne's adaptation rather than Behn's novel, which

[118] Ibid.

160

tells the story of two African lovers![119] Given Southerne's appropriation of Behn in the eighteenth century, then, could there be any greater irony than a sketch from his play appearing on the cover of Behn's (finally) reprinted novel? At its worst, this editorial decision represents a continuing fascination with "miscegenation"—the same fascination that Southerne's play exploited now helps sell copies of Behn's story of African lovers. The book tempts readers with the sensation of a black man murdering a white woman, an event that never takes place in Behn's narrative. In some ways, little has changed since Southerne's eighteenth-century appropriation of Behn, with all this implies about "race" and gender remaining stamped on the cover of the Norton edition.

[119] Margaret W. Ferguson notes this inconsistency as well; see her "Juggling the Categories of Race, Class, and Gender."

FOUR

"Ladies and Fop Authors Never Are at Odds": Colley Cibber, Female Wits

No playwright has been remembered more vividly as a plagiarist than Colley Cibber, a man less famous for his drama than for Pope's rendition of his career in *The Dunciad*. Pope pictures Cibber surrounded by heaps of plays, contemplating his next act of literary theft. The pinnacle of literary duncehood now took the form of plagiarism and Colley Cibber earned this honor so regularly bestowed on women. As British law began to define literary property more precisely, as authorship became increasingly professionalized, and as print culture flourished, intertextual relationships for dramatists changed. The violation of the borders between texts, as Pope's dunce-as-plagiarist demonstrates, emerged as a greater object of scrutiny and sometimes came to signify differences between popular and elite culture. Public scandals around plagiarism and forgery flourished in the eighteenth century. Sterne was the object of attack for his repetition of Burton in *Tristram Shandy*; Theobald became the center of a vicious controversy over *The Double Falshood*, a play he claimed as a new Shakespearean discovery but that others rejected as a forgery by his own hand. Accusations leveled in the battle between the ancients and moderns, which Joseph M. Levine has recently documented so well, commonly took the form of attacks for plagiarism: William Wotton accused Swift of plagiarism; Abel Boyer leveled the same charge against Sir William Temple. Pope insisted that his rival Madame Dacier plagiarized part of her translation of Homer, even though Pope himself,

162

according to Levine, "borrowed from her work without acknowledgment."[1] Plagiarism became one of the central terms through which rival playwrights articulated both enmity and cultural distinction.[2] For Fielding, the efforts of dramatists to *avoid* the charge of plagiarism were excessive enough to merit the satire of Don Tradegio in *The Author's Farce*:

> Yes, Tragedio is indeed my Name,
> Long since recorded in the rolls of fame,
> At Lincoln's Inn, and eke at Drury-Lane.
> Let everlasting thunder sound my praise
> And forked light'ning in my scutcheon blaze.
> To Shakespeare, Jonson, Dryden, Lee, or Rowe,
> I not a line, no, not a thought, do owe.
> Me, for my novelty, let all adore,
> For, as I wrote, none ever wrote before.

Yet the other dead poets in this play-within-the-play complain that "Grub Street harbors as many pirates as ever Algiers did."[3] Similarly, Swift responds to Wotton's accusation of plagiarism with both irony and earnestness. Swift answers several charges in the *Apology* for his *Tale*, but the

---

[1] Joseph M. Levine, *The Battle of the Books: History and Literature in the Augustan Age* (Ithaca: Cornell University Press, 1991), 111, n.79, 209.

[2] Even Congreve endured this accusation in the anonymous *Animadversions of Mr. Congreve's Late Answer to Mr. Collier. In a Dialogue between Mr. Smith and Mr. Johnson* (1698). Although the issue was dramatic propriety, Congreve's adversary attacked him in terms of property. "Those Plays [of Congreve's]," Mr. Smith concludes, "*are little Compounds of the whole Body of Scriblers* . . . But if he has still the itch to steal and publish on, and scan other Men's Prose on his own Unpoetical Fingers, he does it so roughly, they must needs break out to Soreness" (7, 12). The poem prefacing this dialogue repeats this and accuses an unnamed plagiarist:

> Next in desert stands one, a Man of Wit,
> Made so by what he stole, not what he writ.
> But should each Bird pluck from this Crow his own,
> His Plumes would all be lost, and he undone.
> In some years space, Play drops from thieving *Muse*,
> So long a time she takes to pick, and choose.
> Thus while he bears his burthens from the rest,
> His Title's but *The Ass of Wit*, at Best.

[3] Henry Fielding, *The Author's Farce*, ed. Charles B. Woods (Lincoln: University of Nebraska Press, 1966), 3.309–317; 3.204–205.

charge of plagiarism merits the most thorough response: "Surely this must have had some allay of personal animosity at least mixed with the *design* of serving the public," Swift concludes; "and it indeed touches the author in a tender point, who insists upon it that through the whole book he has not borrowed one single hint from any writer in the world; and he thought, of all criticisms, that would never have been one."[4] After refuting the accusation point by point, Swift declares, "I know nothing more contemptible in a writer than the character of a plagiary."[5]

In this context, Colley Cibber built his career at the crossroads of the "Grub Street version of imitation" and gender performances outside of dominant masculinity. This explosive combination catapulted him into both fame and infamy; he became an object of ridicule and fascination for the contradictions he exposed. In some ways, Cibber inhabited a position similar to the women playwrights of his generation; in other ways, his exteriority to dominant masculinity differed significantly from that of female wits. For this reason, I hesitate to describe Cibber as "feminized," for the term not only elides important differences between the two positions (women on the one hand, and men outside of dominant masculinity on the other), but also suggests a passivity inconsistent with Cibber's self-fashioning. Cibber emerges as the quintessential plagiarist of his time, a position that must be understood in the context of gendered subjectivities, Grub Street culture, and the achievements of new generations of women dramatists.

Gender and Cultural Capital

During the early eighteenth century, an age in the process of constructing the values of originality and authenticity, plagiarism became not

[4] Jonathan Swift, *Tale of a Tub and Other Works*, ed. Angus Ross and David Woolley (Oxford: Oxford University Press, 1986), 6.
[5] For the anonymous author of *The Battle of Authors Lately Fought in Covent-Garden, Between Sir John Edgar, Generalissimo on one Side, and Horatius Truewit, on the Other* (London, 1720), plagiarism and writing "without either Learning, Judgment, or Genius, contrary to the express Laws of Parnassus" become the two egregious violations that make Edgar the leader of an army of false wits. (Colley Cibber contends for this position, but merely attains the position of a lower officer.) The accuser insists:

'I have Witnesses here to produce, that will make it out beyond Contradiction, that what goes under [Edgar's] Name, is so far from being his, that if we take away what

only a discourse for occluding those who could not inhabit the subject position of owner, but also one of the worst charges one could level at an author.[6] Dryden and Shadwell had negotiated between two models of property, claiming authorship on the basis of genealogical inheritance and/or Lockean appropriation. By the eighteenth century, however, the Lockean model of property had achieved dominance in the wider cultural arena as well as in dramatic authorship. The Glorious Revolution itself sanctioned the interest of property over dynasty.[7] Undoubtedly there emerged multiple ways of reconceptualizing property, culture, and authority (see, for example, Pocock's revisionist reading), but the legal codification of literary property as well as much public discourse about these issues was, as Mark Rose has shown, relentlessly articulated in Lockean terms of possessive individualism.[8] Perhaps one of the best indicators of the reconceptualization of property ushered in by the revolution has been described by Frank McLynn in *Crime and Punishment in Eighteenth-Century England* and Peter Linebaugh in *The London Hanged.* "Most eighteenth-century law defended property," McLynn argues, "that is to say, it united the elite and middle sectors against the propertyless."[9] The criminal laws, also known as the "Bloody Code," defended property rights during this period with a particular ferocity. In 1688, fifty offenses carried the death penalty; by 1765 the figure had risen to 160. An act in 1706 abolished "benefit of clergy" privilege that allowed those who could prove literacy to escape the gallows. Most of these new capital offenses punished crimes of property: "The increase in commercial ac-

---

belongs to other People, there would not remain ten tollerable Papers to himself; but hear the Evidence.'

In this Place appear'd near a Hundred Witnesses, from whom he had receiv'd a Support of his Purse, and his Reputation. (31)

[6] See Margreta de Grazia, *Shakespeare Verbatim: The Reproduction of Authenticity and the 1790 Apparatus* (Oxford: Clarendon Press, 1991); Susan Stewart, *Crimes of Writing: Problems in the Containment of Representation* (New York: Oxford University Press, 1991); Martha Woodmansee, "The Genius and the Copyright: Economic and Legal Conditions of the Emergence of the 'Author,'" *Eighteenth-Century Studies* 17 (Summer 1984): 425–448.

[7] See Christopher Hill, *The Century of Revolution, 1603–1714* (New York: Norton, 1961).

[8] Mark Rose, *Authors and Owners: The Invention of Copyright* (Cambridge: Harvard University Press, 1992), esp. chap. 5.

[9] Frank McLynn, *Crime and Punishment in Eighteenth-Century England* (Oxford: Oxford University Press, 1989), 215.

tivity after the 'Glorious Revolution' of 1688 led to a plethora of laws on stolen property, receiving, embezzlement, fraud, and the obtaining of goods on false pretenses."[10] This codification of commercially beneficial property rights, as Peter Linebaugh has demonstrated, conflicted, often fatally, with traditional understandings of the laborer's entitlements to perquisites such as leftover cloth, floor sweepings, and wood scraps.[11]

In light of the stark increase in the legal codification of property rights after the revolution and the intense interest in punishing its violators, the Statute of Anne in 1709/10 can be understood as one more act of enforcing the rights of private property through law. Dryden had drawn authorial tropes from the Stuart monarchy: just as Restoration culture worked assiduously to establish political continuity across the divide of the Commonwealth, so Dryden had created parallel genealogical links with pre-Commonwealth dramatic poets. By the eighteenth century, however, Shakespeare had become less of a father to engage, wrestle with, and inherit an estate from than a genuine ancient whose plays required editions rather than revisions.[12] At the same time the word *adaptation,* according to the *OED,* came into its modern use, emerging as a distinct genre, a different kind of project from writing an "original" play. When Cibber adapted *Richard III,* he carefully marked off the material he took directly from Shakespeare with apostrophes, demonstrating a distinct concern with the boundaries between texts. Further, the legal protection of literary property, while benefiting booksellers most directly, also supported the economic transition that enabled poets, novelists, and pamphleteers to build careers without depending on pa-

[10] Ibid., x. Of particular interest is McLynn's engaging chapter on poaching, in which he explores the ways in which new property rights came into violent conflict with older, feudal conceptions of privilege.

[11] Peter Linebaugh, *The London Hanged: Crime and Civil Society in the Eighteenth Century* (Cambridge: Cambridge University Press, 1992).

[12] I have written about this more extensively in "(Re)Writing Lear: Literary Property and Dramatic Authorship," in *Early Modern Conceptions of Property,* ed. John Brewer and Susan Staves (New York: Routledge, 1995), 323–338. For an important study of Shakespeare editions in the eighteenth century, see Margreta de Grazia, *Shakespeare Verbatim.* For Shakespearean adaptation, see Michael Dobson, *The Making of the National Poet: Shakespeare, Adaptation and Authorship, 1660–1769* (Oxford: Clarendon Press, 1992), and Gary Taylor, *Reinventing Shakespeare: A Cultural History from the Restoration to the Present* (Oxford: Oxford University Press, 1989).

trons.[13] Although playwrights had long made a living from their pens, publication increasingly became a source of profit;[14] plays commonly appeared in print, in fact, without ever having seen performance. Print brought not only new opportunities for profit, but also a potential to enhance the cultural status of drama. The dramatist, as Julie Stone Peters has shown in her fine study of Congreve, could become as much a *literary* as a *theater* professional. The form of these changes becomes possible only with an individualistic construction of authorship—a sense in which it is not only possible but also urgent to draw the boundaries between texts. Although we may no longer agree with Ian Watt's statement that "Defoe and Richardson are the first great writers in our literature who did not take their plots from mythology, history, legend or previous literature" after reading the duchess of Newcastle, his general point about the novel as distinct for its self-conscious claim to originality still stands.[15] When the enemies of Cavendish and Behn attacked them for plagiarism, they were more interested in their silence than in their originality (although Behn and Cavendish themselves insisted on originality as a strategy for ownership). A critic of an eighteenth-century plagiarist, however, might understand the codification of a more authentic experience as the preferred alternative. The Lockean paradigm of individualism and property rights in some ways appeared to offer fuller versions of social and political subjectivity than those to which Cavendish had access. Yet the social inequalities that the Lockean configuration of property appears to dispel becomes reinscribed in two relevant ways. First, women, as Carole Pateman argues and as discussed in Chapter 1 never fully inhabit the position of individual. Second, a growing concern to distinguish true authors from hacks, high culture from popular cul-

[13] See Rose, *Authors and Owners;* Alvin Kernan, *Printing Technology, Letters, and Samuel Johnson* (Princeton: Princeton University Press, 1987); and Lyman Ray Patterson, *Copyright in Historical Perspective* (Nashville: Vanderbilt University Press, 1968).

[14] See Shirley Strum Kenny, "The Publication of Plays," in *The London Theatre World 1660–1800*, ed. Robert D. Hume (Carbondale: Southern Illinois University Press, 1980), and Julie Stone Peters, *Congreve, the Drama, and the Printed Word* (Stanford: Stanford University Press, 1990).

[15] See Ian Watt, *The Rise of the Novel: Studies in Defoe, Richardson, and Fielding* (Berkeley: University of California Press, 1957), 14. J. Paul Hunter has recently confirmed this point in greater detail and in regard to a greater variety of fiction of the time. See his *Before Novels: The Cultural Contexts of Eighteenth Century English Fiction* (New York: Norton, 1990).

ture, further divides the rights-bearing individual from those signified as outside of this possibility. Thus, plagiarism becomes the Grub Street version of imitation. When Giles Jacob revised Langbaine's catalog of plagiarists in 1724, in fact, he positioned himself more as an arbiter of culture than as an arbiter of property.[16]

The reconceptualization of writing as property and authorship as ownership met with ambivalence. "Isaac Bickerstaff," for example, parodically imagines the complete erasure of all difference between writing and capital:

> I do hereby forbid all Dedications to any Persons within the City of *London*, except Sir *Francis*, Sir *Stephen* and the Bank will take Epigrams and Epistles as Value received for their Notes; and the *East-India* Companies accept of Heroick Poems for their sealed Bonds. Upon which Bottom our Publishers have full Power to treat with the City in behalf of us Authors, to enable Traders to become Patrons and Fellows of the Royal Society, as well as receive certain Degrees of Skill in the *Latin* and *Greek* Tongues, according to the Quantity of the Commodities which they take off our hands.[17]

"Bickerstaff," of course, satirizes this erasure of distinction and adds to a growing pile of commentary expressing uneasiness with the commodification of writing from a variety of perspectives—some nostalgic, some

---

[16] Like a responsible post-copyright author, Giles Jacob tells the reader in his preface that "the Foundation of the Work is owing to Mr. *Langbain.*" Jacob, however, announces his departure from Langbaine's extremity: "However he [Langbaine] had his Faults, and from particular Prejudices has bore a little too severely upon some of our best POETS; he is a little too fanciful in his Conjectures, from whence Authors drew their PLOTS, and having read much himself, imagin'd that every one else had done so too. What occasional Use I have made of him, I always freely acknowledge." In his examinations of individual writers, Jacob indeed departs from Langbaine with a milder rhetoric about intertextuality. Dryden, no longer the egregious plagiarist, as Langbaine had characterized him, becomes the standard to which contemporaries should be held; Dryden transforms his sources sufficiently to own them. Jacob takes an individualist conception of property as a given: without elaborate metaphors about rough diamonds or uncultivated fields, he states as obvious the fact that sufficient novelty constitutes possession. *The Poetical Register: Or, the Lives and Characters of All the English Poets. With an Account of their Writings*, 2 vols. (London, 1724), 2:74.

[17] *The Lucubrations of Isaac Bickerstaff*, 4 vols. (London, 1737), 1:255–256; *The Tatler*, no. 43.

elitist, some moralistic, some radical, and most an unresolved combination. The author nervously satirizes the proximity of the spheres of literature and commodity circulation: trading heroic poems for bonds satirizes the economic value of poetry on which professional writers depended. The sharper satire, however, lies in the second exchange, in which publishers grant degrees to the best customers. The essay thus articulates the importance of the *consumer*'s position and the dependence of the transaction on what Pierre Bourdieu has called cultural capital.[18] Cultural capital, distinct from but potentially helpful in acquiring economic capital, defines the less tangible assets that demonstrate one's refined taste, depth of learning, and capacity to distinguish appropriately edifying pleasures from fleeting entertainment or transgressive carnivalesque. Cultural capital can enhance, but does not constitute, class status. Thus even aristocrats can be mocked for lacking in this area. (In Bourdieu's terms, aristocrats possess *social* capital.) The representation of cultural capital *as capital* provides the satire in this essay. As James Ralph later observes, if a man "writes like one inspired from Heaven, and writes for Money, the Man of *Touch*, in the Right of *Midas* his great Ancestor, enters his Caveat against him as a Man of *Taste*; declares the two Provinces to be incompatible ... that there ought to be so much draw-back upon Character for every Acquisition in Coin."[19] Professional authorship, however, increasingly demanded both complicity and distinction between touch and taste.[20]

In *The Politics and Poetics of Transgression*, Peter Stallybrass and Allon White argue that Dryden, along with his contemporaries, "re-territorialized" the division between high and popular culture at the end of the seventeenth century in bourgeois terms. This re-territorialization gave cultural capital a new significance in the ownership of literary property. In the early Restoration, for example, the duke of Newcastle could hire professionals to revise his plays without compromising his authorship of them. The duchess, however, differently positioned as an elite yet not fully an owner, never managed to escape suspicion of transgression. At the same time, entry into the marketplace probably remained unthink-

---

[18] See Pierre Bourdieu, *Distinction: A Social Critique of the Judgement of Taste,* trans. Richard Nice (Cambridge: Harvard University Press, 1984).

[19] James Ralph, *The Case of Authors by Profession or Trade Stated. With Regard to Booksellers, the Stage and the Public* (London, 1763), 2.

[20] I discuss this issue at length in "The Author as Ghost in the Eighteenth Century," *1650–1850: Ideas, Aesthetics, and Inquiries in the Early Modern Era*, forthcoming.

able for her; she had little choice but to negotiate her authorship in the terms of elite culture. Even at the Restoration, however, the Newcastles belonged to an earlier generation. Dryden and others remapped the public stage as a potential a site of cultural capital, a designation that carried with it the urgency of its distinction from "low" culture.[21] Dryden represented plays as *dramatic poetry* and devoted the same kind of critical energy to distinguishing among Shakespeare, Jonson, and Fletcher as he did to arguing the relative merits of Homer and Virgil. His career of making distinctions between the heirs to Ben and the heirs to Flecknoe, between refined and barbaric verse, as well as his career-long project of representing dramatic poetry as a high-culture form, make him enormously appealing as a predecessor to eighteenth-century playwrights; he was, according to Giles Jacob, "the greatest Refiner of the *English* Language and Poetical Diction that ever liv'd."[22]

The remapping of elite and popular culture *in some respects* opened literary space to women by providing an alternative to both the elite culture that the duchess of Newcastle had to negotiate and the masculine formulations of ownership that Aphra Behn confronted.[23] The existence of a "high" culture always depends upon a "low" culture;[24] a post-Lockean world, however, demanded the remapping of this difference. The cultural location of a text depended decreasingly on the social position of the author alone; cultural capital or strictures of "taste," however, reinscribed class, gender, and ethnicity as significant factors in different ways. Thus the gendering of dramatic authorship changed in the early eighteenth century. Attacks on women as playwrights—and as novelists, poets, and pamphleteers—proliferated. At the same time, however, women dramatists became a powerful presence. Whereas Aphra Behn really had no women colleagues with sustained public careers and the duchess of Newcastle had to originate the blazing world to see her plays performed, in the 1690s Catherine Trotter, "Ariadne," Mary Pix, and Delariviere Manley each had plays on the public stage; Susanna Centlivre,

[21] See, for example, Peters's account of Congreve's career in *Congreve*.

[22] Jacob, *The Poetical Register*, 2:74.

[23] See Paula R. Backscheider, *Spectacular Politics: Theatrical Power and Mass Culture in Early Modern England* (Baltimore: Johns Hopkins University Press, 1993).

[24] See Peter Stallybrass and Allon White, *The Politics and Poetics of Transgression* (Ithaca: Cornell University Press, 1986).

Jane Wiseman, Mary Davys, and Eliza Haywood followed in the next two decades.[25]

Critics, however, regularly defined cultural capital in opposition to the feminine on the one hand,[26] and to the profitable (as James Ralph points out) on the other. In Charles Gildon's *New Rehearsal,* for example, Alexander Pope and Nicolas Rowe replace Dryden as the objects of satire. Gildon quotes Shaftesbury, complaining that "In our Days, the *Audience* makes the *Poet,* and the Bookseller the Author. . . . We go to *Plays,* as to other *Shows,* and frequent the *Theatre* as the *Booths.*"[27] The commodification of writing makes Sir Indolent Easy uneasy: "Wit now is something like our Paper Credit; the Men of Business agree to give that the force of Money, and the Men of Pleasure, This the force of *Wit.* They are both arbitrary" (12). Easy and Freeman, however, must visit with each other because Sawny Dapper (Pope) won't join them until he has finished his business with the booksellers downstairs.

> SIR IN[DOLENT EASY]: Nay, 'foregad *Sawny* has a very pretty Genius, is very Harmonious, and Writes a great many fine things, ask the Ladies else.
>
> FREE[MAN]: The Ladies are wonderful Judges of Art, indeed, of which

---

[25] For a more complete discussion of women playwrights of this era, see Jacqueline Pearson, *The Prostituted Muse: Images of Women and Women Dramatists 1642–1737* (New York: Harvester Wheatsheaf, 1988), and Nancy Cotton, *Women Playwrights in England, c. 1363–1750* (Lewisburg: Bucknell University Press, 1980). Gendered accusations of plagiarism continued to haunt women's literary careers. Mrs. Davys, for example, sounds much like the duchess of Newcastle when she defends her property rights in the preface to *The Reform'd Coquet* (London, 1724) against anticipated charges that she merely attaches her name to writing actually done by men: "But as this Book was writ at *Cambridge,* I am a little apprehensive some may imagine that Gentlemen had a hand in it. It would be very hard, if their Humanity to me, should bring an imputation upon themselves so greatly below their Merit, which I can by no means consent to; and do therefore assure the World, I am not acquainted with one Member of that worthy and learned Society of Men, whose Pens are not employ'd in things infinitely above any thing I can pretend to be the Author of: So that I only am accountable for every Fault of my Book; and if it has any Beauties, I claim the Merit of them too."

[26] See Catherine Ingrassia, "Women Writing/Writing Women: Pope, Dulness, and 'Feminization' in *The Dunciad,*" *Eighteenth-Century Life* 14 (Nov. 1990): 40–58.

[27] [Charles Gildon], *A New Rehearsal, or Bays the Younger* (London, 1714), preface. Future references are cited in the text.

they know not one Syllable; and as for Nature, it has been so corrupted by a course of ill Diet in Poetics, that they can draw no assistance from thence. (8)

The plays of Rowe, which make heroines out of whores, earn the ironic praise that "the Ladies admire them, the Lords encourage them" (10). Not even the social capital of encouragement from lords earns the respect of these men of taste: only cultural capital will do.

The significance of cultural capital, however, offered advantages to women who wanted to write for a living, for they could now perform the cultural work of staging the drama of "low" culture against which others could define their true taste. If dramatic authorship no longer depended upon claiming the position as heir to Jonson or Shakespeare, and originality competed with the expression of traditional learning as authorial legitimization, then the stage could more easily become another venue for women's writing. Providing the popular culture against which men of taste could define cultural capital, however, involved enduring public ridicule. Two plays, *The Female Wits* and *Three Hours after Marriage*, level vehement attacks against women playwrights, in part for their violations of literary property. In both these plays, not coincidentally, Colley Cibber literally played a prominent role—not as an author but as a performer. Like the women ridiculed in *Female Wits* and *Three Hours*, Colley Cibber provided the cultural forms against which men of taste defined themselves. In these plays, Cibber plays lover to the whore and admirer to the female wit.

The Female Wits, first produced in 1696, again insists upon the connection between women's authorship and sexual transgression so commonly leveled at Aphra Behn: as Mr. Aw'dwell comments, "Who wou'd a kind and certain Mistress choose,/Let him, like me, take one that loves a Muse."[28] Marsilia, the main object of ridicule and a satire of Delariviere

---

[28] *The Female Wits; Or, the Triumvirate of Poets at Rehearsal*, intro. Lucyle Hook (1704; reprint, Los Angeles: William Andrews Clark Memorial Library, Augustan Reprint Society no. 124, 1967), 42. Future references are cited in the text. Similarly, "'What a Pox,'" demands Critick in Charles Gildon's *Comparison between the Two Stages*, "'have the Women to do with the Muses? I grant you the Poets call the Nine Muses by the Names of Women, but why so? not because the Sex had any thing to do with Poetry, but because in the Sex they're much fitter for prostitution. . . . I hate these Petticoat-Authors." *Comparison*, ed. Staring B. Wells (Princeton, 1942), 17.

Manley, strings along several lovers. From this play's modest success—a run of six nights at Drury Lane and publication—it is safe to assume that it articulated a broader hostility to Manley, Catherine Trotter, and Mary Pix, depicted as Marsilia, Calista, and Mrs. Wellfed, than the prejudice of the anonymous author or authors. Writers, of course, pilloried each other all the time during these years, but the actual impersonation and public performance of an author's intimate vulnerabilities, produced by the company for which these women wrote, expresses a particular vehemence. Further, *The Female Wits* may have had real effects on the careers of these women: Manley did not produce another play until 1706; Pix wrote for Lincoln's Inn Fields thereafter; Trotter changed theaters also until a new management took over Drury Lane in 1700.[29] This play, though, also offers testimony as to how important these women had become. The play's full title—*The Female Wits; Or, the Triumvirate of Poets at Rehearsal*—itself reveals this simultaneous recognition and attack, for it puns on the triumvirate of precursors (Shakespeare, Jonson, and Fletcher) as well as Buckingham's play satirizing Dryden, the poet laureate and most prolific dramatist of his time.

The Female Wits attacks Manley, Pix, and Trotter for a range of transgressions against modest desires, from Manley's sexuality to Trotter's learning, to the physical space occupied by Pix's body. The violation of propriety, however, suggests the violation of property. This play, however, places more at stake than the gendered capacity to own language, for the specific violations of the female wits involve their attempts to appropriate the drama of high culture, signified as masculine. Like *The Rehearsal*, *The Female Wits* offers a behind-the-scenes look at a dramatic poet preparing her play for opening night. The play-within-the-play satirizes Manley's *The Royal Mischief*, originally promised to Drury Lane but eventually produced at Lincoln's Inn Fields due to (from the perspective of the satirist) the petulance of the author. The play-within characterizes *The Royal Mischief* as excessive, histrionic, and in violation of even heroic tragedy's generous boundaries of verisimilitude. Predictably enough, *The Female Wits* represents Manley as a plagiarist. While watching the rehearsal to her own play, Marsilia demands of her admirer Praiseall (performed by Colley Cibber) as soon as the first lines have been delivered,

[29] Hook, *The Female Wits*, intro., x. Manley was by no means silenced, however, for she continued as a prolific writer of prose fiction and political pamphlets.

> Mr. *Praiseall*, is not that Simile well carried on?
> MR. PRAIS. To an Extreamity of Thought, Madam,
> But I think 'tis stole. [Aside] (30)

Marsilia expresses her own anxieties about plagiarism in the opening scene, in which she snappishly wonders if Patty her maid is not "vain enough to hope from the fragments of my Discourse you may pick up a Play" (2).

The perception of women's inappropriate appropriation articulated by this play, however, exceeds these standard accusations of plagiarism. After Wellfed and Calista arrive, Marsilia boasts of the triumph of women authors: "Now here's the Female Triumvirate," she declares, "methinks 'twou'd be but civil of the Men to lay down their Pens for one Year, and let us divert the Town; but if we shou'd, they'd certainly be asham'd ever to take 'em up again" (5). These women, according to the satire, have the audacity to think of *themselves* as the modern Shakespeare, Jonson, and Fletcher, threatening to leave no literary space at all for men. The play even attacks them along the same division that critics created for Shakespeare and Jonson: Marsilia becomes a parody of an heir to Shakespeare with her excess and passion; Calista a wannabe Jonsonian with her pretensions to learning. *The Female Wits* creates parallels to high culture in order to represent female wits as its opposite and thus to show the ways these women violate gendered divisions of literary territory. Upon overhearing their conversation on Aristotle, Aw'dwell becomes so dismayed (in spite of his love for Marsilia) that he wishes he could "Conjure up the Old Philosopher, to hear these Women pull him in pieces!" (8).

Marsilia's most egregious violation of literary property lies in her "Design to alter *Cateline's Conspiracy*" (9), making use only of the first speech. Long before actually satirizing *The Royal Mischief*, *The Female Wits* establishes Marsilia's character and crime by her future project of rewriting this play: "Nor wou'd I meddle with that," she declares, "but to let the World, that is so partial to those old Fellows, see the difference of a modern Genius" (9). Calista also participates in this inappropriate appropriation by piping up that she has turned that very speech into Latin, apparently not realizing that Jonson had adapted his play *from* Latin sources. Mr. Aw'dwell wishfully declares that "this Scene will chace her from my Soul" (10); even the sycophant Mr. Praiseall laments Ben Jonson's apparent displacement as he celebrates Marsilia's triumph: "Ah!

Poor *Ben*! Poor *Ben*! You know, Madam, there was a famous Poet pick'd many a Hole in his Coat in several Prefaces.——He found fault, but never mended the Matter.——Your Ladyship has lay'd his Honour in the Dust.—— Poor *Ben*! 'Tis well thou art dead; this News had broke thy Heart" (10). If literary men had frequently rewritten the rough-edged plays of Shakespeare, rarely had anyone altered the learned works of Ben Jonson. Marsilia's plan to compete with Jonson, then, would have resonated to the audience as the most audacious female trespass onto masculine literary property, equaled only by her additional claim to excel Shakespeare: "He is beginning to be jealous," Marsilia comments as she watches her own play in rehearsal, "I dare be bold to say, here's a Scene excells *Jago*, and the *Moor*" (35).

However Manley, Trotter, and Pix understood their literary careers, the author(s) of *The Female Wits* clearly saw them as posing a specifically gendered threat to the masculine province of dramatic poetry. Ben Jonson remained an emblem of this masculinity, and *The Female Wits* represents Marsilia's plan to appropriate *Catiline* as a destruction of her precursor. In the play itself, she intends to "make *Fulvia* a Woman of the nicest Honour; and such Scenes!" (10). Fulvia, then, will become the center of interest in her version as well as the heroine. Marsilia later cannot focus on the conversation during her rehearsal because "My Head was got to *Cataline*" (23). (Re)writing this play gives her a seductive edge over the other female wits (in her own estimation): all three offer parts to Mr. Powell implicitly in exchange for his affection, and Marsilia promises, "Oh, Mr. *Powell*, you shall be *Cataline*, not *Ben Johnson*'s Fool, but my *Cataline*, Mr. *Powell*" (23). Possibly offended at Marsilia's appropriation of Jonson and certainly resentful of her authority, Powell responds, "I'd be a Dog to serve your Ladyship." As a similar representation of Manley's failed attempts to appropriate masculine authority, Marsilia hires two men with weapons to deliver the prologue and frighten the critics. The "puny Fellows" (27), however, cannot carry off this task. Marsilia herself understands these dynamics as gendered: "Sure by this Play," she insists, "the Town will perceive what a woman can do"; it sickens her to hear the dramatic poetry of men praised so often (63). In both acting and writing, women plot to wrest theatrical glory away from men: "Take care, Gentlewomen, as we Poets are fain to do," Marsilia tells the actresses, "that we may excell the Men, who first led the way" (46).

Marsilia encourages the actresses to outperform the actors, but *The*

Female Wits offers little offense to women players. It represents the actresses, in fact, with a surprising dignity at a time when they had become common targets of satirical pens. Marsilia encourages the attentions of Mr. Praiseall, but Mrs. Cross (apparently, like the other actors, playing herself) wittily spurns his annoying advances. The author(s), in fact, represent the actresses as possessing keener judgment than the house management:

> MRS. CROSS. Good morrow Mrs. *Knight*. Pray, dear Mrs. *Knight*, tell me your Opinion of this Play; you read much, and are a Judge.
> MRS. KNIGHT. Oh your Servant, Madam! Why truly, my Understanding is so very small, I can't find the Ladies meaning out. (18)

They go on to point out how often "the Masters" choose the wrong play. Mrs. Cross eventually begs to give up her part in the tragedy, and never does Marsilia become more ridiculous than when she attempts to fill the role herself. This gesture threatens to destroy Aw'dwell's affection: "After such a weakness, I will never see your Face again" (39), he declares. At a time when women actors regularly endured attacks for their lack of modesty, *The Female Wits* allows them to appear chaste, dignified, and sensible, in contrast to the women writers. *The Female Wits* represents the actresses as professionals with only the ambition to make a living and negotiate their way around the managers and poets. In this context, they pose no threat to the system of cultural capital. The play satirizes Marsilia (and to a lesser extent Calista and her pretense to learning) for competing in this realm. As in *A New Rehearsal*, *The Female Wits* opposes the cultural capital of "true" taste, represented here by Mr. Aw'dwell, to the social capital of rank without cultivation, represented by Lord Whiffle, "an empty Piece of Noise" fawned over by Marsilia. Aw'dwell demands Marsilia's respect in the beginning of the play by insisting upon the superior legitimacy of his ownership: "Why are you so ungrateful?" he demands. "Is it from your Lands water'd by *Helicon*, or my honest dirty Acres, your maintenance proceeds?" (12). By representing Marsilia as incapable of earning her living by her literary property, *The Female Wits* "reveals" her ambition as self-indulgence through a presumed accumulation of cultural capital. In *The Female Wits*, women transgress not so much by entering the marketplace (as may have been the case with Aphra Behn), but by their pretension to high culture and masculine literary property. Strange as this may appear with those familiar with

Manley's career as a scandalmonger, *The Female Wits* records a perception of Manley's heroic tragedy as an absurd attempt to locate its author within a lofty tradition. But even Manley's scandalous writing declares a kind of symbolic capital (perhaps more social than cultural), for it records an intimacy with elite men and women at the same time that it exposes their foibles. The burgeoning importance of cultural capital, however, ironically may have enabled the careers of women willing to accept their position as hacks.

The choice to parody *The Royal Mischief* demonstrates the gendered cultural issues at stake. Although one critic has argued that Manley's play "invites parody,"[30] it remains far from clear that this tragedy indulges in any greater extravagances than did many heroic tragedies written in the same era. It does differ, however, in its inscription of several forms of female desire.[31] "The miasma of hot surging sex that hovers over the entire production," as Lucyle Hook puts it, nevertheless emanates primarily from Manley's antiheroine Homais. The offense lies not just in Homais's passionate desire but in the author's representation of this desire on a *heroic* scale. Manley notes in a message to the reader that "the principal Objection made against this Tragedy is the warmth of it";[32] instructively, she insists that her play offers no more offense than Southerne's *Oroonoko*, which pleased the ladies. Manley specifically notes that the dialogue between the Widow Lackitt and her son Daniel offers as much scandal as her own heroine. She fails to observe (deliberately or not), however, that Southerne creates the Widow as an object of ridicule *for* her scandal; Manley, by contrast, attempts to raise the scandalous woman to the level of tragedy, not for her pathos but for the intensity of her ambition. The particular circumstances surrounding the *The Royal Mischief*'s production provide a parallel instance of female hubris: the play began at Drury Lane and ended up at Lincoln's Inn Fields, either because Manley stormed out of Drury Lane in a huff or because the company threw her out for her temperamental behavior.[33] What might

---

[30] Ibid., viii.

[31] See Cynthia Lowenthal, "Portraits and Spectators in the Late Restoration Playhouse: Delariviere Manley's *Royal Mischief*," *The Eighteenth Century: Theory and Interpretation* 35 (Summer 1994): 119–134.

[32] Delarivier[e] Manley, *The Royal Mischief* (London, 1696).

[33] See Lucyle Hook's discussion in the introduction to *The Female Wits* and also Fidelis Morgan, *A Woman of No Character: An Autobiography of Mrs. Manley* (London: Faber and Faber, 1986), chap. 5.

have been written from another perspective as artistic disagreement comes across as pure petulance in *The Female Wits*.

The published edition of *The Royal Mischief* articulates another kind of female (cultural) desire. Hook argues that "the true cause of the attack was the surprising success of the women playwrights" (iii). *The Royal Mischief* makes unprecedented claims about women's dramatic authorship and literary property. In a prefatory poem, Catherine Trotter hails Manley as the female champion who finally forced men to relent some of their empire: "I knew my force too weak, and but assay'd/ The Borders of their Empire to invade./I incite a greater genius to my aid." Here Trotter represents women as engaged in a collaborative project to conquer men and force them to relinquish some of their property:

> Our Title clear'd, nor can a doubt remain,
> Unless in which you'll greater Conquest gain,
> The Comick, or the loftier Tragick strain.
> The Men always o'ercome will quit the Field,
> Where they have lost their hearts, the Lawrel yield.[34]

Similarly, Mary Pix contributed a poem calling Manley the "Pride of our Sex, and Glory of the Stage." Whereas Trotter imagines Manley leading the battle against men for literary territory, Pix places Manley in a tradition of women poets: "Like *Sappho* Charming, like *Afra* Eloquent,/ Like Chast *Orinda*, sweetly Innocent."

Even before the publication of *The Royal Mischief*, Manley had demonstrated enthusiasm for a distinct female literary estate as an alternative, which she expressed in a poem entitled "To the Author of Agnes de Castro" and printed with Trotter's play:

> *Orinda*, and the Fair *Astrea* gone,
> Not one was found to fill the Vacant Throne:
> Aspiring Man had quite regain'd the Sway,
> Again that Taught us humbly to Obey;
> Till you (Natures third start, in favour of our Kind)
> With stronger Arms, their Empire have disjoyn'd,
> And snatcht a Lawrel which they thought their Prize,
> Thus Conqu'ror, with your Wit, as with your Eyes.

[34] Catherine Trotter, "To Mrs. Manley. By the Author of *Agnes de Castro*," preface to Manley, *The Royal Mischief*.

Fired by bold Example, I would try
To turn our Sexes weaker Destiny.[35]

Manley goes on to identify Trotter's accomplishment as an inspiration for her own writing. Trotter echoes this conceit, in which women must launch a war against men for poetic empire, in her praise of Manley's *Royal Mischief*. These women further encourage each other by feminizing the poetic genealogy that served Dryden so well. If Dryden—or, as George Powell calls him, "Old Oedipus"—has his Shakespeare and Jonson, these women insist on their Astrea and Orinda.[36] Astrea and Orinda, however, never become metaphorical mothers the way Shakespeare and Jonson become the fathers in wit for Dryden, a phenomenon that has less to do with different psychology than with gendered property relations. So whereas Aphra Behn pleaded for "the masculine part in me, the poet" and Margaret Cavendish attempted to achieve dominion over literary property through her aristocratic privilege, the published *The Royal Mischief* represents Manley, Trotter, and Pix as united in their insistence on literary space for women playwrights; in retaliation, *The Female Wits* presents disagreements and jealousies among the three, for which there seems to be some evidence as well.[37] Just as Manley's imagined attempt

---

[35] Delariviere Manley, quoted in *Kissing the Rod: An Anthology of Seventeenth-Century Women's Verse*, ed. Germaine Greer et al. (New York: Noonday Press, 1989), 398.

[36] George Powell, *The Fatal Discovery; Or, Love in Ruins* (London, 1698), preface. Powell contends that when Dryden makes his friend George Granville his heir, he forgets "that he had given away his Lawrels upon Record, no less the twice before, *viz.* once to Mr. *Congreve*, and another time to Mr. *Southern*. Prithee old *Oedipus*, expound this Mystery: Dost thou set up thy own *Transubstantiation* Miracle in the Donation of thy Idol Bays, that thou hast 'em Fresh, New, and whole, to give 'em three times over?" Trotter paid tribute to Dryden by contributing a poem to *The Nine Muses*, a collection of elegies on Dryden's death organized by Manley.

[37] On women writers and literary tradition in the nineteenth century, see Sandra M. Gilbert and Susan Gubar, *The Madwoman in the Attic: The Woman Writer and the Nineteenth Century Literary Imagination* (New Haven: Yale University Press, 1979). Early in her career Manley articulates enthusiasm for a distinct women's literary tradition, but she later violently rejects this possibility and attacks her former associates. Trotter, "her sister authoress," becomes the subject of her most bitter slander. In *The Adventures of Rivella*, Manley gives Trotter the name of Calista—the pseudonym from *The Female Wits*—and describes her as "the most of a prude in her outward professions and the least of it in her inward practice." *The Adventures of Rivella*, quoted by Fidelis Morgan, *Woman of No Character*, 95. Manley expresses similar contempt in *The New Atalantis*: "she still assum'd an Air of *Virtue pretended*, and was ever eloquent (according to her

to appropriate and "correct" Ben Jonson's play becomes a cogent threat for the author(s) of *The Female Wits,* so she herself worries in the prologue to her first play about writing in a culture that does not grant women the position of owner:

> Now all ye chattering Insects straight be dumb,
> The Men of Wit and Sense are hither come,
> Ask not this Mask to Sup, nor that to show
> Some Face more ugly than a Fifty Beau,
> Who, if our Play succeeds, will surely say,
> Some private Lover helpt her on her way,
> As Female Wit were barren like the Moon,
> That borrows all her influence from the Sun.[38]

In a revision of Aphra Behn's preface to the *Dutch Lover,* in which an overpowdered, white-faced fop scorns women's dramatic composition, Manley represents the denial of women's wit as a physically unattractive quality. In her preface, she insists that her gender accounts for the play's failure: "I am satisfied the bare Name of being a Woman's Play damn'd it beyond its own want of Merit."[39] Catherine Trotter stopped writing plays when she married and turned to philosophical and theological letters instead. She did, however, produce a stage adaptation of Aphra Behn's *Agnes de Casto* a few years after Southerne produced *Oroonoko,* as if competing with him for Behn's remains.

Mary Pix, satirized in *The Female Wits* less for her forays into masculine property than for her excessive body, seems to have understood the cultural issues at stake, as revealed by her play *Queen Catherine, or, The Ruines of Love* (1698). As argued earlier, women generally avoided trying to appropriate Shakespeare or locate themselves as the heirs to Ben

---

still manner) upon the *Foible* of others. She also fitted her self with an excellent Mask call'd *Religion* . . . But a Husband was *Daphne's* [Trotter's] Business; the only means to prevent her from falling, (when her Youth and Charms were upon the Wing) into extreme Contempt." *The Novels of Mary Delariviere Manley,* ed. Patricia Köster, 2 vols. (Gainesville, Fla.: Scholars' Facsimiles and Reprints, 1971), 1:587–588. Manley further accuses Trotter of an affair with another woman writer and represents her former friend's dramatic career as a failure. *The New Atalantis* represents Sarah Fyge, another erstwhile associate of Manley, as grotesquely ugly and utterly incomprehensible.

[38] Manley, prologue from *The Lost Lover,* in *Kissing the Rod,* ed. Greer et al., 399.
[39] Ibid.

Jonson. Competing with Jonson, in fact, becomes Marsilia's most revealing offense. *Queen Catherine*, however, hesitantly invokes Shakespeare as a precursor but at the same time scrupulously avoids treading on male dramatic turf. In the prologue, Pix writes,

> A heavy *English* Tale to day, we show
> As e'er was told by *Hollingshed* or Stow,
> *Shakespear* did oft his Countries worthies chuse,
> Nor did they by his Pen their Lustre lose.
> Hero's revive thro' him, and Hotspur's rage,
> Doubly adorns and animates the Stage:
> But how shall Woman after him succeed,
> And what excuse can her presumption plead.
> Who with enervate voice dares wake the mighty dead;
> To please you martial men she must despair,
> And therefore Courts the favour of the fair:
> From huffing Hero's she hopes no relief,
> But trusts in *Catherine's* Love, and *Isabella's* grief.[40]

Pix relinquishes the heroic part of history to men as *their* literary property and claims the romantic part of the story that Shakespeare did not tell as appropriate to a woman. Thus she writes a play about Henry V's widow Catherine and her chaste love for Owen Tudor. In Pix's play, Edward plots to overthrow Catherine because she rejects his passionate love of her. If Tate and Dryden claimed and repaired the Shakespearean estate, Pix negotiated her way through the dominant masculine tropes of authorship by telling the "feminine" part of the story that Shakespeare neglected.

While Pix may have escaped the charge of transgressive appropriation, George Powell nevertheless felt free to appropriate one of her plays.[41] After Powell rejected Pix's *Deceiver Deceived* (1698) from Drury Lane, he produced his own *Imposture Defeated*, a play that bears an unmistakable resemblance to Pix's. Pix attacked Powell in her prologue, casting Powell as the real deceiver:

---

[40] Mary Pix, *Queen Catherine, or, the Ruines of Love* (London, 1698).
[41] Powell appears in *The Female Wits* as the actor over whom the women fight. He may have had a hand in this satire.

'Tis t'other House best shows the slight of hand:
Hey Jingo, Sirs, what's this! their Comedy?
Presto be gone, 'tis now our Farce you see

. . .

    Our case is thus:
Our Authoress, like true Women, shew'd her Play
To some, who, like true Wits stole't half away.
We've Fee'd no Councel yet, tho some advise us
T'indite the Plagiaries at *Apollo*'s Sizes?
But ah, how they'd out face a Damsel civil:
Who've impudence enough to out face the Devil

. . .

Therefore to you kind Sirs, as to the Laws
Of Justice she submits her self and Cause,
For to whom else shou'd a wrong'd Poet sue,
There's no appeal to any Court but you.[42]

With apparently no legal recourse for an act of plagiarism, Pix appeals to the audience as the only arbiters of literary property.[43] In Pix's own perception, her position as a woman writer makes her more vulnerable to such an act, for it makes Powell less likely to fear recrimination.[44]

---

[42] Mary Pix, *The Deceiver Deceived: A Comedy* (London, 1698), preface. Also reprinted in *Kissing the Rod*, ed. Greer et al., 418–419.

[43] In all the accusations of plagiarism that I have looked at during this period, not one mentions the possibility of legal action. Plagiarism remained, at least for dramatists, a cultural and not a legal issue.

[44] In a preface to the reader, George Powell dismisses his own play as "only a slight piece of Scribble, . . . being no more than a short weeks work, to serve the wants of a thin Playhouse." *The Imposture Defeated: or, a Trick to Cheat the Devil* (London, 1698). But even "as indifferent as I am to the merit of the Comedy," Powell argues, "I would not willingly be thought so poor a Plagiary, and am far from being guilty of this accusation." He writes that he found the plot in a novel: "'Tis true, such a one she [Mrs. Pix] brought into the House, and made me a Solicitor to the Company to get it Acted, which when I had obtain'd, she very mannerly carry'd the Play to the other House; and had I really taken the Character [of Bondi] from her, I had done her no more than a piece of Justice." Powell's use of such a similar plot and characters, however, could equally be read as an act of aggression against Pix and as an example of gendered differences in the capacity to own. Powell probably expected no consequences, perceiving Pix as occluded from property rights in a text. He might also be indirectly attacking Pix in his prologue to *The Fatal Discovery* (London, 1698):

As when a nauseous Vizor in the Pit,
Grossly abuses, without Sense or Wit,

Pix's last play appeared on stage in 1706. By then, a new generation of "female wits" was publishing plays, poetry, and novels; by 1717, a new play satirized women's dramatic authorship.[45] *Three Hours after Marriage* once again casts Colley Cibber as the collaborator with a transgressive woman playwright. Phoebe Clinket, the dramatic poetess in this play, has been identified with Susanna Centlivre, the countess of Winchilsea, and the duchess of Newcastle.[46] As the only professional of the three, Centlivre seems the most likely immediate object of satire.[47] Although

All justify her merited disgrace,
If they unvail the grievance of the place,
And shew the drab in her own ugly face.
So, Gentlemen, we hope for your excuse,
If in Return of a damn'd dull Abuse,
We pluck the Vizor off from t'other house:
And let you see their natural Grimmaces
Affecting Youth, with pale Autumnal faces.

[45] For women novelists of this time, see Janet Todd, *The Sign of Angellica: Women, Writing and Fiction, 1660–1800* (New York: Columbia University Press, 1989); and Paul Hunter, *Before Novels: The Cultural Contexts of Eighteenth Century English Fiction* (New York: W. W. Norton, 1990). Women's poetry has been anthologized in *Kissing the Rod*, ed. Greer et al., and in Robert W. Uphaus and Gretchen M Foster, eds., *The "Other" Eighteenth Century: English Women of Letters 1660–1800* (East Lansing, Mich.: Colleagues Press, 1991).

[46] *A Key to the New Comedy; Call'd Three Hours after Marriage*, identifies Clinket as Winchilsea but also as a satire of Cavendish. Richard Morton and William W. Peterson, in their edition of the play and the *Key* (Painesville, Ohio: Lake Erie College Studies, 1961), mention the duchess as a possible object of satire but ultimately argue that the figure stands for a generic bluestocking. See also Myra Reynolds, *The Learned Lady in England 1650–1760* (Boston: Houghton Mifflin, 1920), 394–395; and Cotton, *Women Playwrights*, 188–192.

[47] Nevertheless, Fossile's introduction of his niece as one who came "into my House to regulate my Oeconomy; but instead of Puddings, she makes Pastorals; or when she should be raising Paste, is raising some Ghost in a new tragedy" (7) recalls Cavendish's own apology for writing, in which she satirizes her attempts at housekeeping, which end up costing more resources than they save. In an epistle to William prefacing her *CCXI Sociable Letters, Written by the Thrice Noble, Illustrious, and Excellent Princess, the Lady Marchioness of Newcastle* (London, 1664), Cavendish writes: "It may be said to me, as one said to a Lady, *Work, Lady, Work*, let writing Books alone, For surely Wiser Women ne'r writ one; But your Lordship never bid me to Work, nor leave Writing, except when you would perswade me to spare so much time from my Study as to take the Air for my Health; the truth is, My Lord, I cannot Work, I mean such Works as Ladies use to pass their Time withall, and if I could, the Material of such Works would cost more than the Work would be worth, besides all the Time

Centlivre made her reputation as a writer of comedy and Clinket composes a tragedy, Centlivre produced her first tragedy, *The Cruel Gift*, in December, 1716; *Three Hours* appeared in January of 1717.[48] Perhaps her foray into this "higher" genre met with a quick rebuke in Pope, Gay, and Arburthnot's play. Further, John Gay, in his dedication to *The Confederates*, identifies Phoebe Clinket as formerly a performer, which supports the identification with Centlivre.[49] But regardless of the women whom *Three Hours* satirizes in particular—Centlivre, Cavendish, and possibly Winchilsea—it nevertheless satirizes female dramatic authorship in general.[50]

For Pope, Gay, and Arbuthnot, female authorship offends on two fronts: it violates a cultural economy of the ownership and it violates a patriarchal sexual economy. Like Marsilia, Phoebe Clinket writes tragedies in inflated language, designs absurd plots, and insults Ben Jonson.[51] In his dedication to *The Confederates*, Gay laments that Clinket changed from "the agreeable *Dancer*, into the frightful *She-Pedant*" (79), from specular object to writing subject. If Clinket strives for the cultural capital

---

and Pains bestow'd upon it. You may ask me, what Works I mean; I answer, Needleworks, Spinning-works, Preserving-works, as also Baking, and Cooking-works, as making Cakes, Pyes, Puddings, and the like, all which I am Ignorant of." (See no. 150.) Phoebe Clinket's obsession for writing, allegedly like Cavendish's, borders on madness.

[48] Dating of Centlivre, *The Cruel Gift*, from F. P Lock, *Susanna Centlivre* (Boston: Twayne Publishers, 1979); that of *Three Hours* from the Morton and Peterson edition of *Three Hours*.

[49] According to contemporary biographies, Centlivre was an actress in the provinces before she wrote for the stage. Although these biographies are conflicting and unreliable, it was very common to find acting and playwriting in the same career. See, for example, the entry on Centlivre in Thomas Whincop, *Scanderbeg, or, Love and Liberty. To which are added a list of all dramatic authors with some account of their lives and of all dramatic pieces ever published in the English language to the year 1747* (London, 1747).

[50] John Wilson Bowyer contends that Clinket resembles Winchilsea more closely, but he also points out that Centlivre returns the satirists' fire in *A Bold Stroke for a Wife*. Cibber, later realizing the extent to which *Three Hours* made him look absurd, lashed back with allusions to the mummy and the crocodile—an incident that heightened the feud between Cibber and Pope. Observing Pope's sensitivity about this reference, Centlivre alludes to the mummy and the crocodile as well. See Bowyer, *The Celebrated Mrs. Centlivre* (Durham, N.C.: Duke University Press, 1952), 205–206.

[51] To a player's citation of "The famous *Ben. Johnson*," Clinket responds, "Dry." Morton and Peterson, eds., *Three Hours after Marriage*. Future quotations are from the Morton and Peterson edition and are cited in the text.

of the learned author, she also confuses the boundaries of textual property by requesting that Plotwell introduce her play under his name to ensure its production. This gesture blurs the authorial lines between Clinket/Centlivre and Plotwell/Cibber, representing a genuine entanglement, as the next chapter will explore, between the two writers. In *Three Hours*, however, the blurring of textual lines implies the blurring of sexual lines, satirizing Clinket/Centlivre for her lack of propriety and Plotwell/Cibber for his association with unworthy women. Further, Clinket claims originality while practicing appropriation. Her new play takes up "A Subject untouch'd either by Ancients or Moderns, in which are Terror and Pity in perfection" (19). But when Plotwell and Sir Tremendous converse, she alerts her maid: "I perceive here will be a Wit-Combat between these Beaux-Esprits. *Prue*, be sure you set down all the Similes." She and Prue mark down all the men's witty remarks, presumably to be used in some future dramatic composition. Like the other modern plays that Plotwell and Sir Tremendous dismiss, Clinket's presumably also contain "Thefts . . . so open—That the very *French* Taylors can discover them" (17).

Once again, female authorship involves violations not only of property, but also of sexual propriety. Gay's dedication to Clinket marvels at the oddity that "a Person who has got so much Reputation by her *Heels*, should give her self up now to scanning of *Verses*": "For my Part, I should have expected to have seen your *Pinners* stain'd with *Claret*, much sooner than *Ink*, a *Fiddle* carry'd before you, rather than a *Desk*, and another Weapon in that soft Hand, instead of a *Pen*" (79). Rumors of sexual impropriety plagued Centlivre's career, especially from her earlier life. Biographers report that she left home, disguised herself as a boy, and resided with Anthony Hammond at Cambridge.[52] *Three Hours* maintains a running analogy, by now a cliché, between Phoebe's writing and her sexual illegitimacy. Phoebe's play tells a story about a married woman and her lover; her conversation with the critic Sir Tremendous blurs the distinction between discourse and intercourse:

CLINKET. Ah! dear Sir *Tremendous*, there is that *Delicatesse* in your Sentiments!
SIR TREMENDOUS. Ah Madam! there is that Justness in your Notions!
CLINKET. I am so charm'd by your manly Penetration!

[52] See the entry on Centlivre in Whincop, *Scanderbeg*.

185

SIR TREMENDOUS. I with your profound Capacity!
CLINKET. That I am not able—
SIR TREMENDOUS. That it is impossible—
CLINKET. To conceive—
SIR TREMENDOUS. To express—
CLINKET. With what Delight I embrace—
SIR TREMENDOUS. With what Pleasure I inter into—
CLINKET. Your Ideas, most learned Sir *Tremendous!*
SIR TREMENDOUS. Your Sentiments, most divine Mrs. *Clinket.* (18)

When a sailor brings an unknown child to Fossile at the end, Phoebe
appears to take responsibility for it, confessing, "I am not in the least
mortified with the Accident. I know it has happen'd to many of the most
famous Daughters of *Apollo,* and to my self several times" (56). She
speaks of the rejection of her plays, and the authors include other
conversations in which her literary property becomes confused with
literal progeny.

Three Hours further implicates Phoebe Clinket by her similarity to and
alliance with Mrs. Townley, Dr. Fossile's new bride, who has a string of
lovers, past and present. Townley instantly recognizes in Clinket an
important potential alliance: Clinket's play provides an opportunity for
her and Plotwell to kiss, and Clinket excuses Townley's lovers (dressed
as a mummy and a crocodile) to Dr. Fossile by claiming them as her
own masquerade. The most damning parallel, though, emerges through
both of their relationships with Plotwell, played by *and* a parody of Colley
Cibber. Just as Plotwell pursued Townley, so he declares to Clinket that
he will try to get her play produced and that he "should be proud,
Madam, to be a real Father to any of your Productions" (14). Throughout, Plotwell remains identified as the "father" of Clinket's play for his
role in bringing it to the theater: Fossile, for example, intercepts a note
from Clinket to Plotwell saying that "the Child which you father'd is
return'd back upon my Hands" (56). The authors thus represent a
woman's efforts to produce a play in cooperation with a male-manager
as indistinguishable from sexual involvement.[53] Clinket and Townley both
not only have "affairs" with Plotwell, but they also betray Fossile: neither

[53] And as we learn from Cibber's *Apology,* managers were necessarily male. In spite
of Elizabeth Barry's experience, her sex prevented her from becoming a sharer like
the other leading performers. *An Apology for the Life of Mr. Colley Cibber, Written by
Himself,* ed. Robert W. Lowe, 2 vols. (1888; reprint, New York: AMS Press, 1966).

turns out to be who Fossile thought she was when he brought her into the house, and neither fulfills her assigned feminine function there. Townley produces an illegitimate baby; Clinket produces an illegitimate text.

The link between women writing drama and the violation of chastity had become so common by the eighteenth century that we risk simply pointing out instances without pausing to consider the connection between the two positions, beyond perhaps the obviousness that a whore is, in the masculine imagination of the time, one of the worst things a woman can be named and a way of dismissing her. The implications from the Restoration persisted: practicing the most *public* of all literary genres, as Catherine Gallagher argues, women playwrights necessarily sacrificed the kind of guarded life required for a reputation for chastity. They became public women, associated with other public women like actresses and prostitutes.[54] In the context of eighteenth-century professional authorship and Grub Street culture, however, the analogy between writing and prostitution comes to signify not just female unchastity, but a particular *kind* of authorship.[55] As Pat Rogers points out, prostitution becomes the controlling metaphor in the Scriblerian representations of satirized authorship: "Rag Fair, a place infamous for crime, prostitution, poverty and cheap secondhand trading, makes an exact emblem for Pope's artistic point. Grub Street, likewise, is a place notable for literary crime, for poverty of invention, for the prostitution of poetry, and for the retailing of shoddy stolen goods."[56] Beneath the spectacle of Marsilia and Phoebe Clinket's whorishness—their total sexual alienability—lurks the possibility of the alienability of the male body and self with every attempt at authorship. Male hack authorship and female prostitution, in the context of possessive individualism, alienate inalienable rights of self-possession and thus expose the fragility of those promised rights, even for men with education and status. At the same time that the author-as-whore trope articulates the anxiety that anyone, even a full masculine "individual," could suffer complete self-alienation (Aphra Behn, as I have argued, exploits this anxiety by representing Willmore as a whore),

[54] See Chapter 2; also Gallagher, *Nobody's Story: The Vanishing Acts of Women Writers in the Marketplace, 1670–1820* (Berkeley: University of California Press, 1994), chap. 1.

[55] Catherine Gallagher in *Nobody's Story* also explores the analogy between authorship and prostitution at this time, drawing a somewhat different conclusion.

[56] Pat Rogers, *Grub Street: Studies in a Subculture* (London: Methuen, 1972), 44.

it nevertheless performs the important cultural work of suggesting that *some* authors can write without becoming prostitutes.

The word *hack* itself, as Rogers points out, inscribes this distinction: "Johnson's *Dictionary* entry for 'hackney' moves from the sense of a hired horse (with an example from *Hudibras*) to that of a prostitute to 'any thing let out for hire' (both the latter illustrated from Pope) to 'much used or common.' 'To hack' is defined as 'to turn hackney or prostitute.' We notice at once the sexual innuendo in the word and its derivatives: something lost, I believe, to most present-day readers. To be a hack, then, was to traffic commercially in something fundamentally admirable, and thus to sully it. . . . Hence the great advantage to the satirist in being able to suggest that the scribbling profession lived cheek by jowl with the whores."[57] The commodification of selves and of literary expression threatens the possibility of an inalienable self. Further, the "hack" carries class connotations as the second-string horse that would pull a coach for hire, as opposed to the purebred that a gentleman might keep for his own pleasure. Clearly writing and chastity, with their erstwhile aristocratic associations, have become in the eighteenth century crucial areas of bourgeois contestation and distinction.[58] The project of eighteenth-century authorial ideology, like the ideology of exhortations to chastity, is to protect property while at the same time denying that the object of protection *is* property. Hack writers threaten the kind of cultural capital for which Pope aimed by both acknowledging writing as property and failing to demonstrate sufficient respect for claims to the ownership of texts. Plagiarism becomes an egregious violation of the integrity of the self in a commodity culture in which writing and sexuality *potentially* alienate female (or other less-than-full-individual) selves and *potentially* confirm the inalienability of the masculine individual self.[59] The desire

[57] Ibid., 219. Gallagher argues that scandalous women "hacks" came to represent the perceived prostitution of *authorship itself* and in fact succeeded professionally not in spite of but because of being women; my point is that the creation of the whore/hack author became a necessary identity against which "true" authors could define themselves. The cultural work of the author-as-whore trope resides in the implication that *some* authors are not whores.

[58] See Jonathan Goldberg, *Writing Matter: From the Hands of the English Renaissance* (Stanford: Stanford University Press, 1990); and Peter Lazlett, *The World We Have Lost* (London: Methuen, 1965).

[59] In *Writing Matter*, Goldberg demonstrates the ways in which sixteenth-century school textbooks represented writing as elite and masculine, even at the most mechanical level.

for this inalienability that writing potentially provides, however, can emerge from nostalgic elitism, a critique of commodification, or both simultaneously. Finally, the prostitute also signifies, as discussed in the previous chapter, the "picaroon" or the untrustworthy maker of contracts. As John Brewer has recently argued, this kind of trustworthiness took on an extraordinary importance in the early eighteenth century with the emergence of a credit society.[60]

Three Hours articulates an informative ambivalence toward plagiarism. The poets satirize John Dennis's concern for textual property in the character of Sir Tremendous, who exclaims of the modern plays: "O what Felony from the Ancients! What Petty-Larceny from the Moderns! There is the famous *Iphigenia* of *Racine*, he stole his *Agamemnon* from *Seneca*, who stole it from *Euripides*, who stole it from *Homer*, who stole it from all the Ancients before him. In short there is nothing so execrable as our most taking Tragedys"[61] (18). This speech makes fun of plagiarist-hunting, of the assumption that lines can and must be drawn to distinguish literary property. The authors refer specifically to Dennis's own preface to his *Iphigenia* in which he claims that "the subject I choose in order to my design has been handled by several; yet the Fable or Plot is intirely my own."[62] The satirists quite rightly find this passage absurdly self-contradictory: how can the Iphigenia story become entirely his own? Yet the authors of *Three Hours* run into the same contradiction: the very passage that ridicules Dennis's concern *for* plagiarism actually ridicules Clinket *as* a plagiarist, for she has Prue record all of Sir Tremendous's conceits for future use. Unlike the duchess of Newcastle, Pope, Gay, and Arbuthnot assume as natural the difference between plagiarism— stealing necessitated by lack of originality—and imitation, the repetition of familiar, high-culture texts. Strictures against plagiarism, then, cannot be understood outside of the context of cultural capital and the capacity to appropriate. Thus, just as plagiarism is the Grub Street version of imitation, those like Dennis, who fail to note the difference, perform the Grub Street version of criticism.

Three Hours expresses similar ambivalence about collaborative author-

[60] John Brewer, "Commercialization and Politics," in *The Birth of a Consumer Society: The Commercialization of Eighteenth-Century England*, ed. Neil McKendrick, John Brewer, and J. H. Plumb (London: Europa, 1982).

[61] In their introduction to *Three Hours*, Morton and Peterson convincingly identify this character as the critic John Dennis.

[62] Quoted by Morton and Peterson, *Three Hours*, 62.

ship. The play satirizes Clinket for the fluidity of authorial identity between herself and Plotwell; their collaboration becomes explicitly erotic
and the exchange of text is metaphorized as the exchange of body fluids.
The surrender of her body/text becomes violent, however, when Sir
Tremendous and the players start slashing lines: "gash my Flesh, mangle
my Face, any thing sooner than scratch my Play," she protests, while
Plotwell, the supposed author, encourages Tremendous to "blot and
insert wherever you please" (20). Clinket faints at the end of this scene,
and the men leave her in hysterics as Fossile flings her writings into the
fire. Ironically and apparently unself-consciously, this farce, collabora-
tively written by three men, represents the blurring of individual authorial identity as illicitly sexual.

Fop Authorship

In both these infamous satires against women dramatists, Colley Cibber
played a prominent role. But while the women satirized in both plays
endured charges of plagiarism and impropriety, it was Colley Cibber
who emerged as the cultural symbol for compromised authorship. Cibber
achieved everything that Trotter, Manley, Pix, and Centlivre did, only
in greater proportion: if he became an immensely powerful figure in
the theater world and the poet laureate, he also became the most famous
plagiarist of the eighteenth century. Cibber did, of course, repeat and
revise earlier drama, but, like Aphra Behn, not significantly more than
other playwrights of his generation. In spite of the prominence of the
whorish authoress as both object of misogynist attack and figure for the
"prostitution" of letters, Cibber overshadows even Marsilia and Phoebe
as the embodiment of inappropriate appropriation. None of the women
playwrights achieved the cultural visibility of Cibber: Pope attacks Centlivre and Haywood in *The Dunciad*, but clearly did not consider them
sufficiently important for the star position of chief dunce.

This does not mean that Cibber's infamy transcended gender. The
Goddess Dulness herself, as Catherine Ingrassia has recently argued,
genders as feminine all the least admirable qualities of authorship.[63]
Although the replacement of Lewis Theobald with Colley Cibber as the
chief dunce created awkward inconsistencies in terms of the personal

[63] Ingrassia, "Women Writing/Writing Women."

attack on the laureate,[64] it nevertheless generated a new relationship absent in the earlier version. In the revised *Dunciad*, the Goddess and her favorite dunce occupy similar places outside of dominant masculinity, as do Centlivre, Haywood, and others. But to elide Cibber and Centlivre under the general rubric of "feminized" authorship would, I believe, render invisible one of the poem's central points. *The Dunciad*, after all, satirizes *mostly men* for the way they fritter away the potential masculine privilege of full social subjectivity and inalienable selfhood. These men, as *The Dunciad* itself demonstrates, can attract even more impassioned satire than women since they embarrass other men and expose the vulnerability of masculine self-ownership. Cibber fits poetically into *The Dunciad* and remains the ultimate plagiarist for Pope and others because in his fashioned self converge the two figurations of the anxiety and alienation associated with professional authorship: the whore and the hack. Cibber cultivated a position outside of dominant masculinity and flaunted his contamination by commerce.

In Pope's last version of *The Dunciad*, Colley Cibber becomes not just a plagiarist but an actual composite of earlier dramatic literature:

A past, vamp'd, future, old, reviv'd, new piece,
'Twixt Plautus, Fletcher, Shakespeare, and Corneille,
Can make a Cibber, Tibbald, or Ozell.[65]

Pope pictures Cibber in the midst of composition, recalling all his plagiarism:

Next, o'er his Books his eyes began to roll,
In pleasing memory of all he stole,
How here he sipp'd, how there he plunder'd snug
And suck'd all o'er, like an industrious Bug.

---

[64] As Leopold Damrosch, Jr., reminds us, Samuel Johnson pointed out that Pope's replacement creates inconsistency in character. See Damrosch's reading of *The Dunciad* in *The Imaginative World of Alexander Pope* (Berkeley: University of California Press, 1987), 120–135. Pope's own position, of course, was by no means simple or secure. See Helen Deutsch, "The 'Truest Copies' and the 'Mean Original': Pope, Deformity, and the Poetics of Self-Exposure," *Eighteenth-Century Studies* 27 (Fall 1993): 1–26.

[65] Alexander Pope, *The Dunciad* (B), ed. James Sutherland (New York: Oxford University Press, 1943), 290. Future quotations are from this edition and are cited in the text.

> Here lay poor Fletcher's half-eat scenes, and here
> The Frippery of crucify'd Molière;
> There hapless Shakespeare, yet of Tibbald sore,
> Wish'd he had blotted for himself before. (278–279)

Whether from classical, French, or earlier English sources, Cibber becomes a devouring, appropriating monster. Pope had personal reasons that account in part for his hostility toward Cibber,[66] but enmity alone does not explain the *form* that charges against Cibber, from Pope and others, consistently took. In 1704, an anonymous writer included a dialogue "Between Nat. Lee the Tragedian, and Colley C––r the Plagiary" in a collection of *Visits from the Shades*. In this pamphlet, Cibber's lack of cultural capital parallels or even produces his habit of literary theft: upon Cibber's mention of Homer and Virgil, Lee demands that he "leave of[f] insipid Encomiums upon Authors you are wholly a stranger to, for it's as impossible for you to make an adequate Judgment on those two Divine Poets, as to decipher a Letter from China, or write a Play without being a Plagiarist." When Cibber defends himself by insisting on the originality of the texts in question, Lee characterizes him as "Aesop's Crow, [who] strut[s] with the spoils of another's Labour."[67] Another assault on Cibber, *The Theatre-Royal Turn'd into a Mountebank's Stage* (1718), similarly represents Cibber as plagiarist and tasteless in the context of its political attack. (Cibber had revised Molière's *Tartuffe* as *The Non-Juror*; the writer, as a nonjuror, protests this satire.) The "Nonjuror" author associates Cibber with lack of cultural capital, lower-class taste, ethnic inferiority, and another famous "hack" playwright when he revises an attack on D'Urfey to fit Cibber:

> Thou Cur, half *Dane*, half *English* Breed,
>   Thou Mongrel of *Parnassus*,
> To think leud Lines grown up to Seed,
> Can ever tamely pass us.
>
> Thou write *Nonjurors*, and be damn'd!
>   Write Anagrams for Cutlers;
> None with thy Frippery will be shamm'd
>   But Chamber-maids and Butlers.

---

[66] See Damrosch, *Imaginative World*.

[67] *Visits from the Shades: Or, Dialogues Serious, Comical, and Political* (1704), facsimile, ed. Arthur Freeman (New York: Garland, 1972), 22, 26.

In t'other World expect dry Blows,
   No Tears can wash the Stains out,
MOLIERE will pull thee by the Nose,
   And SHAKESPEARE dash thy Brains out.[68]

Cibber clearly *does* base his *Nonjuror* on Molière, but his accuser contradicts himself on the nature of the crime. In some places, he attacks Cibber for having lazily invented nothing, calling him a "pilfering Maroder" who "purloins all [Molière's] incidents" (17). Elsewhere, however, he complains that Cibber ruins the play by changing it so much. Cibber's crime emerges in this attack as not just plagiarism, but as a more generalized transgressive appropriation. This sort of charge crops up throughout Cibber's career, from the early *Visit from the Shades* to satire in *The Battle of Authors* (1720) to the later *Apology for the Life of Mr. T. . . .C. . . ., Comedian* (1740), possibly written in part by Fielding.[69] One satire against Cibber compares the laureate to an ape in order to expose his plagiarism, pandering to low taste, and his sycophantish behavior before elite society:

Keyber! distinguish'd for his *Monkey Rhimes*,
Keyber! the reigning Chief of *Pantomimes*!
Why quit'st thou, *Colley*, thy Dramatic Shape,
T'expire in Ode, and die a *laurel'd Ape*?
Well has thy subtle Nature play'd its Part,
To please thy Own, but gall the *Sharer*'s Heart;
Inimitable *Ape*! but let it pass,
Thou'st play'd the *Courtly Monkey*, he the *Ass*.[70]

What makes Cibber such a consistent object of plagiarism charges when so many of his contemporaries used earlier texts for their plays as well? Surely these attacks have less to do with the quantification of novelty and repetition than with the particularity of Cibber's cultural location.

To a significant extent, Cibber constructed this vulnerable but nevertheless lucrative position himself as part of his strategy for appropriation.

[68] *The Theatre-Royal Turn'd into a Mountebank's Stage* (London, 1718), 12.

[69] For examinations of Cibber's career, see Helene Koon, *Colley Cibber: A Biography* (Lexington: University Press of Kentucky, 1986), and Richard Hindry Barker, *Mr. Cibber of Drury Lane* (New York: Columbia University Press, 1939).

[70] "Court Monkies. Inscrib'd to Mr. Pope" (London, 1734).

Cibber offends his detractors not just for his financial success, but for his apparent lack of interest in the accumulation of cultural capital. Cibber, in fact, parades naked profit motivation: "I wrote more to be Fed," he announces, "than to be Famous."[71] In his "Letter to Mr. Pope," he addresses the charge of plagiarism before anything else, urging first the authority of Dryden in revising earlier plays and asking, "Is a Tailor, that can make a new Coat well, the worse Workman, because he can mend an old one?"[72] Cibber deploys his popularity as well as financial success against Pope's claim to cultural capital, suggesting that his career has offended Pope so much because he, with "such inferior Talents . . . was admitted to as good Company as you, with your superior, could get into." Cibber lords his social capital over Pope, but at the same time commonly folds aristocratic attention into his general claim to popularity. Cibber strategically aligns himself with popular taste as opposed to "a set of well-dress'd merry-making cricks, that call themselves the *Town*, whose private wit was continually insulting the publick diversion." He reports how he once planted himself in the audience of his own play and observed with pleasure "the generality of the audience, in a silent, fix'd attention, never failing by their looks or gestures, to discover those pleasing emotions of the mind, which I was always confident would rise from so elevated a subject."[73]

In fact, Cibber on occasion even sacrifices a chance to represent himself as well connected to a chance to exalt his role as businessman and entertainer. Although his *Apology* allows a pinch of sympathy for the "ingenious Indigent" who attempts to convince him to produce an unmarketable play, he mocks the indignation of such amateurs: "immediate Want was not always confess'd their Motive for Writing; Fame, Honour, and *Parnassian* Glory had sometimes take a romantick Turn in their Heads; and then they gave themselves the Air of talking to us in a higher Strain—Gentlemen were not to be so treated!"[74] Cibber even contributed

[71] "Letter from Mr. Cibber to Mr. Pope, Inquiring into the MOTIVES that might induce him in his SATYRICAL WORKS, to be so frequently fond of Mr. CIBBER's Name" (London, 1742), 9.

[72] Ibid., 32–33.

[73] Colley Cibber, Preface to *Ximena*, in *The Dramatic Works of Colley Cibber, Esq* (1777), facsimile reprint, 5 vols. (New York: AMS Press, 1966) 3:105. Future references are cited in the text.

[74] Cibber, *Apology*, 2:250. Future references are cited in the text. Others repeated such self-representations. An anonymous writer defending Pope, for example, sarcasti-

to the battle between the "ancients" and "moderns" in his "Rhapsody Upon the Marvellous" (1751), both advocating the moderns and praising his arch-rival for his high-culture achievements. The laureate reasons that if the ancients made such grave errors in their pagan religion, surely they made similar errors in poetry. He pits Milton and Dryden against Homer and Virgil, admitting that

> Even our Pope, who tho' from *Horace*,
> He plainly Plans of Satire borrows,
> In new-mill'd Coin the Loan repays,
> And mends the Weight of *Roman* Lays;
> In stronger Strokes, and Tints of Nature,
> His Fools and Knaves enrich the Satire,
> And sound his Sense in more harmonious Metre.
> (This Praise must Conscience on him fix,
> Tho' oft' the Loon the *Laureate* licks!)[75]

Even for Cibber, Pope's literary repetition adds to his stock of cultural capital rather than revealing his similarity to Grub Street plagiarists.

Cibber's claim to literary property meets with censure, then, not because he repeats previous texts so much more than anyone else, but because he capitalized on his status as "hack." But this status, along with its potential compromise of literary property rights, threatened all professional authors. The "dunces," in fact, often attack Pope in the *same terms* that he attacks them. Just as Gildon satirizes Pope for his negotiations with booksellers in *The New Rehearsal,* so James Ralph pictures

> Sawney, a mimick Sage of huge Renown,
> To *Twick'nham* Bow'rs retir'd, enjoys his Wealth,
> His Malice and his Muse.
>
> . . .
>
> —Fam'd among Fops and Beaus,
> For Poetry and Sense, or, in effect,

---

cally encourages young men to leave the university for the stage, where Cibber and others make "twice three thousand clear" annually. This attack on Cibber's financial success appears, appropriately, in a pamphlet entitled *The Man of Taste. Occasion'd by an Epistle of Mr. Pope's on that Subject* (London, 1733).

[75] Colley Cibber, *Rhapsody upon the Marvellous* (London, 1751), 7–8.

For *stealing* other Mens; he next usurps
A Sovereign Rule, and, in *Apollo*'s stead,
Becomes the Tyrant of his fellow Bards
Hemn! he begins, attend ye Critics, hear
Ye Poets what by him the *God* ordains.
" *'Tis hard to say if greater want of Skill
Appears in writing, or in* stealing *ill.*"[76]

For Ralph, Pope can just as easily inhabit the position of hack and thus plagiarist. In Pope's construction of cultural capital, however, strategic repetition of canonical texts enhances authorial value. Cultural capital greatly complicates property in writing, constantly recreating the contingencies of ownership already inscribed in possessive individualism. Surely Pope's victory in positioning Cibber as one of the most famous plagiarists of all time owes much to Pope's comprehension of the importance of suppressing the economic as well as to Cibber's gleeful revelations.[77] Pope's own interest in the literary marketplace has been well documented;[78] eighteenth-century authorship, however, comes to depend upon a simultaneous insistence upon and denial of the material property status of writing.[79]

Thus, Cibber earned his place as the greatest plagiarist of all in part for his exposure of the economics of authorship, a gesture that threatens the emergent formation of an independent aesthetic sphere.[80] Yet Cibber also inhabited another position familiarly outside of the potential to own by configuring his public self as outside of proper masculinity. As mentioned above, Cibber played the would-be lover of Marsilia and the erotic collaborator with Phoebe Clinket, the latter offering both parody and self-parody. (The character Plotwell satirized Cibber, yet some con-

---

[76] James Ralph, *Sawney. An Heroic Poem. Occasion'd by the Dunciad* (London, 1728).

[77] At the end of his career, Cibber backpedals on this image somewhat. See his *The Egotist: Or, Colley upon Cibber, Being His Own Picture retouch'd, to so plain a Likeness, that no One, now, would have the Face to own it, but Himself* (London, 1743).

[78] See David Foxon, *Pope and the Early Eighteenth-Century Book Trade*, ed. and rev. James McLaverty (Oxford: Clarendon Press, 1991); and Rose, *Authors and Owners.*

[79] See my "Author as Ghost in the Eighteenth Century."

[80] For a fuller discussion of the way this tension plays out in the late eighteenth century and beyond, see Raymond Williams, *Culture and Society 1780–1950* (New York: Columbia University Press, 1958). More recently, Terry Eagleton takes up this problem in *The Ideology of the Aesthetic* (Cambridge, Mass.: Basil Blackwell, 1990).

temporaries insist on Cibber's obliviousness to this joke.) But in spite
of the prominence and popularity of Pix, Manley, Trotter, and Centlivre,
Cibber mentions none of them in his *Apology* and Aphra Behn only once
in reference to a revival of *Abdelazar*, "poorly written, by Mrs. *Behn*"
(1:195). Cibber's gender performance, then, consists less of an identification or sympathy with women than a location outside of dominant
masculinity, with its claims to full individuality, property rights, and
sexual inalienability. As Kristina Straub has shown, Cibber's career as
actor during the first half of the eighteenth century in itself would have
placed his sexual identity under suspicion.[81] Like Mary Pix and Aphra
Behn, Cibber understood certain forms of cultural capital as unavailable
to him. And like many women playwrights, Cibber defended himself
against the charge of plagiarism by claiming originality. In his dedication
to *Love's Last Shift*, for example, he insists: "Here, SIR, I must beg leave
to clear myself from what the ill wishes of some would have the world
believe, that what I now offer you is Spurious, and not the product of
my own labour. . . . . This DEDICATION were little better than an affront,
unless I could with all sincerity assure you, SIR, that the fable is entirely
my own; nor is there a line or thought throughout the whole, for which
I am wittingly oblig'd either to the dead, or living" (*Works*, 1:17–18).

Cibber's most consistent strategy for defining himself outside of dominant masculinity, however, was his cultivation of his role as fop. The fop
became Cibber's signature role: he wrote and performed Sir Novelty
Fashion in *Love's Last Shift*; Clodio, "a pert Coxcomb" in *Love Makes a
Man: or, the Fop's Fortune*; Lord Foppington in *The Careless Husband*;
George Brilliant in *The Lady's Last Stake*, and Witling in *The Refusal*. Cibber
mobilized this construction on the stage, on the page, and anywhere else
he might attract notice.[82] When Cibber defends the "Comforts of Vanity"
in *The Egotist*, for example, his interlocutor Frankly accuses him of
repeating the "stoical Nonchalence of that modish Philosopher my Lord
Foppington." Cibber responds by asking, "Why, how do you think I
could have given you so finish'd a Coxcomb, if I had not found a good
deal of the same Stuff in myself to make him with?"[83] While Restoration

---

[81] Kristina Straub, *Sexual Suspects: Eighteenth-Century Players and Sexual Ideology*
(Princeton: Princeton University Press, 1992). Cibber's gender position, however,
did not prevent him from also constructing his masculinity as dominant over Pope's
(Straub, 75).

[82] Ibid., 59. See also Koon, *Colley Cibber: A Biography*.

[83] Cibber, *The Egotist*, 38.

and eighteenth-century fops vary widely, Cibber's version of the fop disturbed emergent sexual binaries: "Cibber makes a spectacle of himself in a public sphere increasingly hostile to male spectacle and increasingly nervous about male homoerotic displays," Straub argues. "Cibber's tropes mediate—not always successfully—between class-based definitions of gender and oppositional models of gender and sexuality."[84] Thus, his gender construction takes its meaning less from any likeness to women than from its exteriority to dominant masculinity and its disruption of the heterosexual gendering of specular subject and object.

Significantly, the position of the fop converges with the position of plagiarist, for the fop does not inhabit the masculine position of ownership but takes the social world as text from which to borrow.[85] He incessantly copies his "betters," a quality that defines the fop or "pretty fellow" for the *Tatler*. After describing the perfect behavior of the true gentleman Sophronius, the *Tatler* turns to his shadow: "In imitation of this agreeable Being, is made that Animal we call a *Pretty Fellow*; who being just able to find out, that what makes *Sophronius* acceptable, is a natural Behavior, in order to the same Reputation, makes his own an artificial one. *Jack Dimple* is his perfect Mimick, whereby he is of course the most unlike him of all Men living."[86] Robert Gould explicitly characterizes the fop's borrowing of fashions as the equivalent of his plagiarism:

> Here *painted Ladies*, there *gay-Coxcombs* throng,
> Who, in a soft Voice, charm 'em with a *Song*;
> Their own, you may be sure, for none but such
> Can write what cou'd delight that *Sex* so much
> Some *few French words* (which plainly does express
> Their *Wit* is as much borrow'd as their *dress*)
> Does set 'em up for Poets; their whole time
> Is but one dull Fatigue of *Love* and *Rhime*.

---

[84] Straub, *Sexual Suspects*, 54.

[85] Fops, as Susan Staves points out, nevertheless become increasingly "normalized" into heterosexuality as the boundaries of gender themselves shift in the early eighteenth century. One effect of this might be, as Straub speculates in *Sexual Suspects*, to "subsume the fop's potential for sexual liminality within those ideologies and differentiate him from an increasingly visible gay male identity" (55). See Susan Staves, "A Few Kind Words for the Fop," *SEL* 22 (Summer 1982): 413–428.

[86] *Tatler*, no. 21, 28 May 1709.

These are the Women's Men, their *Demy Gods*,
For *Ladies* and *Fop-Authors* never are at odds.[87]

The author of *The Pretty Gentleman* further characterizes fops by their
replication: they display "such a Sameness . . . in all their Words and
Actions, that the Spirit of the *One* Seems to have passed into the *Other*."
Fops, like the women they gather around, eschew learning, for "there
is something in the Drudgery of *Masculine* Knowledge, by no means
adapted to Youth of so *nice* a frame."[88] The fop, then, resembles the lady
or the "hack" in his relationship to literary property: his (re)writing
necessarily appropriates inappropriately.

Nevertheless, the fop persona proved, as Kristina Straub asserts, "enabling to a public man excluded, by profession [as an actor], from
dominant models of masculinity." But it also "proved hard to shake.
Cibber's small body and high, squeaky voice discouraged him from
venturing into romantic hero parts, but it also seems likely that audiences
typed him after Sir Novelty and simply would not take him seriously in
heroic or romantic roles."[89] Like the women writers, and quite possibly
learning *from* the women writers, Cibber turned his marginality into a
position from which to establish his authorship. Further, Cibber took
advantage of opportunities unavailable to the women he both satirized
and supported: by becoming a manager, he became one of the most
successful men in the theater of his generation. On the other hand, the
constant implications of plagiarism demonstrate that he, like the women,
never entirely inhabited the position of full individual.

The position of fop articulates economic and class tensions as well as
gender and sexual ones.[90] Although the "dunces," as Pat Rogers has
argued, may not originally have come from classes any lower than did
the writers who attacked them, detractors commonly mobilized a rhetoric
that characterized the "dunces," their publishers, and their audience as
inhabiting the lower-class world of irrationality, a position that would

---

[87] Robert Gould, "A Satyr against the Play-House," in *Poems. Chiefly consisting of
Satyrs and Satryical Epistles* (London, 1688/89), 167.

[88] *The Pretty Gentleman; or Softness of Manners Vindicated, from the false Ridicule exhibited
under the Character of William Fribble, Esq.* (1747), ed. Edmund Goldsmid (Edinburgh,
1855), 12, 13.

[89] Straub, *Sexual Suspects*, 56.

[90] Ibid., chap. 3.

disqualify them from proper possessive individualism.[91] The fop frequently and unflatteringly represents a distinctively gendered form of irrationality as well as a class upstart. Etherege's classic Sir Fopling Flutter, after all, is *not* the "man of mode," but rather a country bumpkin who mimics sophistication. Cibber's Lord Foppington purchased his title just as he purchases his women; Lord Morelove describes him as "the pert coxcomb that's just come to a small estate, and a great periwig."[92] The proportion of estate to wig here characterizes Foppington, who made an advantageous marriage but does not understand the ways of the true gentleman.

Witling in *The Refusal*, however, most explicitly exposes the class instabilities associated with the fop. When the more sympathetic characters Frankley and Granger ask Witling where he gets all his money, he informs them that he earned it in the stock market: "Every Shilling, Sir; all out of Stocks, Puts, Bulls, Rams, Bears, and Bubbles" (4:23). The lady Frankley courts, in fact, has already been promised to Witling in a capitalist version of the traffic in women. Although Sir Gilbert likes Frankley, he confesses that "I am under Contract to give one of the greatest Coxcombs upon Earth the Refusal of marrying which of my Daughters he pleases" (4:20). Witling invites Frankley and Granger to join him at his favorite scene of pleasure and profit, which levels all social distinctions:

> I never go [to the Alley], but it puts me in mind of the Poetical Regions of Death, where all Mankind are upon a level; there you'll see a Duke dangling after a Director; here a Peer and a Prentice haggling for an Eighth; there a Jew and a Parson making up Differences; here a young Woman of Quality buying Bears of a Quaker; and there an old one selling Refusals to a Lieutenant of Grenadiers.
> FRAN. What a Medley of Mortals has he jumbled together?
> WIT. O here's no such fun in the Universe! (4:24)

Whereas other playwrights—Lillo comes to mind—represent participation in commerce as a form of civic virtue, Cibber creates a character

---

[91] Again, I rely here on C. B. Macpherson's reading of Locke in *The Political Theory of Possessive Individualism, Hobbes to Locke* (Oxford: Oxford University Press, 1990).

[92] Cibber, *The Careless Husband*, in *Works* 2:21.

who embodies the potential promiscuous and illicit mixing of classes through an unstable market.[93]

If the fop commonly attempts to inhabit a class position for which he possesses the money but not the "true gentlemanliness," then he expresses this lack of comprehension specifically through his clothes. Etherege's *Man of Mode* provides the best example of this in the classic scene in which Sir Foppling Flutter enumerates every item of his apparel to the amusement of the ladies. Robert Gould parodies the same vanities in members of the audience. In his satire, the fop is so oddly dressed that

> You'd think God mean 'em for a standing Jest,
> Ap't into Men for pastime to the rest:
> Observe 'em well, you'll think their Bodies made
> To wait upon the motion of the Head:
> Their Cravat-strings and Perukes so refin'd,
> They dare not tempt their Enemy, Wind:
> Of the least slender puff each Sot afraid is,
> It kills the Curls design'd to kill the Ladies.
> So still they are, in all parts ty'd so strait,
> 'Tis strange to me the blood shou'd circulate.[94]

Straub, in fact, has observed that the fop indulges such great vanity that he potentially disrupts the emergent dichotomy between the male spectator and the female object of the gaze by positioning himself as specular object. The fop's clothes disrupt not only the visual economy, but also the gendered positions within a commercial economy. As Laura Brown has recently argued, early eighteenth-century writers commonly represented women as the quintessential consumers and embodied the conception of commercialism in the figure of the woman.[95] The fop disrupts this gendered dichotomy as well as the visual one; Cibber's fops in particular expose the connection between the pretty fellow and

---

[93] See J. G. A. Pocock, *Virtue, Commerce, and History: Essays on Political Thought and History, Chiefly in the Eighteenth Century* (Cambridge: Cambridge University Press, 1985).

[94] Gould, "A Satyr," 169.

[95] Laura Brown, *The Ends of Empire: Women and Ideology in Early Eighteenth-Century English Literature* (Ithaca: Cornell University Press, 1993), see esp. intro. and chap. 6, "Imperial Disclosures: Jonathan Swift."

consumer pleasure. In *Love's Last Shift*, Sir Novelty, perhaps Cibber's most famous fop, boasts of the way his indulgence in luxury contributes to the economy: "I must confess, madam, I am for doing good to my country: for you see this suit, madam—I suppose you are not ignorant what a hard time the ribband weavers have had since the late mouring: now my design is to set the poor rogues up again, by recommending this sort of trimming . . . By the way, madam, I had fifteen hundred guineas laid in my hand, as a gratuity to encourage it: but, i'gad, I refus'd them, being too well acquainted with the consequence of taking a bribe in a national concern" (1:39). Like Southerne's Oroonoko, Sir Novelty Fashion boasts of his loyalty to the property relations of capitalism. But unlike Oroonoko and Lillo's Trueman, Sir Novelty crudely exposes economic relations, foregrounding the potential irrationality of the market itself. In his position as speculator, Witling further unites the vagaries of fashion with the vagaries of the market. Thus the eighteenth-century fop performed the part of the male consumer out of control, the specter of the propertied gender having no ability to distinguish between trinkets and solid investments. The fop role that Cibber cultivated so well became such a successful object of fascination in part because the fop embodies the anxieties that J. G. A. Pocock argues emerge as central at this time: "it was the hysteria, not the cold rationality, of economic man that dismayed the moralists."[96] To embody this irrationality in the figure of a woman performed the grotesque; to embody this irrationality in the liminal but nevertheless masculine Cibberian fop both seduced through a sheer pleasure in commodity fetishism rarely permitted to sympathetic female figures *and* fascinated through invoking the deeper threat of male economic hysteria.[97] Irrational consumer indulgence in women attracts the relentless satire of Jonathan Swift;[98] irrational consumer indulgence in a man self-positioned outside of dominant masculine gender identity attracts public fascination.

---

[96] Pocock, *Virtue, Commerce, and History*, 113.

[97] While Cibber's fops fall outside of dominant masculinity, though, they are rarely despicable characters. Both Kristina Straub and Susan Staves point out, in fact, that Cibber represents his fops more sympathetically than did most playwrights. See Straub, *Sexual Suspects*, and Staves, "A Few Kind Words."

[98] See Brown, *Ends of Empire*; Felicity A. Nussbaum, *The Brink of All We Hate: English Satires on Women, 1660–1750* (Lexington: University Press of Kentucky, 1984); Ellen Pollak, *The Poetics of Sexual Myth: Gender and Ideology in the Verse of Swift and Pope* (Chicago: University of Chicago Press, 1985).

Colley Cibber, then, became the biggest plagiarist of the Augustan age in part because he exploited liminal gender and economic positions that advanced his career but nevertheless cast suspicion on his ability to inhabit the position of owner. For whatever reason—his physical appearance, his foreignness, his status as actor (which made a dissociation with the marketplace and popular culture impossible)—Cibber built a career at the confluence of Grub Street and the feminine. His authorial strategy sometimes comes closer to that of the early women playwrights than it does to that of his male contemporaries. In his simultaneous appropriation and claim to originality, he resembles Cavendish; in his consciousness of the gendered authorial body behind dramatic performance, he resembles Behn; and in his negotiations around the dominant masculine high culture, he resembles Susanna Centlivre, as we will see in the next chapter. Further, he almost literally paraded his Grub Street complicity with the popular and the profitable. But to end here would tell only one part of Cibber's career. Unlike many Grub Street authors, Cibber achieved great success and a measure of respectability: he became the poet laureate and teased Pope for attacking him out of a jealousy that Cibber traveled in more elite circles with less talent.[99] And if he adopted some of the strategies for owning literary property that women had discovered, he was nevertheless not a woman, nor was he particularly sympathetic toward female authorship. Even becoming the star of *The Dunciad* granted a kind of cultural importance to Cibber's career that was unavailable to Cavendish, Behn, Manley, or his less famous but equally talented contemporary, Susanna Centlivre.

[99] "Letter from Mr. Cibber to Mr. Pope."

FIVE

Writing (as) the Lady's Last Stake: Susanna Centlivre

Susanna Centlivre achieved neither the fame nor the notoriety of Colley Cibber, although she did become a significant force on the London stage during the first quarter of the eighteenth century. Her plays continued to be popular long after her death; David Garrick, in fact, chose the lead in her *Wonder* as his farewell performance.[1] Measured by stage longevity, Centlivre led the most successful career of all the women who began writing for the stage at the century's end.[2] Her popularity, however, did not preserve her from attack: although Pope aimed the bulk of his satire in the *Dunciad* at other men, he devoted a line in his catalog of dunces to Centlivre and Eliza Haywood. Pope elsewhere satirized Centlivre as one of Curll's hacks:[3] Centlivre (like Haywood) not only wrote, but wrote

---

[1] For Centlivre's career, see F. P. Lock, *Susanna Centlivre* (Boston: Twayne, 1979). Additional details about the stage history of Centlivre's plays accompany Richard C. Frushell's facsimile edition of *The Plays of Susanna Centlivre* (New York: Garland, 1982).

[2] Jacqueline Pearson, *The Prostituted Muse: Images of Women and Women Dramatists, 1642–1737* (New York: Harvester Wheatsheaf, 1988), 202. Pearson speculates that Centlivre combined the Orinda and Astrea types, with her racy past but quiet married life. Further, Pearson names Centlivre "the greatest comic playwright of the eighteenth century" (255).

[3] In Pope's *A Full and true Account of a Horrid and Barbarous Revenge by Poison on the Body of Mr. Edmund Curll, Bookseller,* he imagines that Curll remembers Centlivre in his will: "He clos'd the Book, fetch'd a Groan, and recommended to Mrs. *Curll* to give Forty Shillings to the Poor of the Parish of St. *Dunstan's,* and a *Week's Wages* Advance to each of his Gentlemen Authors, with some small Gratuity in particular to Mrs. *Centlivre.*" Quoted by John Wilson Bowyer, *The Celebrated Mrs. Centlivre* (Durham, N.C.: Duke University Press, 1952), 191.

unabashedly for money. The most thorough attack on Centlivre (as well as women playwrights in general) was leveled by way of the character Phoebe Clinket of *Three Hours after Marriage*. Centlivre was portrayed as absurd, obscene, plagiaristic, and so desperate for exposure that she would attempt to slip her plays to the public under Plotwell/Cibber's name. The irony of this accusation is rich: Cibber seems to have used her rejected manuscript as the foundation for a play in much the same way that Powell used Mary Pix's. Years before *Three Hours*, however, Centlivre was already fighting the charge of plagiarism. As she objected in her dedication to *The Platonick Lady*, "Some have arm'd themselves with resolution not to like the Play they paid to see; and if in spite of Spleen they have been pleas'd against their Will, have maliciously reported it was none of mine, but given me by some Gentleman: Nay, even my own Sex, which shou'd assert our Prerogative against such Detractors, are often backward to encourage a Female Pen."[4] In spite of accusations of taking a man's play and attempting to pass it off as her own (the opposite of what *Three Hours* charges her with, but both remain part of the discourse of plagiarism), Centlivre constructed her authorship in terms of originality. She even became known for her skillful plotting and innovative contrivances.[5]

While writing for the stage—and acting on it as well—would have threatened Centlivre's reputation, she nevertheless earned a living and even gained a certain kind of respect as a popular and clever inventor of comic plots. Centlivre seems to have recognized the type of career possible for a professional woman writer and carefully negotiated the boundaries of literary property. For many critics of her generation, the phrase "female hack" was redundant; Centlivre, however, exploited the institution of cultural capital by claiming a position outside of it. Unlike Delariviere Manley, who found herself ridiculed for her imagined pretense to excel Shakespeare and Jonson, Centlivre seems to have understood that a woman such as herself, who had run away from home as a teenager, who played both male and female characters on stage, and who could not even claim Manley's upper-class background, would best

[4] Dedication to *The Platonick Lady* (1707), in *The Plays of Susanna Centlivre*. Future references to Centlivre's plays are from this facsimile edition and are cited in the text.

[5] Giles Jacob, *The Poetical Register: Or, the Lives and Characters of the English Dramatick Poets*, 2 vols. (London, 1724), 2:32–33.

survive by aiming her ambitions toward the popular.[6] Only one side beckoned in the battle between the ancients and moderns. In spite of the vast differences in class and political perspectives (Centlivre remained a dedicated Whig), her career in some ways recalls that of Margaret Cavendish, for both found ways to circumvent masculine literary property as a strategy for claiming their own.

Centlivre absorbed a range of authorial strategies from women playwrights before her. She adopted the name "Astrea" as well as the possessive individualism of Aphra Behn without the longing for a world without it; she found, like Cavendish, that originality best ensures women's property, although she could not claim the duchess's aristocratic singularity; she located herself, like the "female wits," in a context of women writers, but alternately pleaded for sex-blind and sex-conscious evaluation. In the context of the emergent eighteenth-century paradox of authorship in which writing had to both become and transcend property, Centlivre claimed possession in part by relinquishing the cultural capital that could provide the basis for transcendence. Her most reliable strategy might be called a "feminist individualism," for she remained committed to Whig politics, Lockean individual rights, and some freedoms for women. She claimed to own by innovating, making little pretension to an elite poetic genealogy. Her attempt to inhabit the position of individual, however, gave rise to contradictions in her authorship; her plays themselves explore similar contradictions faced by women characters. Centlivre's career and plays reveal the contradictions inherent in a feminist individualism that seeks ways for women to inhabit the (masculine) position of full social subjectivity. In her own career, Centlivre acted in male drag and sometimes wrote anonymously; her published plays sometimes indicate a male author. The plays themselves further expose both the possibilities and the limitations of a feminism founded on liberal individualism. Her drama tends to insist upon certain freedoms for women, but at the same time reveals, under the guise of romantic love, little more than a rejection of a paternal form of patriarchy in favor of a fraternal version of the same. With no absolutist order to secure privileges for *some* women (as in Cavendish) or even a nostalgic

[6] Manley, of course, had the reputation of being a notorious hack herself. Part of the scandal that Manley was able to stir up, however, depended on her sometime access to elite society.

longing for a heroic monarch (as in Behn), upon the comic closure of marriage the women in Centlivre's plays find themselves with little to call their own.

Authorial Strategies

Centlivre may not have articulated anxiety over plagiarism and insisted on originality with the same obsessive passion as Cavendish, but she shared—or perhaps even emulated—Cavendish's consciousness of women's differing capacity to appropriate. Like her precursor, Centlivre experimented with the fluidity of gender identity; but whereas the duchess dressed extravagantly out of pleasure, Centlivre's performative and authorial transvestisms were professional. For the most part, Centlivre avoided obvious appropriation when writing under her own name; in masculine disguise, however, she rewrote more freely. When publishing incognito, she celebrated intertextuality; when publishing as a woman, she insisted on her originality. Her first play, *The Perjur'd Husband*, was produced at Drury Lane in 1700 and published under her then-name, Susanna Carroll. Apparently the play met with disapproval, for the printed edition includes a biting message "To the Reader" complaining that "the Beaux usually take a greater liberty with our sex than they wou'd with their own, because there's no fear of drawing a Duel upon their hands." Like Aphra Behn, Centlivre found herself accused of sexual freedoms that would have passed unnoticed in a male author. Her next play (*The Beau's Duel: Or a Soldier for the Ladies*, 1702) includes a prologue ascribed to "a Gentleman" that contemplates Centlivre's gendered relationship to literary property and cultural capital:

What Hazard Poets run, in Times like these,
Sure to Offend, uncertain whom to please:
If in a well-work'd Story they aspire,
To imitate Old *Rome*'s or *Athens*' Fire,
It will not do, for strait the Cry shall be,
'Tis a forc'd heavy piece of Bombastry.
If Comedy's their Theam, 'tis Ten to one
It dwindles into Farce, and then 'tis gone.
If Farce their Subject be, this Witty Age

Holds that below the Grandeur of the Stage.
Our Female Author, tho' she sees what Fate
Does the Event of such Attempts still wait;
With a true Brittish Courage ventures on,
Thinks nothing Honour, without Danger won.

Unlike Marsilia and Calista, Centlivre studiously avoided the imitation of Rome and Athens, finding greater possibilities "below the Grandeur of the Stage" for most of her career. Many of her plays—including the *Beau's Duel*—in fact border on farce. This prologue, though not necessarily written by Centlivre, articulates a consciousness of the dangers of female authorship, but in particular of any woman who would attempt to make the discourse of the ancients her own. Since this prologue prefaces a farcical comedy, its author articulates a preference for the popular culture risk of falling below the stage's "grandeur" to the high-culture risk of poorly imitating the fires of Rome and Athens.

After the *Beau's Duel*, Centlivre produced her most explicit appropriations: an adaptation/translation of Molière called *Love's Contrivance* and a revision of Thomas May's *The Heir* as *The Stolen Heiress*. Neither, however, appeared under Centlivre's name, offering instead the impression of a male author. The prologue to *The Stolen Heiress* reports that "Our Author fear[s] his success" and the preface to *Love's Contrivance* complains that "a Man may write to please the Town, but 'tis uncertain." Centlivre exposes her own appropriation for *The Heiress* on the title page, along with the futility of originality: "Nihil dictum quod non ante dictum." The preface to *Love's Contrivance* also freely admits the author's adaptation of another play: "Some Scenes I confess are partly taken from *Molier*, and I dare be bold to say it has not suffer'd in the Translation: I thought 'em pretty in the French, and cou'd not help believing they might divert in an English Dress." In publishing *The Gamester*, her first popular success, Centlivre continues to write as a man and continues to represent her authorship as appropriative: "Part of it I own my self oblig'd to the *French* for, particularly the Character of the *Gamester*; but he is intirely ruin'd in the *French*: whereas I, in Complaisance to the many fine Gentlemen that Play in *England*, have reclaim'd him, after I have discover'd the ill Consequence of Gaming, that very often happens to those who are too passionately fond of it; I shall not inlarge upon the Alteration, but refer Your Lordship to the Original." In this masculine persona, Centlivre develops a swaggering superiority to the French as well as an imperialistic reclaiming of this character on behalf of her countrymen. When publishing as a man, Centlivre exposes the process of appropriation.

When Centlivre reveals herself as a woman (again), her authorial strategies become both gender-conscious and reticent about intertextuality. She energetically defends women's authorial legitimacy, sometimes by demanding equality, sometimes by pleading that women can inhabit the masculine position of authorship in the absence of men, and sometimes by expressing amazement and disappointment that the promised parity of individualism collapses into a hierarchy of gender. Before one play, for example, she pleads that the audience endure her text in the absence of a man's:

> Since War, and Places claim the Bards that write,
> Be kind, and bear a Woman's Treat to Night;
> Let your Indulgence all her Fears allay,
> And none but Woman-Haters damn this Play.[7]

Women's plays deserve a fair hearing, but remain a wartime substitute for the writing of true authors. Elsewhere Centlivre appeals to women in the audience to support her efforts and forgive her flaws. The prologue to *The Wonder* announces that the author "fears the Criticks of the Stage/ Who like Barbarians, spare nor Sex, nor Age." Centlivre sues to a few *"Candid Judges"* and

> To the bright Circle of the Fair, she next,
> Commits her Cause, with Anxious Doubts Perplext.
> Where can she with such hopes of Favour kneel,
> As to those Judges, who her Frailties feel?
> A few Mistakes, her Sex may well excuse,
> And such a Plea, No *Woman* should refuse:
> If she succeeds, a *Woman* gains Applause,
> What *Female* but must favour such a Cause.

She optimistically dedicates her *Platonick Lady*, which itself honors learned women, to *"all the Generous Encouragers of* Female Ingenuity" and in the dedication attacks assumptions of women's literary illegitimacy:

[7] Centlivre, prologue, *"By the Author of* Tunbridge-Walks," in *The Busy Body* (1709).

"A Play secretly introduc'd to the House, whilst the Author remains unknown, is approv'd by every Body: The Actors cry it up, and are in expectation of a great Run; the Bookseller of a Second Edition, and the Scribler of a Sixth Night: But if by chance the Plot's discover'd, and the Brat found Fatherless, immediately it flags in the Opinion of those that extoll'd it before, and the Bookseller falls in his Price, with this Reason only, *It is a Woman's*. Thus they alter their Judgment, by the Esteem they have for the Author, tho' the Play is still the same." In authorship as in reproduction, only a *father*, she protests, can grant legitimacy.[8] Here Centlivre articulates a consciousness that the promised equality of possessive individualism collapses with the revelation of gender.

In constructing her defense of women's authorship, Centlivre echoes both Behn and Cavendish, although she ultimately forges a feminist individualism alien to both of them; she remains loyal to this philosophy, but nevertheless notices and sometimes protests its contradictions.[9] She recounts, much as does Behn in her preface to *The Dutch Lover*, how a "Spark" saw her *Gamester* three or four times and "having bought one of the Books, ask'd who the Author was; and being told, a Woman, threw down the Book." She echoes the duchess in her separation of poetic capacity from learning: "And why this Wrath against the Womens Works? Perhaps you'll answer, because they meddle with things out of their Sphere: But I say, no; for since the Poet is born, why not a Woman as well as a Man? Not that I wou'd derogate from those great Men who have a Genius, and Learning to improve that Genius: I only object against those ill-nature'd Criticks, who wanting both, think they have a sufficient claim to Sense, by railing at what they don't understand" (dedication to *The Platonick Lady*). Like Cavendish, Centlivre represents genius as inborn and independent of access to the masculine discourse of learning; unlike Cavendish, she identifies a distinct women's tradition: "would these profest Enemies but consider what Examples we have had of Women that excell'd in all Arts; in Musick, Painting, Poetry; also in War," raising Queen Anne herself as the final argument for the possibility

[8] As Mark Rose argues, paternity remained a popular if problematic metaphor for authorial property in the early eighteenth century. See *Authors and Owners: The Invention of Copyright* (Cambridge: Harvard University Press, 1993), 38–39.

[9] See Pearson's chapter on Centlivre in *The Prostituted Muse*. Pearson explores the extent to which Centlivre's insistence on women's individual liberty emerges from her Whig commitments.

of female greatness.[10] Like the women before her, Centlivre observes
and protests the refusal to grant women property in their writing; she
objects that some maliciously report, as mentioned earlier, that her plays
are "none of mine, but given me by some Gentleman." Although early
in her career Centlivre found safety in anonymity and male disguise,
she later publicly insisted on her property and her identity. For Centlivre,
perhaps a woman can only truly own her plays by owning them.

Granting that women writers benefit from models of excellence, Centlivre, like Cavendish, nevertheless insists that female authorship must
ultimately be self-creating. It may seem odd to find the same strategies
for women's writing in a "Tory absolutist" and a Whig individualist, yet
both women recognized their gendered exteriority to full social and
political subjecthood within those ideologies (nonetheless remaining
doggedly loyal to them). In her masculine authorial identity, Centlivre
translates and appropriates Molière; in her feminine identity, however,
she avoids and veils most rewriting.[11] While she modestly complains that
"the Muses, like most Females, are least liberal to their own sex," Centlivre
identifies the single advantage of her feminine position as a greater
capacity for originality: "All I dare say in Favour of this Piece is, that the
Plot is entirely New, and the Incidents wholly owing to my own Invention;
not borrowed from our own, or translated from the Works of any foreign
Poet; so that they have at least the Charm of Novelty to recommend
'em."[12] She repeats this insistence in verse:

> To Night we come upon a bold Design,
> To try to please without one borrow'd Line:
> Our Plot is new, and regularly clear,
> And not one single Tittle from *Molière*:

[10] Centlivre's female authorial persona includes tropes of modesty as well, especially
in dedications. In her dedication of *A Bold Stroke for a Wife* to Philip, duke and marquis
of Warton, she wishes, in sharp contrast to her previous masculine positions, that "I
were capable to cloath the following Scenes in such a Dress, as might be worthy to
appear before Your Grace." Being a woman, however, prevents this perfection: "The
Muses, like most Females, are least liberal to their own Sex."

[11] It is not clear that Centlivre always would have had control over whether or not
her name appeared on her published plays; she does, however, seem to have gone
through a period when she preferred anonymity.

[12] Centlivre, dedication to *A Bold Stroke for a Wife.*

O'er bury'd Poets we with Caution tread,
And Parish Sextons leave to rob the Dead.[13]

The prologue also flirtatiously exploits the author's feminine identity
by referring to "Our Female Wit," who has such warm feelings about
soldiers that she made one the hero of her play. The parsimony of the
Muses, the claimed intimacy with soldiers, and the resolution to tread
cautiously around dead poets converge in Centlivre's authorial self-positioning as outside of masculine appropriation and cultural capital. She
wrote mostly comedy, and in the epilogue to *The Busy Body* explicitly
rejects "Sowr Critics, [who] Time and Breath, and Censure waste,/ And
baulk your Pleasure to refine your Taste." Thus she avoids both inappropriate appropriation and claims to original genius through the overly
modest configuration of her work as trivial novelty.

Whether or not Centlivre's plays actually *were* more original, she succeeded in acquiring this reputation (as well as, contradictorily, a reputation for plagiarism). Male critics, however, carefully distinguished her
innovation from original genius. Giles Jacob, who revised Langbaine's
Account, identifies Centlivre's talent as "Comedy, particularly in the Contrivance of the Plots and Incidents" and finds sources for only three of
the eighteen plays that he lists.[14] Steele explicitly associates Centlivre's
talent for plotting with her gender: "On Saturday last was presented,
THE BUSY BODY, a comedy, written . . . by a woman. The plot and
incidents of the play are laid with the subtilty of spirit which is peculiar
to females of wit, and is very seldom well performed by those of the
other sex, in whom craft in love is an act of invention, and not, as with
women, the effect of nature and instinct."[15] Steele writes condescendingly
of Centlivre and gives her no credit for an artistic product; at the same
time, however, he only repeats her own self-fashioning.[16] Centlivre, like

[13] Centlivre, prologue to *A Bold Stroke for a Wife*. This prologue is attributed to "a
Gentleman," but the sentiment matches Centlivre's own in the dedication so closely
that she may have been complicitous in, if not the author of, this poem.
[14] Repeating Centlivre's own representation, Jacob calls *Love's Contrivance* a "Translation from *Molière*" and *The Gamester* "an improv'd Translation of one under the
same Title in *French*." Of *The Cruel Gift*, he writes, "for the Story of this Play, see
Signismonda and *Guiscarda*, a Novel of *Boccace*." *The Poetical Register* 2:33–34.
[15] [Sir Richard Steele], *Tatler*, no. 19, 1709. Quoted by Bowyer, *The Celebrated Mrs.
Centlivre*, 98.
[16] Generally, Steele praised Centlivre, if condescendingly, for they found themselves aligned as fellow Whigs. See Lock, *Susanna Centlivre*.

Cavendish, often disavowed her intertexuality; unlike Cavendish, however, she wrote professionally and without claim to genius. Cavendish's struggle to own her texts parallels her struggle to possess full, as opposed to specifically feminine, aristocratic privileges. Centlivre insists on her ownership from a feminist individualist perspective, eschewing claims to cultural capital. She negotiates her ownership of literary property by—when she writes as a woman—disavowing appropriation.

Centlivre encountered the contradictions of her feminist individualism in politics as well as in literary property. In spite of her enduring dedication to the Whigs and literary activism in their favor,[17] Centlivre also represents herself as outside the political world of men. She makes this claim in the prologue to *Marplot* (1711, sequel to the popular and hilarious *Busy Body*), describing her own comic art as artless:

> The Men of Wit do now their Brains fatigue
> So much with Politicks and State-Intrigue!
> That there's not one Male-Poet of the Age
> Will condescend to labour for the Stage.
> Therefore our Author, tho' no *Rules* she knows,
> What Nature prompts, with Artless Hand bestows.

She characterizes her composition as a trivial entertainment compared to the political work of men, and also compares writing for the stage to sexual availability: "For once, then, break old Custom; be not e'er-nice,/ But let the *self-same* Woman please you *Twice*." The prologue to *The Perplex'd Lovers* makes a similar claim to both skillful erotic scheming and political innocence: the author "plots, contrives, embroils, foments Confusion,/ And yet to Politicks makes not the least Allusion"—although here the irony lies in the author's comparison of the play to its notorious epilogue flattering Prince Eugene of Savoy and the duke of Marlborough, recently dismissed from his post and greatly out of favor with the Tories.[18]

---

[17] See Bowyer, *The Celebrated Mrs. Centlivre*, esp. chap. 7. Centlivre composed several poems praising Whig leaders.

[18] Although Centlivre frequently claimed originality, she wrote a preface after the stage failure of *The Perplex'd Lovers* claiming she took "very little Pains" with it, "most of the Plot being from a Spanish play." Curiously, though, she fails to name this play, and as F. P. Lock points out in *Susanna Centlivre*, no Spanish play has yet been identified as her source (89). Perhaps she fabricated appropriation in this instance as a way to deny responsibility for and property in this unpopular text.

The theater managers suppressed these verses, first because they had been unable to obtain a license in time and later because a rumor spread that Centlivre had written a "notorious[ly] whiggish epilogue."[19]

In response to attacks on her political participation, Centlivre comically agrees to relinquish her ownership and implicitly her individuality: she supplied replacement verses abdicating life, liberty, and literary property. To deliver them, Mr. Norris appears in mourning, announcing that the audience's rejection caused the death of the author. Nevertheless, he explains, she has "left you all her Heirs":

> First to the Ladies, she bequeaths her Spouse;
> To th'Beaus, some Copies of soft Billet-doux.
> She knew that few of them, alas! love thinking,
> Their chiefest Talent lyes in Dress and Winking.
> To th' Plyant Girles, and Gamesters of the Pit,
> If they can find it out—she leaves her Wit.
> To all the Soldiers, when the Wars shall cease,
> She leaves her Pen, to purchase Bread in Peace.
> Her Plots, Contrivances, and Stratagems,
> She leaves t'intreaguing Wives of Citizens.
> Dramatick Rules, and Scraps of Poetry,
> She leaves those—ay, ay, those she leaves to me.

Like Steele, Centlivre represents her own form of innovation as an extension of inborn feminine wiles: she erases the difference between sexual negotiations and the plotting of a play, wit on stage and wit amongst masks and gallants, billets-doux written for published collections and those treasured by beaux.[20] The pen, left to hungry soldiers, transforms these negotiations into commodities. Once again, Centlivre configures her authorship as safely "artless," giving away to the audience

---

[19] Lock, *Susanna Centlivre*, 23.

[20] The prologue to *The Cruel Gift*, written by Mr. Sewell, makes a similar argument on Centlivre's behalf:

> Our *Woman* says, for 'tis a *Woman's* Wit,
> (That *single Word* will fain us half the *Pit*)
> This is her first Attempt in *Tragick-Stuff*;
> And here's *Intrigue*, and *Plot* and *Love* enough.
> The Devil's in it, if the *Sex* can't write
> Those Things in which *They* take the most Delight.

and actors all claims to inhabit the position of owner.[21] Thus, Centlivre's feminist individualism takes the form of temporary claims to inhabit the position of individual and owner, as well as a preparedness to back off from those claims when confronted with their gendered limitations. In an age in the process of defining the author as a proprietor, Centlivre represents herself as dead to ownership.

Even when Centlivre does claim the authority of her own literary property, she locates it outside of cultural capital or "taste," defining herself as a writer for bread. Unlike many of her male colleagues, Centlivre did not publish a collection of her plays; one did not appear, in fact, until almost forty years after her death. She frequently proclaims in prefaces and dedications a greater concern for performance; a printed volume signified a kind of prestige that Centlivre avoided asserting.[22] Dedications, which demand the poet's praise of the patron's taste, presented a particular problem that Centlivre twice resolved by pleading that her gender excused her from such evaluations. In the dedication to *The Busy Body*, she writes: "And here, my Lord, the Occasion seems fair for me to engage in a Panegyrick upon those Natural and Acquired Abilities, which so brightly Adorn your Person: But I shall resist that Temptation, being conscious of the Inequity of a Female Pen to so Masculine an Attempt." In her dedication to *The Man's Bewitch'd*, she similarly argues that "To attempt your Grace's Character, is the superiour business of a Masculine Pen."

Finally, when the problems of gender, patronage, and literary property converge in her plea to Charles Joye for stock, Centlivre represents herself as an unabashed hack, yet modestly avoids an unseemly desire

---

[21] Centlivre similarly represents herself as curious about but nevertheless alien to the complexities of science. In a complimentary poem to Anne Oldfield, she marvels at the idea of a

> *Plurality of Worlds!* Such Things may be,
> But I am best convinc'd by what I see;
> Yet tho' *Philosophers* such Schemes pursue,
> And *fancy'd Worlds* in every *Planet* view;
> They can but *guess* at Orbs *above* the Skies,
> And *darkly paint* the Lakes and Hills that rise.

Published in William Egerton, *Faithful Memoirs of the Life, Amours, and Performances of that Justly Celebrated, and most Eminent Actress of her Time, Mrs. Anne Oldfield* (London, 1731), 59. Quoted in Bowyer, *The Celebrated Mrs. Centlivre*, 149.

[22] On the prestige of print, see Julie Stone Peters, *Congreve, the Drama, and the Printed Word* (Stanford: Stanford University Press, 1990).

for compensation by assuring this potential donor that all such cravings belong to her husband alone. Like Cavendish, Centlivre uses her subordination to her husband as an apology for writing. But while the aristocratic duchess signs over all her literary property to the duke as part of his conjugal estate and privileges, Centlivre assures this potential patron that any desire for money must be understood as a desire for domestic harmony. In her verse "Letter from Mrs. C--e, to Mr. *Joye*, Deputy-Governour of the SOUTH-SEA," first published separately and later included in a collection of poems, Centlivre attempts to attract the deputy-governor's patronage by reminding him of her persistent loyalty to the Whig cause. Whig leaders, she gently complains, have failed to reward those who promoted them: "*Whigs* in Place have still been known/ To help all Parties but their own:/ To *Charles* the Second's Maxim kind,/ Advance your Foes, your Friends ne'er mind."[23] On the one hand, Centlivre positions herself in one of the most commonly satirized authorial positions: the hack for party politics. Yet Tories tease her because the party she writes for ignores her:

> Yet, Madam, are you unprovided?
> You, who stickled late and early,
> Against the wicked Schemes of H--y;
> And clearly prov'd by Dint of Reason,
> To name the *Chevalier* was Treason;
> Why, Faith, I think it very hard,
> So brave a *Whig* is not prefer'd.
> One might have thought this Golden Age,
> You'd left off Writing for the Stage;
> And from *South-Sea* got Gold—true *Sterling*,
> Enough to keep your Coach, or *Berlin*. (1:178)

On the other hand, she also denies any desire for material reward. The modest living she ekes out of the stage, she responds to this imagined attack, suffices for her: "Not that I want for wholesome Diet/ Bread, and

---

[23] Susannah Centlivre, "Letter from Mrs. C--e," in *A Miscellaneous Collection of Poems, Songs, and Epigrams*, 2 vols. (Dublin, 1721), 1:175–84, 178. Future references are cited in the text. Originally entitled "A Woman's CASE: in an Epistle to CHARLES JOYE, Esq; Deputy-Governor of the *South Sea*" (1720). Bowyer reprints passages from this poem in *The Celebrated Mrs. Centlivre*, 226–229.

my Muse, with Peace and Quiet:/ I would prefer, were I to chuse." But
her husband,

> who understands
> Nought to be good, but Bills and Bonds,
> The ready Cash, or fruitful Lands,
> Begins new Quarrels every Day,
> And frights my dear-lov'd Muse away.

Mr. Centlivre, not Susanna, desires patronage to supplement the meager
income from his wife's drama:

> Duce take your Scribbling Vein, quoth he,
> What did it ever get for me?
> Two Years you take a Play to write,
> And I scarce get my Coffee by't:
> Such swinging Bills are still to pay,
> For Sugar, Chocolate, and Tea,
> I shall be forced to run away. (1:179–180)

If she prevails, however, Mr. Centlivre vows "to be the best of MEN": "In
this, if you advance my State,/ I'll be your constant Loving Mate" (1:183).

Even the degraded individuality of a party hack, then, becomes discur-
sively available to Centlivre only intermittently. She comically represents
her husband as both tyrannically opposing her stage career *and* using his
influence to encourage her to seek patronage. What this poem reveals,
however, is less the individual oppression of a wife by a husband (Centlivre's career, in fact, flourished after this marriage) than Centlivre's
recognition of the unseemliness of requesting money on her own behalf.
Centlivre in this instance negotiates her position by representing a desired material exchange as the ambition to excel as a wife; she uses her
husband's posited desires to justify an exchange that epitomizes the hack
relationship. Further, Centlivre carefully represents her own writing as
merely supplying a modest but sufficient way of procuring bread: hacking
provides the interdependent opposition not only to cultural capital, but
also to working in order to satisfy any taste for luxury of her own. She
merely asks for the stock out of a desire to please her husband's longing
for small indulgences. Rather than attempting to convince Joye that

patronizing her advances knowledge, learning, and British culture, Cent-livre appeals to him to help her become a better wife.[24]

Centlivre and Cibber: Intertextual Tensions

Colley Cibber grew rich, famous, and powerful as a flamboyant hack, a position made possible by both his gender and the gender anxieties he provoked. Hostile fascination fed his career. Centlivre, however, did not become the most famous plagiarist of the eighteenth century, positioning herself instead as both a wife and a common hack who invented plots and contrivances with feminine skill. Cibber and Centlivre did not share the complex and documented history that Aphra Behn shared with Killigrew, nor did Cibber openly appropriate one of her plays the way Southerne did *Oroonoko*. Their intersecting careers, however, reveal both literal and symbolic tensions over their differing, gendered positions in relation to literary property. In one incident, Cibber seems to have plagiarized a play that Centlivre submitted to Drury Lane and that he rejected. In several others cases, however, he less directly rewrote Cent-livre's plots, taking advantage of her acute ear for popular themes but revising her feminist individualist representation of property.

When Centlivre submitted her *Love at a Venture* to Drury Lane, she had no personal reason to satirize Cibber in particular as a fop author. She would soon acquire one. Cibber rejected *Love*, but produced *The Double Gallant*—a play with striking similarities—under his own name shortly thereafter. Centlivre's eighteenth-century biographer, in fact, reports that she "used to complain" that Cibber "had taken in the greatest Part of her Play."[25] Unlike Mary Pix, however, Centlivre found some vocal supporters, perhaps as a result Cibber's reputation for plagiarism. Enemies leaped at the chance to charge Cibber once again with a viola-

---

[24] Bowyer implies that this poem probably did not result in patronage since Cent-livre mentions "A *Quondam South-Sea* Director" as one of the living dead in *The Artifice*, act 5. Bowyer, *The Celebrated Mrs. Centlivre*, 229, n.16. Her satirists John Gay and Alexander Pope, by contrast, each received gifts of South-Sea stock from James Cragg.

[25] John Mottley, *A List of All the Dramatic Authors, with some Account of their Lives; and of all the Dramatic Pieces ever published in the English Language to the Year 1747.* Appended to Thomas Whincop, *Scanderbeg, or, Love and Liberty* (London, 1747). Quoted in Bowyer, *The Celebrated Mrs. Centlivre*, 80.

tion of literary property, in spite of his greater power relative to Centlivre. Barton Booth wrote to Aaron Hill that "as soon as the good-natur'd Town found [Cibber] out, they resented his calling [*The Double Gallant*] a new Play, and *hounded* it in a most outrageous Manner."[26] Booth identifies Cibber's sources as plays by Burnaby and by Centlivre. Although such a response must remain in the context of Cibber's own self-positioning as a fop-author and the consequent eagerness to identify him with plagiarism, and although Cibber himself clearly did not respect Centlivre's capacity to own, she nevertheless appears to have achieved enough popularity to earn recognition for her ownership from others. Centlivre, in fact, did not invent the eponymous double gallant—a man who courts two women by pretending to be two men (played by Cibber himself in his *Double Gallant*)—for this device appears in Corneille's *Le Galant double* and Calderon's *Hombre pobre todo es trazas*. Booth, however, implicitly attributes this character to Centlivre.[27] Decades later, the anonymous author of *The Laureat* specifically represents the incident as the theft of Centlivre's property:

> There was at this Time a certain *Poetess* in *Rome*, called *Fulvia* [Centlivre], who had sometimes succeeded in Characters of Humour on the Stage; she offer'd a Play to the Perusal of *Aesopus* [Cibber]; in this Play she had drawn the Character of a very impudent Fellow, who in the same Play acted under his own Appearance two different Persons, and persuaded his Mistress to believe him not to be himself in Opposition to her Senses; this Character *Aesopus* scouted extremely. Why, Madam, said he, this would be putting upon the Audience indeed; they will never bear it; 'tis extravagant, it is outraging Nature, it is silly, and it is not ridiculous. The poor Lady was beat out of her Design; but as our Corrector had the Play left sometime in his Hand, he culled out this very Character, mix'd it with some other Felonies of the same Nature, which he had committed, and had it acted as his own the very next Year.[28]

Perhaps in response to such attacks, Cibber acknowledges his intertextuality several times but never mentions Centlivre. The prologue to

---

[26] Barton Booth to Aaron Hill, *A Collection of Letters, Never before printed: Written . . . To the Late Aaron Hill, Esq.* (London, 1751), 80. Quoted in Bowyer, *The Celebrated Mrs. Centlivre*, 82.

[27] For Centlivre's foreign sources, see Bowyer, *The Celebrated Mrs. Centlivre*, 78–79.

[28] *The Laureat: or, The Right Side of Colley Cibber* (London, 1740), 111–112; quoted in Bowyer, *The Celebrated Mrs. Centlivre*, 80.

The Double Gallant claims both originality and the lack of it, arguing that although "from former scenes some hints he [Cibber] draws/ The ground-plot's wholly chang'd from what it was," hoping the audience will find "enough that's new,/In plot, in persons, wit, and humour too:/ Yet what's not his, he owns in other's right."[29] In his autobiography, however, Cibber represents Centlivre's plot (without naming Centlivre) as waste matter and therefore open to salvaging efforts: *The Double Gallant*, he writes, "was a Play made up of what little was tolerable in two or three others that had no Success, and were laid aside as so much Poetical Lumber; but by collecting and adapting the best Parts of them all into one Play, the *Double Gallant* has had a Place every Winter . . . these Thirty Years."[30] While Restoration revisers represent earlier texts as raw material, Cibber here recognizes Centlivre's play as an artifact (not nature), but nevertheless as one whose low quality does not merit ownership. In his assumption that personal and socially contingent judgments of taste determine the proprietary status of a text, Cibber contributes to the emergent eighteenth-century distinction between the status of an artifact signified as an aesthetic object and one signified as "merely" commercial.

Having defined Centlivre's efforts as common (in both senses), however, Cibber immediately backs off from any claims to cultural capital, comparing himself to a cobbler who "may be allow'd to be useful though he is not famous: And I hope a Man is not blameable for doing a little Good, tho' he cannot do as much as another?" Cibber closes this case by returning to his self-representation as a hack, resigning himself to the fact that "Twopenny Criticks must live as well as Eighteenpenny Authors."[31] In spite of their profoundly entangled professional careers—Cibber, for example, acted in Centlivre's next play—the laureate never mentions Centlivre's name in regard to *The Double Gallant*, as if to reject the possibility that one could benefit from a woman writer. While he does not, like Southerne, rewrite the plot to disinherit his female precur-

[29] *The Dramatic Works of Colley Cibber, Esq.*, 5 vols. (London, 1777), facsimile (New York: AMS Press, 1966), 3:5. Future references to Cibber's plays are from this edition and are cited in the text.

[30] *An Apology for the Life of Mr. Colley Cibber, Written by Himself,* ed. Robert W. Lowe, 2 vols. (London, 1889; reprint, New York: AMS Press, 1966), 2:3.

[31] Cibber, *Apology*, 2:4. Lowe points out that "eighteenpence was for many years the recognized price of plays when published."

sor—in fact, he barely rewrites it at all[32]—his neglect witnesses a lack of obligation even to dispute borders.

It is tempting to speculate that Centlivre added the foppish, plagiarizing character of Wou'd-be to *Love at a Venture* in response to Cibber's appropriation.[33] Whether or not this character appeared in the version of *Love* that she first submitted, the upstart poet embodies many characteristics attributed to Cibber by his enemies. Centlivre commonly distinguishes her own works as more original and thus her own; Wou'd-be, however, trails around after gentlemen of fashion and literally takes notes on their clothes in order to have his tailor reproduce them. He even scribbles down their witty comments for the dialogue of his next play, a practice the gentlemen protest:

BELL[AIR]: I hope, you are not one of those Spungy-Brain'd Poets, that suck something from all Companies to squeeze into a Comedy, at Acting of which, the Pit and Boxes may laugh at their own Jests.
NED.: Where each may claim his share of Wit.
BELL.: And by my consent, shou'd claim a share of the Profits too, ha, ha.
WOU'D. This is a Gentleman of an intellectual Sublimity—No, Sir, I contemn the Terrene extraction of those poor Animals, whose Barren-Intellects thrusts such spurious Brats abroad; when I write, it shall be all my own, I assure you. (27)

Wou'd-be's literary and sartorial plagiarism become parallel expressions of his limited capacity and resources; Wou'd-be's attempts at gentlemanly language ("Dear, Sir *William*," he says, "my Stars are superabundantly propitious, in administring the seraphick Felicity of finding you alone.") fail just as absurdly and foppishly as his attempts at gentlemanly appearance. Thus Bellair finally advises him to "leave off this foolish Whim of Mimicking" (the true gentleman) Sir William, who has a "plentiful Fortune. . . . you, whose slender Allowance from a Father's Hand, admits of no profuseness—to imitate him is Madness" (62). Centlivre's satire on the literary and cultural ambitions of some men differs from misogynist

[32] See Bowyer, *The Celebrated Mrs. Centlivre*, 80–83, for an instructive comparison of passages.

[33] Centlivre's *Love at a Venture* was first performed at Bath in 1706. According to eighteenth-century theater historian John Mottley, credited with writing the *List of All Dramatic Authors*, which was appended to Thomas Whincop's *Scanderbeg*, Centlivre acted in this play herself. See Bowyer, *The Celebrated Mrs. Centlivre*, 77–84.

attacks on female authorship in that she argues against, rather than encourages, gender-based generalizations about the capacity to create literary property. Wou'd-be's fashions and authorship both appropriate transgressively—a point, as we have seen, that belongs to broader anxieties about the professionalization of authorship. But it is also important to Centlivre's feminist individualism to insist that paltry talents and overblown self-conception appear just as commonly among men as women. In the dedication to her next play, for example, she reminds audiences not to reject women authors out of hand since "we have had some Male-Productions . . . void of Plot and Wit."[34] In her most optimistic moments of feminist individualism, then, men and women share equal capacities to excel, appropriate, plagiarize, and scribble.

Cibber and Centlivre both thematized gendered literary property through the trope of the learned lady and gendered alienability through the trope of gambling. Ladies and fop authors, as it turns out, actually *were* in Cibber's case at odds, for learned or scribbling women became common objects of his satirical energy. As his prominent roles in *The Female Wits* and *Three Hours* suggest, Cibber's own exteriority to dominant masculinity did not create in him sympathy toward women writers (although he does seem to have been generous toward women actors).[35] Cibber's appropriation of *Love* provides the most obvious example of his unwillingness to recognize his female colleague's capacity to own; his revisions of Centlivre's liberal feminist plots elsewhere demonstrate their differing and complex relation to the position of ownership. Two sets of plays, possibly in dialogue with each other, reveal these differences. Centlivre's *Platonick Lady* appropriates and revises the popular trope of the learned lady, possibly responding to Thomas Wright's *Female Vertuoso's*. Centlivre, however, also satirized the learned man. In an echo of *The Platonick Lady* and *The Female Vertuoso's*, the problem of women who know too much later appears in Cibber's *Refusal*. Differences further become apparent in three gambling plays: Cibber's *The Lady's Last Stake* and Centlivre's *The Gamester* and *The Basset Table*.

The epilogue of Centlivre's *Platonick Lady*, written by Thomas Baker, represents the author not only as male but also as misogynistic: "What

[34] Centlivre, dedication to *The Platonick Lady*.

[35] See also Kristina Straub's chapter on Colley Cibber's daughter, Charlotte Charke, in *Sexual Suspects: Eighteenth-Century Players and Sexual Ideology* (Princeton: Princeton University Press, 1992), chap. 7.

mighty pains our Scribling Sot has shown," an actress recites, "To Ridicule our Sex, and Praise his own." But in spite of Baker's epilogue, Centlivre actually represents her platonic lady quite sympathetically in a clear revision of the "learned lady" genre. More typical, and possibly providing a subtext and source for *The Platonick Lady*, is Thomas Wright's *The Female Vertuoso's*, which satirizes learning as a sign of lust in women: "A Woman's Wit," Wright's Sir Maurice Meanwell complains, "was always a Pimp to her pleasures."[36] Meanwell insists that women should study only to please their husbands and instruct their children: "The Women of Old did not read so much, but lived better, Housewifry was all the Knowledge they aspired to; now adays Wives must Write forsooth, and pretend to Wit with a Pox."[37] Typically, Centlivre both repeats and attempts to refute cultural prejudices: she holds her platonic lady Lucinda up for admiration, but has this very same character satisfy the popular desire to ridicule learned women by joining in the scorn of Mrs. Prim, "the Poetical She-Philosopher, whose Discourse and Writings are fill'd with Honour and the strict Rule of Virtue" (17) that she does not follow herself. Lucinda, however, derides Mrs. Prim's hypocrisy, not her learning itself.

If in Locke full individuality, as Macpherson argues, is achieved at the expense of other men, full individuality in Centlivre is (temporarily) achieved by some women at the expense of other women. Even this individuality, however, often becomes compromised in some way by the end of the play. At the same time, however, *The Platonick Lady*'s Lucinda distinctly disrupts the trope of the learned lady. Combining a love of learning with a Platonism that recalls the earlier court culture in which Cavendish participated, Centlivre's Lucinda not only escapes the generic ridicule but also inadvertently prevents a disaster through her chaste philosophy. Belville loves and courts Lucinda, but she makes him swear only to "admire the Beauties of [her] Mind—without regarding those of [her] Person" (17). Meanwhile Isabella, who had been contracted by her father to marry Sir Charles (who loves Lucinda) but had also made her own contract to marry Belville, returns in various disguises to tempt Belville back into her arms. Lucinda's broad knowledge provides her with the first clue that Belville might have another love, for she recognizes

[36] Thomas Wright, *The Female Virtuoso's* (London, 1693), 26. Wright's play was itself inspired by Molière's *Femmes savantes*, which Centlivre and Cibber clearly knew also.
[37] Ibid., 25.

the poem he courts her with: "what Lady have you lavish'd your Wit upon this Morning," Lucinda demands, "that you are forc'd to Trade upon other Mens Stocks?" (16). In a curse that recalls Centlivre's Horatian epigram from *The Stolen Heiress*, Belville rails against "these Poetical Rogues, they publish every pretty Thought, that a Gentleman's forc'd to borrow to express his own Notions" (17). Belville's curse not only echoes the author's commitment to originality, but it also demonstrates one kind of usefulness of literary learning to a lady. Belville clearly did not expect Lucinda to recognize the lines. This scene, in fact, repeats an accusation that Centlivre herself makes to "Celadon" in one of her published love letters: "Let *Celadon* consider if I ought not to be angry after his affecting the wholsome food of Plaindealing, he should offer me the fragments of Flattery from the Table of another. . . . Learning, Wit, and Eloquence are your inseparable Companions; therefore borrowing is as unpardonable in you as in a Miser. You ought rather to enrich the Publick, than encroach upon it. . . . I must tell you there's not one word in that Letter could be apply'd to me."[38] Not only does Lucinda's learning make her a more savvy lover, but her platonism, which restrains her from offering Belville so much as a kiss, also saves them both from incest. When Lucinda's uncle, Sir Thomas, finally reveals Belville's true identity as Lucinda's *brother*, she platonically turns her affection into "a Sister's Fondness" (69) and recommends him to Isabella.

The risky efforts of Isabella, Lucinda's rival for Belville, suggest that Centlivre may even have had in mind a liberal feminist intervention not just into the learned lady in general, but into Thomas Wright's play in particular. In her desperation to win Belville, Centlivre's Isabella (disguised as Donna Clara) tells Lucinda that she had married, and been abandoned by, Belville, after which she gave birth to his son. In spite of her own love for Belville, Lucinda pities "Donna Clara" and vows to protect her. Isabella turns to this last resort out of love and resistance to her childhood betrothal to Sir Charles: "I own I have gone beyond my Sex and Quality," she confesses, "but it was to purchase Liberty, and break a forc'd Contract with that perfidious Man who paid his Vows to [Lucinda]" (66). In the process, however, she places her reputation in jeopardy. A similar device appears in *The Female Vertuoso's*, but in Wright's

[38] Abel Boyer, "Letters of Wit, Politicks, and Morality" (London, 1701), 335–356. Nevertheless, "Astrea" adds a postscript, admitting that "I fear I shall go to the Play. I believe *Astrea* would be well enough pleas'd to find *Celadon* there."

play a *servant* undertakes this risk *on behalf* of her lady. Here the maid Lucy fakes a pregnancy by Witless, an upstart pretender to both learning and numerous rakish conquests, as part of a plot to free the heroine Mariana for marriage to her true love Clerimont. Witless, however, uses Lucy "just as he do's his Books; for as he quotes every day Passages out of 'em, which he never read, so he boasts of Favours of mine he never enjoy'd" (4). Lucy takes pleasure in trapping Witless, who does not object even when he discovers Lucy's identity. Centlivre's rewriting, however, turns a servant's clever machinations into a lady's high-stake risk of her reputation. Wright's play has the servant scheme for her lady's sake, leaving Marianna herself relatively passive; in Centlivre's version, the lady herself risks her reputation and puts her faith in the good will of another woman.[39]

Thus, not only does Centlivre's *Platonick Lady* appropriate and rewrite the learned lady trope in feminist individualist terms, but it also represents Isabella as breaking a paternally arranged marriage contract and making one of her own choice. In order to accomplish this, however, she must adopt several disguises and plot to turn his affections away from another woman. And while we feel that poetic justice has nevertheless been served by the marriage of Isabella and Belville, the fate of the platonic lady herself remains enigmatic. Astonished at Belville's previous marriage to "Donna Clara" (Isabella), his apparent initial refusal to acknowledge this marriage *and* Isabella's deceit of *her,* Lucinda cries out, "What, am I then a Property, am I a Person fit to be Abus'd?" (67). In true platonic fashion, she vows to "renounce Mankind" (67). She does not, however, get away with this renunciation, even for a moment. Her uncle, Sir Thomas, insists, "Faith and Troth but thou shalt not" (67); soon after revealing Belville's identity, he and Belville agree to advance the interest of Sir Charles with Lucinda. Lucinda does not respond to this agreement between men, but the ending implies that between paternal insistence and fraternal coaxing, Lucinda will give in to marriage. At best, Centlivre's heroines negotiate for a better contract and greater individual choice. Unlike Cavendish, her more radical yet less liberal precursor, Centlivre does not imagine alternatives to marriage or even less traditional kinds of marriages. Perhaps the authority of aristocratic rank opens up these possibilities more readily. But whereas Thomas

[39] Centlivre's plays stand out in this period for their positive representation of friendship between women. See also, for example, *The Wonder.*

Wright, following his French source, represents women's learning as a hypocritical excuse for shrewishness, petty domineering, lust, and transgressive appropriation, Centlivre represents Lucinda's contemplative inclinations as dignified. Wright's Lady Meanwell and her friends, by contrast—the "Sappho's of our Age" (16)—seek power and have the audacity to set themselves up as the arbiters of literary value: "Our Society shall be as the Inquisition, a Tribunal without Appeal, or Mercy; where, with a Sovereign Authority, we shall Judge of all Books that come out: No Authors shall write well, but those we approve of; and no body pretend to Wit, but we, and our Friends" (16). Lady Meanwell rejects Clerimont as a possible husband for her daughter because, among other reasons, he has failed to pay attention to her own literary accomplishment: she will not "admit into my Family a Despiser of Wit, one who knows well enough I'm an Author, and never had the manners to ask me to read any of my Works to him" (49). In Centlivre's play, however, Lucinda realizes that, in spite of her attempts to reject all men in favor of philosophy, "a real Passion cannot be disguis'd" (67), which humanizes her and endears her to the audience. At the same time, the Platonism that prevents her from acting on this passion also saves her from incest.

Cibber's *Refusal* most distinctly repeats Wright's *Female Vertuoso's*, but it also engages Centlivre's portrait of female Platonism and the specter of women's authorship in general. In Cibber's *Refusal*, women's learning and/or writing only disguise hypocrisy or unbounded acquisitiveness. Cibber turns the awkwardly sympathetic and bookish lady in Centlivre into an expression of vicious misogyny, for Sir Gilbert suffers the torments of a wife far more learned than he. Lady Wrangle raises her daughter Sophronia "half mad with her Learning and Philosophy" (4:9); she resembles Centlivre's platonic lady in her apparent rejection of physical desire. Sophronia snobbishly considers sex fit only for "Cookmaids and Footmen" (4:28), while drifting off into rape fantasies. But Frankley, suitor to Sophronia's more willing sister Charlotte, reveals that Lady Wrangle has only trained the young women in Platonism out of her own desire to prevent their marriages and thus appropriate their fortunes. Female education in Cibber becomes a strategy for the mother to expand her possession of both language and money.

While Lady Wrangle's desire to educate her daughters may spring from unsavory motives, her enthusiasm for her own authorship proves genuine and perhaps even provides Cibber with the opportunity to ridicule his female competitors. But as in *The Female Wits*, the pretension to the highest cultural capital, not writing or reading in themselves, proves to be the genuine transgression: Charlotte's reading of the *Tatler* teaches her "natural" manners, while Sophronia's reading of Latin literature turns her into a harridan. Lady Wrangle, however, goes so far as to translate Latin poetry—an effort that the cook literally skewers ("what a Life's here about a Piece of foul Paper," the cook puns, 4:60). Lady Wrangle runs mad with provocation when she discovers the maid has given the cook her poems as scrap, and the cook will not return them for fear of burning his roast beef. Upon hearing his wife's exclamations of horror, Sir Gilbert Wrangle suspects a murder; he relaxes and dismisses her outrage upon learning that she only protests the loss of her literary property. Lady Wrangle probably does not satirize Centlivre or any other woman writer in particular, but she represents (like Phoebe Clinket) the mutually implicating literary and proprietary transgression of learned women. By contrast, her virtuous daughter Charlotte never falls for the trap of learning; even Sophronia, who at first indulges in learned literature, eventually gives it up for "plain, naked, natural Love" (4:93). Thus the play ultimately endorses Sir Gilbert's conclusion about Lady Wrangle's learning. Sir Gilbert locates Lady Wrangle in the subordinated position of Prospero's Caliban when he implies the similarity of the wife's and the slave's relationship to language: "All the use I find of her Learning, is, that it furnishes her with more words to scold with" (4:62).

The satirized learned lady becomes a fixture in early eighteenth-century drama. And while a range of authors attack pedantry in general, Centlivre offers alternatives to the shrewish learned lady with both dignified learned women and with the absurd "learned man."[40] Attacks on male pedantry do not necessarily signal feminism; Centlivre's learned men, however, reveal their absurdity in gendered contexts. In her attack on the masculine learning to which she has no access, Centlivre once again echoes Cavendish. But whereas the duchess advances her aristocratic singularity, Centlivre opposes an elite masculine reliance on the authority of books to a savvy comprehension of the world that distinguishes many of her women characters and also describes her own authorial self-representation. Sancho in *The Stolen Heiress*, for example, represents Centlivre's elite scholar who knows nothing of human machi-

---

[40] Centlivre's satire of male literary and scholarly ambition has the most relevance here, but her comedies poke fun at a range of masculine foibles.

nations.[41] Thus Francisco, who wants to marry the woman to whom Sancho has become engaged, tricks Sancho into pretending to know nothing of books and everything of the social world as a way to impress Lavinia. Lavinia's father and his stubborn insistence that his daughter marry a scholar, regardless of her affections, becomes the object of Centlivre's potent satire. Centlivre upholds the love between Lavinia and Francisco as more valuable than the father's hypocritical and elitist fascination with Sancho and his learning. Sancho earns some sympathy for his naive simplicity; he speaks an epilogue about the inadequacy of learning:

> Tho' the Learn'd Youth, can all the Sages Quote,
> Has *Homer, Hesiod,* and the rest by roat;
> Yet what's all this to Picquet, Dress or Play?
> Or to the Circle, on a Visiting-Day?[42]

Attached to a different play, these lines could read as yet another satire on a society too frivolous to honor learning. In the context of *The Stolen Heiress,* however, they leave genuine doubt about the superiority of Homer and Hesiod to visiting or the theater. Centlivre slyly opposes masculine rote learning of classical poets to the feminine world of fashion and drama.

The erudite Periwinkle cuts a similar figure in her *Bold Stroke for a Wife.* In order to marry Ann Lovely, Colonel Fainwell in this play must gather permission from each of three idiosyncratic guardians, including Periwinkle, "a kind of a silly *Virtuoso.*" Periwinkle cares only for "scientific" curiosities from the distant past and from around the world. As in *The Stolen Heiress,* however, the lover outsmarts the scholar: the Colonel pretends to share Periwinkle's interests and earns his good will by offering him a girdle that he claims will render its wearer invisible. In both these plays of Centlivre's, the learned man blocks and thus structurally stands in opposition to a woman's happiness. Most of Centlivre's plays,

[41] This opposition between knowledge of books and knowledge of the world became a central part of eighteenth-century thought, perhaps best articulated by Samuel Johnson in "The Vanity of Human Wishes." For a brilliant deconstruction of this division, see Joel Weinsheimer, *Imitation* (London: Routledge & Kegan Paul, 1984).

[42] In fact, when Lavinia makes a desperate move to get out of marrying him by claiming pregnancy, Sancho generously takes public responsibility for the child to save her honor.

in fact, feature young couples who plot against tyrannical fathers or guardians in order to marry. Her plays consistently protest fathers or guardians who treat women as property and celebrate the men and women who outmaneuver them. The marriage contract remains the goal; Centlivre's women, however, attempt to position themselves as makers rather than objects of this contract.

Cibber's and Centlivre's gendered relationships to property become perhaps most apparent, however, in their representations of gambling. Gambling attracted attention as a vice in the early eighteenth century,[43] but moralists and satirists expressed particular anxieties about women playing games of chance. Perhaps most memorably, the card game provides the scene of Bellinda's jeopardy in Pope's *Rape of the Lock*; as in Pope's poem, most of the attacks on women and gambling represent the loss of chastity as the greatest danger to betting women. The sarcastic author of *The Womens Advocate* identifies the staking of virtue as every man's anxiety over his wife's gambling: "There she sits from after dinner, till one, two, three, four a clock i'the morning, day after day, night after night, consuming and wasting her fine Portion, till she begins to prey upon the main stock. And this is a parlous grievance . . . . One cries, *I think my wife will play away her A——*."[44] *Mundus Mulierbris* identifies the same danger:

> To play at *Ombre* or *Basset*,
> She a rich *Pulvil* Purse must get,
> With Guineas fill'd, on Cards to lay,
> With which she fancies most to play:
> Nor is she troubled at ill fortune,
> For should the bank be so importune,
> To rob her of her glittering Store,
> The amorous Fop will furnish more.
> Pensive and mute, behind her shoulder
> He stands, till by her loss grows bolder,
> Into her lap *Rouleau* conveys,

[43] See, for example, *The Gamester Law* (London, 1708).
[44] [M. Marsin], *The Womens Advocate; or, Fifteen Real Comforts of Matrimony . . . Written by a Person of Quality* (London, 1683), 107–108. The author comforts husbands: "there's the thing gone, which is many times the cause of all his fears, jealousies and disturbances. How many men are there, that curse their wives tayls? which if the women have a faculty to play away, there's a fair riddance of the mens discontent" (108).

The softest thing a Lover says:
She grasps it in her greedy hands,
Then best his Passion understands;
When tedious languishing has fail'd,
Rouleau has constantly prevail'd.[45]

As *The Guardian* similarly concludes, "The husband has his lands to dispose of, the wife her person."[46] The trope of the female gambler takes on a life of its own, embodying more than the general concern for women's chastity. The lady in *Mundus Mulierbris* begins as a possessor and circulator of gold, but her body becomes a vessel for holding coins when she runs out. In the course of the poem, the gambler changes from a controller of property into property herself, as a prostitute but also as a body penetrated by and indistinguishable from money. So while satires against women gamblers warn against gambling's risk to chastity, they also repeat as a trope the fluidity of boundaries for women between circulating property and becoming property. For *The Guardian*, the possibility of circulating property without becoming property remains masculine; women who gamble thus earn sarcastic praise because they "acquire such a boldness, as raises them near the lordly creature man. . . . Their natural tenderness is a weakness here easily unlearned; and I find my soul exalted, when I see a lady sacrifice the fortune of her children with as little concern as a Spartan or a Roman dame."[47] The discourse of gambling thus reveals the ideology of post-Lockean representations of gender and ownership, for it consistently depicts female sexuality and self-possession not only as alienable, but also as constantly in danger of alienation. A lady's last stake differs from a gentleman's. Gambling *also*, however, potentially offers women the (temporary) position of possessor rather than possessed, although rarely in the drama can a woman keep from folding when a man calls her bluff.

Colley Cibber's gambling play, *The Lady's Last Stake, or, The Wife's Resentment* (1707), followed Centlivre's first two popular successes, *The*

---

[45] *Mundus Mulierbris: Or, the Ladies Dressing-Room Unlock'd, and her Toilette Spread in Burlesque* (London, 1690), 4–5. Attributed to Mary Evelyn. The appended "FOP-DICTIONARY" defines "rouleau" as "Forty Nine Guineas, made up in a Paper Roll, which Monsiery F–– Sir J–– and Father B–– lend to losing Gamester, that are good Men, and have Fifty in Return."

[46] *The Guardian*, 2 vols., London, 1714, no. 20, 2:193.

[47] Ibid., no. 174, 2:503.

Gamester (1705) and *The Basset Table* (1705), to which I will return. Both of Centlivre's plays, as their titles indicate, address the issue of gambling. Although *The Lady's Last Stake* does not repeat Centlivre quite as explicitly as *The Double Gallant*, produced the same year, it certainly engages and responds to its Lincoln's Inn Field rivals. Cibber's rewriting of the learned lady reveals his patriarchal complicity; the unstable economy of gambling, however, prompts an exploration of the instability of gender. Like Centlivre's plays, but also like so many other texts at the time, *The Lady's Last Stake* locates money and sexuality in the same economy of risk: alienable sexuality is the lady's last stake, the ultimate prize she finds she must offer in order to pay off her debts. Cibber states his own purpose as exposing folly "to the Fair Sex in its most hideous Form, by reducing a Woman of Honour to stand the presumptuous Addresses of a Man, whom neither her Virtue nor Inclination would let her have the least Taste to" (2:196). Yet throughout the play and the dedication it becomes apparent that this promise of a moral for the ladies also becomes a vehicle through which Cibber expresses an array of anxieties over what Pocock calls the "mobility of property."[48] Cibber specularizes, with a combination of glee and horror, consumer culture's potential capacity to threaten naturalized gender differences. Locke's treatises may represent women as outside the position of ownership, but as Pocock points out, "a case might be made for the view that women could expect more mobility, and even active agency, from a commercially conceived society than from the alternative model of the masculine and self-contained classical patriots."[49] A gender ideology representing the alienability of women's sexuality, as opposed to the inalienability of male sexuality, commonly emerges to offset this potential for equality. Cibber playfully and provocatively calls attention to this economy's potential "feminization" of men and "masculinization" of women. One would not have to see the play to guess the substance of the lady's "last stake"; in the

[48] J. G. A. Pocock, "The Mobility of Property and the Rise of Eighteenth-Century Sociology," in *Virtue, Commerce, and History: Essays on Political Thought and History, Chiefly in the Eighteenth Century* (Cambridge: Cambridge University Press, 1985), 103–124. Although Cibber declared himself an adamant Whig in his *Apology*, the politics in his plays often theatricalize popular anxieties rather than stake out an explicit position. See John Loftis, *The Politics of Drama in Augustan England* (Oxford: Clarendon Press, 1963), 56. Loftis points out Cibber's dependence on Tory ministers in the early part of his career.

[49] Pocock, *Virtue, Commerce, and History*, 118.

dedication, however, Cibber represents *himself* as down to his last stake in the gamble of theater: "Great Sums have been ventur'd upon empty Projects, and Hopes of immoderate Gains; and when those Hopes have fail'd, the Loss has been tyranically deducted out of the Actors Salary" (2:196). Cibber's (not necessarily conscious) parallel between the actor/manager's and the lady's last stake further complicates the stated moral against women gamblers, for risky forms of financial circulation destabilize both gender positions and economies of desire that only differing capacities for self-alienation can reinscribe.

The creature to whom gambling unfortunately exposes Lady Gentle in *The Lady's Last Stake* is Sir George Brilliant, Cibber's nastiest fop. George Brilliant confesses to Lord Wronglove that he has reason to hope for the favors of the virtuous Lady Gentle because he has discovered her "over-fondness for play" (2:214). When she plays herself into debt she cannot repay, George tempts her into staking her body against all her losses. George, however, violates the gambling contract and cheats to ensure his victory. Further, when enough money mysteriously arrives to excuse Lady Gentle from her sexual obligation, George refuses to accept it and attempts to rape her. Once Lady Gentle enters the irrational economy of the gaming table, she, like the actors subject to the whims of managers and investors, becomes vulnerable.

On the one hand, then, Cibber counters Centlivre's gambling plays with a lesson about the extraordinary risk that women undertake once they enter such an unstable economy, but the play also suggests the danger of gambling to naturalized ideologies of masculinity. All of Cibber's fops, as Kristina Straub argues, express fluid sexual identities; George Brilliant, however, makes the most explicit declaration of homoerotic desire when he returns the greeting kisses of Lord Wronglove: "And kiss, and kiss again, my Dear," he responds, "By *Ganymede* there's Nectar on thy Lips."[50] As Straub further observes, at an historical moment of the emergence of bipolar oppositions between hetero- and homosexual identity, as well as the bipolar reification of masculine and feminine identity, Cibber's Brilliant comically destabilized both oppositions.[51] Like

---

[50] Straub, *Sexual Suspects,* 59. See also Susan Staves, "A Few Kind Words for the Fop," *SEL* 22 (Summer 1982): 413–428.

[51] For a good discussion of the construction of feminine identity in the early eighteenth century, see Katherine Shevelow, *Women and Print Culture: The Construction of Femininity in the Early Periodical* (London: Routledge, 1989).

other fops, George's self-consciousness associates him with feminine consumer vanity. In intriguing gender-crossing symmetry, Lady Conquest, George's former lover, dresses up as her brother, John Conquest, in a bid to foil George's conquest of Lady Gentle. Mrs. Conquest accomplishes as a man what she cannot as a woman: s/he rescues Lady Gentle from George's advances and insists on fighting him to revenge the damage to his/her "sister's" reputation.

In the Mrs. Conquest plot, the gendered division between alienable and inalienable sexuality nearly collapses in the context of irrationally mobile finances. Mrs. Conquest ultimately makes a "conquest" of George Brilliant by putting him in the same financial and thus sexual position as he placed Lady Gentle. And while Lady Conquest achieves this by appearing to risk her own body and finances, she nevertheless takes this risk in male guise and uses it to manipulate Brilliant into marriage. When George arrives to fight "John" Conquest, robbers seize him and attempt to strip him of his clothes and money. They appear to wound "John" Conquest mortally, and when the surgeon reveals the gender of the injured patient, George promises to marry his former lover. Yet Lady Conquest has set up the whole plot, simultaneously staging her own vulnerability to the robbers *and* letting George think that *he* has become just as vulnerable to an illicit and violent economy as had Lady Gentle herself. Lady Conquest appropriates him as a husband just as he had tried to appropriate Lady Gentle as a lover. Gender *positions* remain the same, for Lady Conquest frightens George in male disguise and hires other men to help. *The Lady's Last Stake*, however, forces the feminized George himself down to his last stake: he gives himself (albeit in marriage) after a frightening encounter with men who would rob and strip him. Cibber's play thus raises the unnerving possibility that, in the context of an irrational economy, men might have a "last stake" as well.

While Cibber captures contemporary anxieties about gender difference and the mobility of property in the context of a lesson for women gamblers, Centlivre finds in this popular trope a range of feminist possibilities. In her successful *Gamester*, Centlivre uses gambling to suggest the alienability of male sexuality without, as in Cibber's play, "feminization"; in her *Basset Table*, she uses it to represent the related possibility of women as equally able to circulate property. Through the extreme mobility of gambling, Centlivre finds support for the very feminist individualism that Pocock suggests. At a time when the specter of the woman gambler embodied so many anxieties about gender and financial instability, Susanna Centlivre wrote her first big commercial success about a *man* who can't stop gambling. In *The Gamester*, Centlivre's Valere places himself in sexual danger by his gambling—not exactly in the same way as do women in so many representations, but enough to invite comparison. Valere loves Angellica, at least—as his servant Hector notices—when his luck turns down. Angellica loves him, but fears his bad gambling habit; her wealthy sister, however, loves him as well. Valere's father has grown so impatient with his son's gambling that he threatens to disinherit him. Gambling, then, stands in the way of Valere's marriage to Angellica not only because she dislikes his addiction, but also because he becomes vulnerable to the advances of any woman who can offer him money.

With limited money from his father, Valere finds he can use his masculine charms to secure loans from women. In the first act, he flatters and flirts with Mrs. Security, but becomes indignant when she will not extend credit to him. Lady Wealthy, Angellica's rich sister, declares the profligate Valere unsuited to Angellica's small fortune, but thinks he would make a good match for her and the vast estate her dead husband left her. Both women offer gifts: Angellica seals her promise of love with her portrait; Lady Wealthy sends Valere money. Lady Wealthy represents herself as powerful, masculine, and sexually aggressive when she positions herself as Jove in this transaction: "I confirm my words," she writes, "in a Golden showr" (44). Valere knows that "when a Widow parts with Money, 'tis easie to read the valuable Consideration she expects"; he feels that his "Virtue's staggering." So although gambling does not expose Valere to literal rape, it turns him into a kind of prostitute and stands in the way of his affective choice in marriage.

Centlivre calls attention to her revisions of sexuality and commodification in part through her repetition and appropriation of Aphra Behn. Like Behn, she hangs out the sign of Angellica, who loves, as Lady Wealthy calls him, "the Gay, the Rover, the unconquer'd Rambler" (47). Centlivre, however, has collapsed the figure of the attractive prostitute and the marriageable lady in her Angellica. Like Hellena, she relentlessly pursues her rover, but like Angellica Bianca, she fully comprehends sexual commodification and attempts to establish a relationship outside of it. But whereas Behn's Angellica cannot escape the commodification of her sexuality in the Rover's eyes, Centlivre's Angellica directly intervenes to prevent Valere's temptation to cast her into the market. Armed with Angellica's picture and Lady Wealthy's hundred pounds, Valere heads to the gaming house and gradually begins to lose his money. At this point, both women have endangered their reputations by trusting him with symbols of their affection. Betting Lady Wealthy's money potentially commodifies *her*, and she becomes greatly distressed when she learns that rumors have begun to circulate about her payment. Angellica decides she must intervene before Valere can circulate the even more dangerous token of her affection, the picture that signifies the potential alienability of her sexuality. She appears at the gaming house disguised as a man, wins all Valere's money from him, and tempts him into staking her own portrait, which she wins as well. Through this intervention, Angellica insists that Valere cannot both have her and commodify her, for once he uses her picture as capital—in the way that he has been using their impending marriage as capital by borrowing against it—he no longer possesses proof of their constant love. Nevertheless, using Angellica's portrait as capital erases any difference between their relationship and Valere's potential prostitution to Lady Wealthy after accepting and losing her money. Further, he would have symbolically prostituted Angellica by staking her portrait to another man. Forced into this recognition by Angellica's trick and overcome with regret, Valere finally vows to leave off gambling. Lady Wealthy escapes commodification as well, for her admirer Lovewell falsely and gallantly claims that he had, out of jealousy, spread a spurious rumor that the lady had given money to Valere, compromising his own reputation to save hers. Centlivre, then, uses the symbolic economy of gambling to suggest the equal vulnerability of men and women to sexual alienability. In order to merit a happy marriage, Valere must learn not to commodify Angellica, but he must also escape commodification himself. In spite of the sexual vulnerability of both Angellica and Valere, however, the ending of the play, like so many "reformed rake" plots, creates as much ambivalence as it resolves. The end leaves us not so much with the specific anxiety that Valere will return to the gambling table, but with an uneasiness about Angellica's marriage to a man who was willing to stake her picture, her reputation, and thus her very self. Sexual commodification threatens both characters, but gender differences nevertheless remain apparent through Valere's capacity symbolically to "sell" Angellica. She can claim no property in him, and therefore has no such equivalent power. Angellica can rescue herself only by buying herself back, and she can do that only by temporarily inhabiting the position of masculine individual at the gaming table.

Following up on the success of *The Gamester*, Centlivre next wrote *The Basset Table*, a play that addresses the popular moral concern with women and gambling. *The Basset Table* resembles Cibber's *Lady's Last Stake* and may indeed have provided a source for it. Centlivre's Lady Reveller stays up all night gambling, eventually loses money, and must borrow from Sir James Courtly. Courtly then demands her body in exchange for his money, insisting that no woman can claim virtue who spends so much time at the basset table. Reveller's true love, Lord Worthy, apparently saves her from Courtly's rape attempt, and she swears off gambling thereafter. Cibber finds in Centlivre's plot the potential to specularize anxieties about the mobility of property and the instability of gender; *The Basset Table*, however, maintains confidence in possessive individualism, for her characters never truly face the bodily alienation that Cibber proposes. In this play Centlivre responds to the gendered positions of self-ownership by attempting to refute difference more optimistically: her lady cannot lose her "last stake." Further, Centlivre includes in this play a subplot about the lady scientist Valeria, whose intellectual interests cheerfully, comically, yet somewhat ambivalently suggest the potential for women's equality and full individuality.

Cibber specularizes a mobile economy's potential destabilization of masculine selfhood in the context of assumptions that gambling endangers female virtue. From this perspective, women cannot fully inhabit the position of "individual" because they remain constantly available, willingly or not, to contracts of sexual (and self) subordination. In *The Lady's Last Stake*, then, it is not so much that gambling simply turns sexual access to Lady Gentle *into* a commodity; rather, sexual integrity is assumed to be alienable and open to contracts—her last piece of property, but one that is not even properly hers to stake.[52] In *The Basset Table*, however, Centlivre explores the possibility of women's sexual selves as inalienable: Lady Reveller and Valeria provide sharply and comically contrasting versions of femininity, but they nevertheless have in common a struggle over sexual self-ownership. Sir Richard Plainman, who battles to control his niece Lady Reveller and his daughter Valeria, swears that he will "find a way to humble" Reveller's insolence and berates her for gambling. Centlivre, however, gives Lady Reveller the most advantageous position from which to counter her uncle: that of a rich widow. "Widdows are accountable to none for their Actions," the lady's servant Alpiew

[52] Perhaps this is why male chastity provides such a good joke for Fielding in *Joseph Andrews*: men have inalienable property in their bodies, and commodify nothing by violating their virtue.

236

declares (5). Lady Reveller laughs at her uncle's warning that "For she whose Shame, no good Advice can wake,/When Money's wanting, will her Virtue Stake" (6). Centlivre theatricalizes the pure pleasure Lady Reveller takes in manipulating money, and even though Sir James slips her extra money when she loses her own, Lady Reveller never actually gambles down to her "last stake." Cibber's Lady Gentle knows she has staked her virtue; Lady Reveller, on the other hand, refuses to recognize her virtue as vulnerable to being staked. She receives James's gift as the "Genteelest Piece of Gallantry" and becomes incredulous when he expects sex in return: "Basest of Men," she cries indignantly, "I'll have your Life for this Affront" (56). Sir James declares Lady Reveller's virtue a commodity that he now owns: he offers her another fifty guineas and insists, "You are mine; nor will I quit this Room till I'm Possest." Her lover Lord Worthy rescues her from the other man's advances, where-upon Lady Reveller accepts Worthy for her husband. In her understand-ing of the scene (which, as we will see, is not the only one available), Sir Richard never humbles her, she chooses her own husband, and her virtue remains inalienable.

In spite of Centlivre's clearly feminist intervention into the lady gam-bler trope, the ending of *The Basset Table* nevertheless reveals the inherent limits of her feminist individualism as the exchange of one form of patriarchy for another. Lady Reveller rejects the traditional patriarchal-ism represented by Sir Richard, but unwittingly embraces the fraternal patriarchalism of Sir James and Lord Worthy. When Sir Richard's bully-ing tactics fail to keep his niece away from the gambling table, Lord Worthy and Sir James hatch a plot of their own. Gambling alone stands in the way of Lady Reveller's acceptability as a wife to Lord Worthy. Thus the two men stage her loss at the table, the loan from Sir James, James's threat to her body, and Lord Worthy's opportunity to rescue her. What appears to her as a free choice to relinquish gambling and marry her lover appears to the audience as the successful manipulations of two men. With her marriage to Lord Worthy, she gives up the indepen-dence and self-ownership of a widow and subordinates herself (and her property) to a man in exchange for his protection of her from other men. True, Centlivre has Lord Worthy confess his manipulations, giving Lady Reveller the "choice" to marry him or not with full knowledge of his actions. Yet the threat that the two men stage persists, and individual-ism for Lady Reveller turns out to mean the willing exchange of obedi-ence for protection.

Theatricalizing similar tensions between traditional patriarchy and liberal individualism, Lady Reveller's cousin Valeria openly defies her father. Though indulging in science rather than literature, Valeria represents the generic learned lady, who becomes an object of satire in the early eighteenth century. But just as Phoebe Clinket appears to invoke the woman author in general as well as Centlivre in particular, so Valeria bears a distinct resemblance to the duchess of Newcastle, with whom Centlivre shares, as argued earlier, authorial strategies. Centlivre creates in Valeria a female virtuoso consumed by a passion for science who nevertheless, like the duchess, loves a soldier who supports her intellectual endeavors. The other characters consider Valeria mad, but Centlivre draws this female eccentric with sympathy.[53] Valeria loves both her ensign and her experiments, which she will not leave even to run away with her lover. Sir Richard, in a gesture that expresses his refusal to believe that Valeria can own anything, smashes his daughter's specimens and orders the servants to clean out her laboratory. Sir Richard's patriarchalism remains ineffective in this household, however, for Valeria knows that the servants will not obey. Nevertheless, he has also taken the liberty to choose the rough-edged Captain Hearty for Valeria's husband, insisting that they produce a fleet of sons. Valeria, though, completely baffles the Captain with her learned language; she dismisses him as an "irrational creature," claiming the position of rational creature for herself.

Through Ensign Lovely, Valeria's true love, who tolerates her scientific projects, Centlivre not only suggests an alternative, more egalitarian relationship, but also finds the opportunity to satirize Sir Richard's conception of masculinity. When Lovely proves insufficiently manly for Sir Richard's approval, Captain Hearty helps him mimic virility: "mehap a Woman may not like me," the gentle Lovely declares, disguised as the manly Captain Match, "I am Rough and Storm-like in my Temper, unacquainted with the Effeminacy of Courts" (44). Centlivre's plot, however, ultimately allows Valeria to marry her lover without actually defying her

[53] Valeria differs from Cavendish in her interest in experimentation, as opposed to the duchess's preference for reason. Valeria's desire to establish a college for women also recalls Mary Astell. See Ruth Perry, *The Celebrated Mary Astell: An Early English Feminist* (Chicago: University of Chicago Press, 1986). As Perry argues elsewhere, however, Astell more fully recognized the place of women in possessive individualism. See her "Mary Astell and the Feminist Critique of Possessive Individualism," *Eighteenth-Century Studies* 23 (1990): 447–457.

father, for she weds "Captain Match" at Sir Richard's command. This plot, like the Lady Reveller plot, both parodies and reinscribes the alienability of women's sexuality, for the two men fool Sir Richard into believing that he owns Valeria, can trade on her sexual destiny, and can use her body as a vessel through which to produce grandsons. Once again the fraternal patriarchy triumphs over the traditional patriarchy, leaving Valeria both inside and outside of contractual relations.

Lady Reveller's self-ownership in widowhood provides the conditions for her circulation of money; similarly, Valeria struggles with her father for self-ownership as the foundation of her claim to intellectual property. While boastful of his daughter's immunity to the basset table, Sir Richard expresses extraordinary hostility to Valeria's philosophical interests. Centlivre, however, renders him powerless to stop either of these women. As in *The Platonick Lady*, Centlivre finds feminist possibilities in the same mind/body opposition that provides for Locke the basis for several forms of self-alienation. Sir Richard understands Valeria as a body that he owns, a mechanism for creating more men (implicitly under his command): "Oh! such a Son-in-Law—how shall I be Blest in my Posterity? Now do I foresee the Greatness of my Grand-Children; the Sons of this Man shall, in the Age to come, make *France* a Tributary Nation" (44–45). Valeria, however, insists on the inalienability of her heart and soul, distinct from her body:

> VAL. . . . Oh my Dear *Lovely*!—We were only form'd one for another;—thy Dear Enquiring Soul is more to me—than all these useless Lumps of Animated Clay: Duty compels my Hand,—but my Heart is subject only to my Mind,—the strength of that they cannot Conquer; . . . I here protest my Will shall ne're assent to any but my *Lovely*.
>
> SIR RICHARD. Ay, you and your Will may Philosophize as long as you please,—Mistress,—but your Body shall be taught another Doctrine,—it shall so—Your Mind,—and your Soul, quotha! Why, what a Pox has my Estate to do with them? Ha? 'Tis the Flesh Huswife, that must raise Heirs,—and Supporters of my Name. (46)

From the perspective of paternal authority, Valeria can do anything she wants with her heart and soul. A husband's possession, however, must be more profound. When Sir James suggests to Lord Worthy that he merely carry Lady Reveller away, Lord Worthy refuses:

LORD. That Way might give her Person to my Arms, but where's the Heart?

SIR JAMES. A Trifle in Competition with her Body.

LORD. The Heart's the Gem that I prefer. (42)

Although Cavendish and Centlivre both find feminist potential in versions of Platonism, the division of the true self from the body takes on a different meaning in Centlivre's post-Lockean individualism. By insisting that everyone owns his own body, Locke represents an owning self distinct from the body. The (masculine) ownership of the body provides the basis through which other forms of ownership become possible, but it also provides the capacity to alienate labor. In her feminist individualism, Centlivre insists that women possess themselves in this same way. Yet clearly in this play self-possession cannot be constructed in a gender-neutral way, for what part of Valeria would be left free if Sir Richard gave her to Captain Hearty to produce grandsons? Centlivre never truly challenges Sir Richard's ownership of Valeria, but merely allows the young men to trick him. For the husband, on the other hand, the sexual/marriage contract clearly has at stake more than a woman's body, for Lord Worthy responds to Sir James's suggestion to rape Lady Reveller not with indignation over the violation of her personhood, but with the observation that rape simply would not satisfy his desire.

Further, in Centlivre's liberal individualism, even the compromised potential self-ownership of Lady Reveller and Valeria does not extend to Mrs. Sago, the citizen's wife who keeps losing money that she does not have. Mrs. Sago functions in a similar way to George Brilliant: as an embodiment of the dangers and anxieties of finance capitalism. If Centlivre allows the unmarried, wealthy ladies various degrees of self-ownership, she also inscribes Mrs. Sago's body and wealth as the property of her husband. Mrs. Sago's unlucky gambling, in fact, parallels her affair with Sir James, for both steal from Mr. Sago. Mrs. Sago draws cash out of her husband through various underhanded manipulations of the credit system. In one instance, she leads her husband to believe that he has bought her a diamond ring, which she returns, keeping his note for basset. She cheats at cards (although it doesn't help her win) and gets credit against her husband's assets without his knowledge, partly by sending herself gifts on his account and using those gifts to pay back her gambling debts. Thus she has "Imbezell'd," as Mr. Sago accuses her at the end, from the household accounts. Mrs. Sago clearly owns none of the marital property, nor does she have inalienable property in her sexuality: "For that Fair Face," Mr. Sago declares after he has been arrested for debt, "if I turn you out of Doors, will quickly be a cheaper Drug than any in my Shop" (62). Sir James pays Mr. Sago's debts, apparently out of generosity. But in doing so, James not only returns money he won from Mrs. Sago at cards, but also pays her off for her sexual services. Thus, Mrs. Sago's combined status as citizen's wife and married woman keep her from even the compromised individuality that Lady Reveller and Valeria achieve. Married women, which our heroines will soon become, have little to call their own.

In spite of Centlivre's feminist attempts to imagine some women as self-owners and consequently as owners of material and immaterial property, then, *The Basset Table* ultimately demonstrates the limits of Lockean individualism for feminists. Mrs. Sago can only manipulate property illegitimately. As Macpherson and Pateman have in various ways shown, Locke predicates his theory of property on the assumption of an unequal society. Centlivre's feminism allows her to reimagine the division between owners and non-owners somewhat differently from Locke, but her women characters still never truly achieve the equal status as individuals that they commonly insist upon for themselves. They defy tyrannical fathers for benevolent lovers, but remain both makers and objects of their marriage contracts. Those contracts themselves, even in Centlivre, usually exchange obedience for protection. Further, not all women can attempt even this level of autonomy. Perhaps, then, gambling becomes such a popular trope in Augustan drama not only because it dramatizes the risk of finance capitalism, but also because the basset table is literally a zero sum game. Mrs. Sago can never win, Lady Reveller can sometimes win, and Sir James Courtly can always win. In Locke as in basset, property is both finite and mobile: every time somebody wins, somebody else—ideologically inscribed as a non-owner—loses.

Authorship for Centlivre participates in this economy as well. In the dedication to the upholders (undertakers) prefacing *A Bickerstaff's Burying*, Centlivre represents her own ownership of literary property as made possible by the same material/immaterial split that allows Valeria to resist her father's attempts fully to appropriate her. "Gentleman," she comically declares, "I honour you tho' I have no Desire of falling into your Hands, but I think we Poets are in no Danger of that, since our real Estate lies in the Brain, and our personal consists in two or three loose Scenes, a few Couples for the Tag of an Act, and a slight Sketch for a Song, and as I take it, you are not over-fond of Paper-Credit, where there is no Probability of recovering the Debt: So wishing you better Customers, I expect no Return." Authorship consists of the ownership of immaterial property. Comically and morbidly, Centlivre locates her inalienable self-ownership in the brain; as for her body, a skimpy income provides little incentive for the upholders to look forward to possessing it. But even though writing generates immaterial property, authorship nevertheless resembles other games of chance:

> The Gamester Ventures, to improve his Store,
> And having lost, he Ventures on for more.
> The *London Punk*, in Garret shut all Day,
> At Night, with last half Crown she Ventures to the Play.
> The Amorous Cully, meeting with the Miss,
> Ventures at Water-Gruel for a Kiss.
> Since every Man, Adventures in his way,
> Hither our Author ventur'd with her Play.
> And hopes her Profits will her Charge defray,
> If that bright Circle Ventures to adorn her Day.[54]

Everyone circulates what he or she has in the hope of accumulating more. In authorship as in gambling, some improve on their property, some find their estates in ruin, and others cannot get into the game in the first place.

[54] Centlivre, prologue to *Love at a Venture* (1706).

EPILOGUE

As promised, I have not actually defended any playwrights against the charge of plagiarism. Rather, I have attempted to defamiliarize the term itself in the context of late seventeenth- and early eighteenth-century transformations in authorship and conceptions of property. While a range of writers found themselves accused of the illegitimate appropriation of texts, gender and cultural positioning made a significant difference in the way these accusations circulated. (This does not mean, however, that Aphra Behn, Margaret Cavendish, and Colley Cibber did not rewrite, sometimes changing surprisingly little from the earlier text.) I have also tried to show that the same playwrights accused of plagiarism have at once been some of the most passionate advocates for originality. Since contemporary histories of criticism as well as histories of literature have tended to be written without recognizing women's full participation, we have been left with the idea of original composition as "originally" articulated by Romantic poets, the first to wrestle themselves free of the burden of the past and plunge into the anxieties of influence. But a critical history that includes women and also writers who locate themselves in popular culture reveals that "originality" had, at least since Margaret Cavendish, been used as a strategy of appropriation by those who found themselves outside of elite literary traditions. Cavendish and others constructed from originality the possibility of a subject position from which to own literary property.

But just as I have not defended these writers from the charge of plagiarism, so I have also resisted concluding that feminists should return to the humanist values of originality and genius and claim them for women, even though we *should* recognize the ways in which women contributed to these ideals. To participate in the critique of those values, however, does not seem to me to undermine the impulse of what was one of the initial projects of modern feminist criticism: the recognition of women's simultaneous occlusion from and participation in literary

243

culture. While earlier contributions to the field concentrated too heavily on the limits under which women labored, we have in recent years rejected those arguments so vehemently in our reluctance to see women as victims that we risk neglecting to account for the genuine challenges faced by those who inhabited positions other than that of the full, rights-bearing individual. I have attempted to steer between the Scylla of victimization and the Charybdis of neglecting difference through all kinds of weather and, no doubt, with uneven navigational skill. I have found it helpful to think about the cultural category of gender more centrally than the category of women writers, and the emerging divisions between "high" culture and "popular" culture as equally important to those between amateurs and professionals. These divisions, however, carry their own hazards. Although the category of gender helps us see the complications of literary property for John Dryden as well as for Aphra Behn, I have nevertheless taken not only as a given but also as an important political observation that some humans become signified as "women" and others as "men." These significations work differently in different times and cultures; I have been interested in the ways in which late seventeenth- and early eighteenth-century English culture interpellated different subject positions through ideologies of gender, property, class, "race," and sexuality.

Finally, then, who *does* get to inhabit the position of the full, rights-bearing individual? In researching this book, every time I thought I had identified the stable, dominant male figure whom women had to negotiate—John Dryden, Alexander Pope, Colley Cibber, Thomas Killigrew, Thomas Southerne, Charles Gildon, Gerard Langbaine—each turned out, upon closer inspection, to have his own complex, even embattled relationship with the ownership of literary property. In some ways, the position of dominant masculinity and true authorship that posited ladies and fop authors as its negative opposition remained itself empty, or only inhabitable temporarily and contingently. There was, then, no exemplary figure who escaped all suspicion of plagiarism through masculine authority: the search for Aphra Behn's privileged brother remains just as futile as the search for Shakespeare's sister. Nevertheless, women clearly experienced a different relationship to this provisional position than did men. Ladies and fop authors became the necessary others to an emergent canon of literary worthies that had no stable constitution; canonicity remained an elusive position rather than anyone's assured identity. The demand for an "other," however, accounts in part for the financial and popular success of some of those who found themselves trapped in the lines of *The Dunciad, The Female Wits,* and *Three Hours after Marriage.* While the work of these playwrights found admiration in places ranging from the commercial stage to private readers to closet theatrics to the blazing world, they have long been received as little more than practitioners of the Grub Street version of imitation. In this book I have offered an alternative possibility.

Index

Actors, 31, 232
  men, 49, 54, 107, 181n41, 204, 214.
    See also Cibber, Colley: as actor
  represented in *The Female Wits,*
    175–176
  women, 9, 77n56, 79, 87, 88, 95,
    117n34, 157, 186n55, 187, 215n21,
    222. *See also* Centlivre, Susanna: as
    actor
Adam and Eve, 29–30, 113
Adaptation, 33, 43, 49, 55, 69, 166. *See
  also* Appropriation
Ancients vs. moderns, 63, 195
  appropriation by, 11–12, 15, 17–18,
    55, 107, 162–163, 166, 189
  in women's writing, 103, 185, 206, 208
Anne, Queen (of Great Britain and Ireland), 210–211
Appleby, Joyce Oldham, 24
Appropriation
  fabricated, 213n16
  of foreign vs. British works, 51–52
  legitimacy of, 4, 10, 189
  as masculine, 44, 49, 212
  selectively approved by Langbaine, 37,
    52, 55
  transgressive, 31, 173–175, 181, 190,
    222
  and women, 38–40, 70, 182, 213
  writing as, 12, 20, 22–23
  See also specific writers; Ancients vs. mod-
    erns: appropriation by; Intertextu-
    ality; Lockean appropriation; Pla-
    giarism
Arbuthnot, John. *See Three Hours after Marriage*
Ariadne (pseud.), as playwright, 170
Astell, Mary, 238n55
Astrea, 108, 178, 179, 204n2, 206,
  224n38. *See also* Behn, Aphra
Authorship, 3–5, 16n6, 21, 31

amateur (elite), 18, 32, 37, 120, 130
  vs. child-bearing, 78–79, 186–187
  claimed, 42, 45
  and class, 199–200
  hack, 5–6, 108n6, 167, 187–188, 191,
    192, 196, 199, 203, 216; women prac-
    ticing, 177, 188n57, 205, 215–217,
    245
  vs. marriage, 77–78
  as ownership, 9, 104, 168, 242
  and patriarchy, 45, 47
  professional, 7, 31–34, 105, 142, 167,
    169, 187
  and race, 143n87
  See also specific writers; Women writers

Ballaster, Ros, 137
Barkan, Leonard, 124
Barthes, Roland, 21
Battersby, Christine, 19–20, 22
Baudrillard, Jean, 139
Behn, Aphra, 48–49, 116n28
  accused of plagiarism, 37–38, 105, 107,
    167; answers to charge, 4–5, 105–
    106, 107–108
  accused of sexual impropriety, 109,
    110–111, 159–160
  eroticized, 113–114
  espionage of, 105, 118, 130
  on imitation, 106–107, 124n52
  and (T.) Killigrew, 117–119
  as owner of literary property, 105, 109,
    113, 116, 131, 142–143, 144, 159
  as professional playwright, 9, 105, 130,
    170
  signified in Southerne's *Oroonoko,*
    158–160
  and theatre companies, 117, 119, 143
  as widow, 116–117
  Abdelazar, 197
  Agnes de Casto, 180

Index

Centlivre, Susanna, 211n10, 215n21
  accused of plagiarism, 212; answer to
    charge, 205
  accused of sexual impropriety, 185, 207
  as actor, 183–184, 205, 206, 221n33
  apology for writing, 209, 216
  and cultural capital, 205–206, 212–
    213, 215, 217
  feminist individualism, 6, 206, 209,
    210, 213, 215, 222, 225, 233, 237,
    240–241
  as hack writer, 215–217
  marriage, 216–217
  and originality, 205, 206, 207, 211,
    212, 213n18, 224
  and ownership, 213–215, 241–242
  patronage, 215–218
  as professional playwright, 204–205,
    207, 213
  publication, 206–209, 211, 215, 223
  satirized, 171, 183–187, 204–205
  The Basset Table, 222, 231, 233,
    235–241
  The Beau's Duel: Or a Soldier for the La-
    dies, 207–208
  Bickerstaff's Burying, 241–242
  A Bold Stroke for a Wife, 184n50,
    211n10, 212n13, 228
  The Busy Body, 212, 213, 215
  The Cruel Gift, 184, 212n14, 214n20
  The Gamester, 208, 210, 212n14, 222,
    231, 233–235; appropriation from
    Behn, 234
  "Letter from Mrs. C--e, to Mr. Joye,"
    216–217
  Love at a Venture, 221–222, 242; appro-
    priated by Cibber, 218–221, 222,
    231
  Love's Contrivance, appropriated from
    Molière, 208, 212n14
  The Man's Bewitch'd, 215
  Marplot, 213
  The Perjur'd Husband, 207
  The Perplex'd Lovers, 213
  The Platonick Lady, 205, 209–210, 222–
    226, 239; compared to Wright, The
    Female Vertuoso's, 224–225, 226
  The Stolen Heiress, 224, 227–228; appro-
    priated from May, 208
  The Wonder, 204, 209

Charles I (king of England), 36, 136
Charles II (king of England), 33, 45, 73, 118
Chastity, 91, 157, 176, 181, 223, 236n52
  and gambling, 229–230
  and literary property, 70, 79–80,
    187–188
Chaucer, Geoffrey, Troilus and Criseyde,
    appropriated, 55
Child-bearing
  vs. authorship, 78–79, 186–187
  in works by women writers, 97, 128,
    239
Christensen, Jerome, 16n6
Churchill, John (first duke of Marlbor-
    ough), and Centlivre, 213
Cibber, Colley
  accused of plagiarism, 6, 162, 191–193,
    196, 203, 218–219; answer to charge,
    192, 194, 197, 220
  as actor, 172, 173, 186, 196, 203, 219,
    220
  appropriation of Shakespeare, Richard
    III, 166
  and cultural capital, 192, 194, 195–
    197, 220
  feud with Pope, 184n50, 192, 194
  and foppery, 197, 198, 199, 201,
    202n97, 218–219, 221, 222,
    232–233
  as hack writer, 191, 195, 195n74, 203,
    218, 220
  satirized, 193; in The Dunciad, 162,
    190–192, 203; in Love at a Venture
    (possibly), 218, 221; in Three Hours,
    183, 184n50, 185, 186, 196–197
  and women writers, 164, 183, 185, 199,
    203, 218–220, 222
  An Apology for the Life of Mr. Colley Cib-
    ber, 186n55, 194, 197
  The Careless Husband, 197, 200
  The Double Gallant, appropriated from
    Centlivre, 218–221, 222, 231
  The Egotist: Or, Colley upon Cibber,
    196n77, 197
  The Lady's Last Stake, or, The Wife's Re-
    sentment, 197, 230–233, 236
  "Letter from Mr. Cibber to Mr. Pope,"
    194
  Love Makes a Man: or, the Fop's Fortune,
    197

Index

Index

Ownership (*cont.*)
   and genius, 19–20
   Locke on, 25–28
   as male, 24, 47, 49, 120, 152–153
   in *Oroonoko* (both), 131, 133, 146, 150, 151, 152–153, 159
   See also Property; Self-ownership/-possession

Parker, Patricia, 41n62
Pateman, Carole, 27, 167
   on Hobbes, 28–29, 30
   on Locke, 26, 28–29, 241
   on prostitution, 111–112
Patriarchy, 24–25, 28–30, 83, 122, 152, 184, 231
   and authorship, 45, 47
   M. Cavendish and, 73, 81, 82, 86
   traditional vs. fraternal, 206, 237–238, 239
Patronage, 7, 8, 52, 166–167
   by Charles II, 33, 45, 118
   for men, 53–54, 132n68, 146, 218n24
   for women, 61, 114, 215–218
Payne, Deborah C., 114
Payne, Linda R., 77n57
Pearson, Jacqueline, 141n86, 146n94, 204n2, 210n9
Pepys, Samuel, re Dryden's *Sir Martin Mar-All*, 54
Performance, 96, 202, 215
   gender, 77, 87, 100, 164, 197, 207
   women and, 77n56, 87, 97
Perry, Ruth, 238n55
Peters, Julie Stone, 9, 167
Peterson, William W., 183n46
Phallocentrism, 21–22
Phallus, and genius, 19
Philips, Katherine, 42, 116n28
   Letters from Orinda to Poliarchus, 42
Pix, Mary, 178, 179
   as playwright, 170, 173, 183
   satirized, 173, 180
   The Deceiver Deceived, appropriated by Powell, 181, 182n44
   Queen Catherine, or, The Ruines of Love, 180–181
Plagiarism, 3, 8n15, 10–14, 243
   and class, 34–35, 36–37
   vs. imitation, 7n13, 13–14, 16, 67, 189
   Langbaine's accusations, 33–38, 51–52

in Renaissance art, 7–8
   term, 7n13, 10
   women charged with, 10, 38–41, 108, 171n25, 174
   See also specific writers; Appropriation; Intertextuality
Platonism, 89, 104, 223–226, 240
   eroticism of, 91, 102–103
Pocock, J. G. A., 5, 25, 123n51, 202, 231
Poetic genealogy, 45–47, 51, 64, 69, 165–166, 206
   feminized, 178–179
   Jonson as literary ancestor, 45, 47, 172, 174, 180–181
   as justification for appropriation, 49–50, 57
   Shakespeare as literary ancestor, 49–50, 172, 174
Poetry, 5, 7, 8, 75
   dramatic, 9, 170, 175
   women accused of appropriating, 39–40
Pollak, Ellen, 26n33
Pope, Alexander, 5n8, 171, 187, 218n24
   appropriations by, 195
   feud with Cibber, 6, 184n50, 192, 194
   satirized, 195–196
   Account of a Horrid and Barbarous Revenge by Poison, 204n3
   The Dunciad, 162, 190–191, 203, 204, 245
   The Rape of the Lock, 229
   See also Three Hours after Marriage
Powell, George, 179n36
   as actor in *The Female Wits*, 181n41
   The Fatal Discovery, 182–183n44
   The Imposture Defeated: or, a Trick to Cheat the Devil, appropriated from Pix, 181, 182n44
Property, 28
   authorial, 2n1, 165, 210n8. *See also* Property: literary
   crimes of, 165–166
   Hobbes on, 14, 104
   human. *See* Slavery
   literary, 3, 6, 14, 23, 37, 102, 182, 188; claims to, 22–23, 42, 45, 54, 195; as masculine, 175–176; and originality, 69, 243; protected, 70, 79, 165–166; violated, 17, 32, 34, 65–66, 106–107, 172, 174–175; women owning, 4,